GOLF CLINIC

PLAY BETTER GOLF

GOLF CLINIC

PLAY BETTER GOLF

BEVERLY LEWIS

Illustrations by Ken Lewis

CLB

CLB 3060
This edition published in 1995
© 1993 Colour Library Books Ltd, Godalming, Surrey
All rights reserved
Printed and bound in Italy
ISBN 1-85833-117-X

Beverly Lewis

PLAY BETTER GOLF

Contents

5 Curing Common Faults

6 How to Break 90

CHAPTER ONE

What are we trying to achieve?

There is a saying in golf: 'drive for show, and putt for dough'. Now while there may be more than a grain of truth in that adage, there is little chance of putting for too much dough, i.e. money, if driving is the weak part of your game. Naturally, even among the best players in the world, there are those renowned for their driving skills, and others who are better known as superb putters, but you cannot expect to achieve your best scores if the first shot on each hole lands in the rough, a bunker, lake or forest. The best putter in the world is going to be hard pressed to salvage a decent score.

Anyone who has been to a professional golf tournament will undoubtedly have been impressed by the standard of driving – not only the power but also the accuracy. Time and time again, the top professionals' super-smooth swings

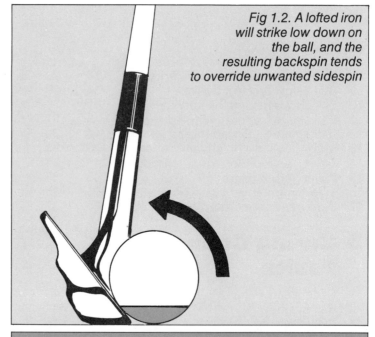

Fig 1.2. A lofted iron will strike low down on the ball, and the resulting backspin tends to override unwanted sidespin

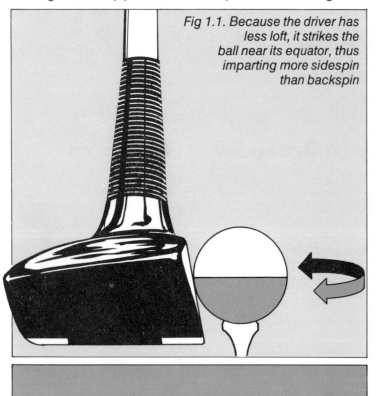

Fig 1.1. Because the driver has less loft, it strikes the ball near its equator, thus imparting more sidespin than backspin

produce shots that seem to explode off the clubface and travel hundreds of yards to the optimum point in the fairway. To be able to reproduce shots of such high quality is probably every club golfer's dream, and in writing this book I have tried to highlight the most important factors that permit professionals to achieve these exhilarating shots, and hope that by integrating them into your game you will start to emulate the skills of your heroes or, indeed, heroines.

The drive that is struck powerfully from the middle of the clubface to the middle of the fairway, is not only extremely satisfying, but sets up a possible birdie chance and makes par much more of a formality.

But why is it that this department of the game can cause such misery to many players, who, although they may not be very low handicap golfers, are able to hit a high proportion of their other shots to an acceptable standard? Well, the problem arises with a driver mainly because of its lack of loft on the clubface, and it is this factor that accentuates any flaws in the swing. When using other clubs, the additional loft will tend to offset these imperfections to a

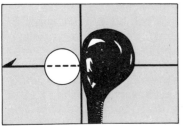

Fig 1.3. At impact, the clubhead should be swinging directly towards the target, with the club face square to the target

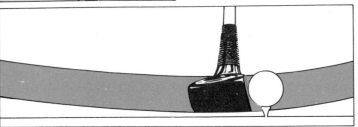

Fig 1.4. The clubhead should approach the ball on a shallow arc

▶ it must be travelling at a shallow angle of attack (Figs 1.3 & 1.4);

▶ the ball must be struck from the middle of the clubface.

To produce this set of circumstances, the swing-path has to be from in-to straight to-in. Now if the implications of that statement are not totally clear, let me explain further, using the clock face to give you a better picture of the situation.

Imagine that as you address the ball, it is in the centre of a clock face. You are standing at 6 o'clock, with 3 o'clock on your right, and 9 o'clock on your left (Fig 1.5). As you swing the clubhead away from the ball, for a short distance it will travel towards 3 o'clock. Then, as your body continues to turn, so the clubhead will leave that straight line and start to swing inwards and upwards between 3 and 4 o'clock. Ideally you will then swing it down again on a similar line, strike the ball while the clubhead is travelling directly towards the target at 9 o'clock, and then, as the body continues its turn, the clubhead will start to swing inwards to 8 o'clock.

Throughout the book I will refer to this clock face system of describing the clubhead swing-path, since not only is it an easy system from an instructional point of view but it is also a simple method of analysis that you can take onto the course to help during your round.

certain extent, and you are able to proceed around the golf course in a fairly direct manner. The driver, due to its straight face, strikes the ball on its equator, and thus any hint of sidespin is emphasised (Fig 1.1). A more lofted club will strike the ball lower down, and create more backspin which, to a certain extent, tends to balance unwanted sidespin (Fig 1.2). Do not ignore the fact that the driver has the longest shaft of all the clubs, and this can seem rather unwieldy, and therefore harder to swing in a controlled manner. And control does seem to desert many players when they take the driver in their hands. When using their irons, if a 6 iron will not hit the ball far enough, they quite happily take a 5 iron for the shot, knowing that there is a limit to how far they can hit each iron. However, when it comes to the driver, many golfers seem to think that infinity is their limit. They thrash away with the club, hoping beyond all reality that they will suddenly be able to hit the ball an additional 50 yards if they launch everything into the shot. What does happen is that any hint of smoothness and good timing disappear, and the ball goes nowhere.

Poor driving can send you scurrying to unchartered parts of the course and totally ruin your round, but improve this department of your game and who knows how low your handicap may become. To produce a long straight drive:

▶ at impact the clubhead must be travelling at speed directly towards the target;

▶ the clubface must be at right angles to this path;

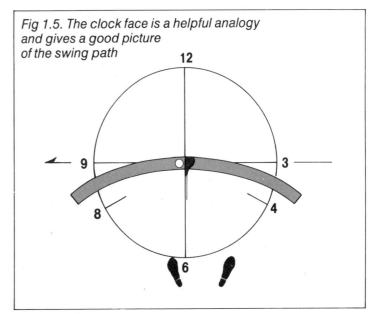

Fig 1.5. The clock face is a helpful analogy and gives a good picture of the swing path

CHAPTER TWO

The right equipment

Before I explain any more about the swing, I think that a few points about equipment would be helpful. Many people believe that you cannot go into the professional's shop and 'buy' success, but you can buy and use equipment that can either help or hinder your game, and this is never truer than with the driver.

The driver face

There are several aspects to consider when choosing a driver, and one of the most important is the amount of loft on the club. As I have already pointed out, the less loft on a club, the more it will impart sidespin – wanted or not – on the ball. So if you are someone who viciously hooks or slices the ball, you should choose a driver with plenty of loft. The better the player you become, the more able you will be to use a club that is relatively straight-faced, and thus benefit from the extra distance that can be gained from such a club. So how should you select the right loft? Most drivers will have a loft of between about 9 and 12 degrees, and it is one that is 12 degrees that is the easier to hit. If your driver is straight-faced, it is better to use the more lofted 3 or 4 wood in the set, until such time that you can hit reliably (Fig 2.1). Your driver will gain you maybe 10 to 15 yards, but that is no use if it sends the ball too far off line – better to sacrifice distance for accuracy.

A deep faced driver is also more difficult to use, so check that aspect of the club as well, since if it is deeper than one-and-three-quarter inches it will be difficult to use. If you hook the ball, you may find that a slightly open faced club would help to hit the ball straighter (Fig 2.2), whereas the player who slices the ball consistently, would be better suited to one that sits a little closed (Fig 2.3). Do not expect to be able to judge these angles and lofts with an untrained eye, so always ask your professional for advice. He (or she) might ask you to hit a few shots and will help in your final choice.

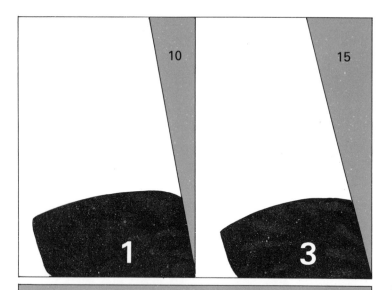

Fig 2.1. The higher numbered woods have more degrees of loft and can help to hit the ball with less sidespin, and therefore straighter

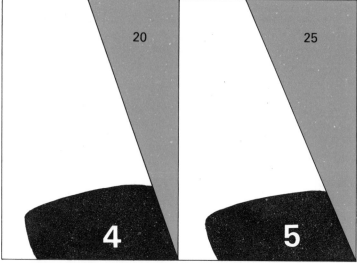

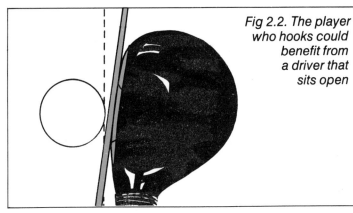

Fig 2.2. The player who hooks could benefit from a driver that sits open

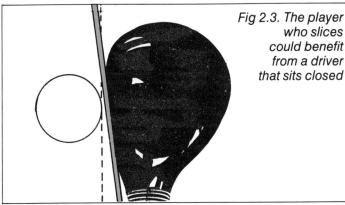

Fig 2.3. The player who slices could benefit from a driver that sits closed

Swing-weight	C0-C5	C6-C8	C9-D2	D3-D5
Shaft	L	L or R	R	S or XS
Category of Player	Lady beginner and average lady player. Slow swing and hand action.	Strong lady and weaker man. Reasonable hand and club speed. Man may feel that a lighter club is easier to control and L shaft helps clubhead speed.	Strong lady and average man. Good hand action and clubhead speed.	Strong man. Very fast hand action and clubhead speed.

Fig 2.4. This table shows which swing weight and shaft flex suit the different categories of golfers

The swing weight

Along with the various flexes of shaft to consider, you must also select a club that is the correct swing weight for you. Swing weight is a system of measuring the balance of a club, and it also helps to indicate how heavy a club feels when it is swung. The scale starts at the light end for ladies, which is anything from C0 to C9, continuing into the men's range which overlaps the ladies' heavier club in the C8 to C9 category up to D5 and onwards at the heaviest end (Fig 2.4).

A man's average driver could be at the light end of the scale D0, progressing to D2 as a medium weight, with D4 onwards being considered quite heavy. Some professionals, since they create very fast clubhead speed, can use clubs that would register about D5 or D6, but they would also use a stiff, or very stiff shafted, club to control this extra weight. However, they are exceptional and most men would be best suited to a club that will not feel too heavy to swing when they are nearing the end of a round and beginning to feel tired. The less athletic woman may find a club of around C3 most suitable, whereas a stonger player, perhaps someone who has excelled in other sports, may find that this weight of club is like a wand in her hand. She would need a heavier club in the ladies' range, or maybe discover that a men's lightweight club suits her better. In recent years, there have been many more lightweight clubs on the market, and for the stronger woman, or weaker man, these can prove ideal.

The shaft

Most men should use a driver with a man's regular shaft. It is only the stronger player, who hits the ball a long way and tends to draw or hook the ball consistently, who might benefit from a stiffer shaft. Alternatively, I know many men who, accepting that they are not as strong as they used to be, get on better and gain some length by using lighter whippier ladies' clubs. Most ladies should use ladies' clubs (often they inherit their husbands' cast-offs, which are totally unsuitable). It is only those who are stronger than average who should be considering a man's driver. Since men's clubs are longer, they are generally heavier to swing, and if you are not sufficiently strong to control that extra weight and to cope with the stiffer shaft, then there is no benefit from the club.

The lie

The lie of the club is the angle between the shaft and the base, or sole, of the club. When buying a set of irons, this is one of the most important aspects to consider, since a club with an incorrect lie can affect the shot. However, when using a driver the ball is on a tee peg, so the lie is not so important. But if, for instance, you are five foot tall, and use a man's length driver, make sure that the lie is not too upright.

Grip thickness

One further point to consider is the thickness of the grip. Ideally, when the left hand is closed around the handle, the last three fingers should be quite close to the base of the thumb (Fig 2.5). Too great a gap will probably deny you enough hand action and control. Alternatively, grips that are too thin may not allow the club to sit snugly in your left hand

and then one of two things may happen: you might grip the club just in the fingers of this hand, instead of the palm and fingers; or, trying to place the club correctly across the palm, you will find the fingers tending to 'run into' the base of the left thumb, preventing a solid grip. Remember, however, that if you change the grip thickness on your clubs, a thinner grip will make the club feel heavier to swing whereas thicker grips will lighten it. Thinner grips will also encourage more hand action, while thicker ones will have the reverse affect.

Consult the expert

I am sure that your local professional will be only too pleased to help you choose a driver, but you should always tell him your handicap and the characteristics of your game. Ideally, he can watch you hit a few shots, and then he can better assess the right club. These days we are spoilt for choice, with drivers now being made not only in wood but also in carbon and metal, and with either carbon or metal shafts, so you can see why you should seek professional advice.

Summary

So to summarize club choice, the most important factors are the loft, how the face lies, the shaft flex, swing weight and grip thickness. It takes some professionals years to find exactly the right driver, and when they have done so, they guard it with their lives. So do not be too hasty in buying the first one you see – ask your professional what will suit your ability, and go from there.

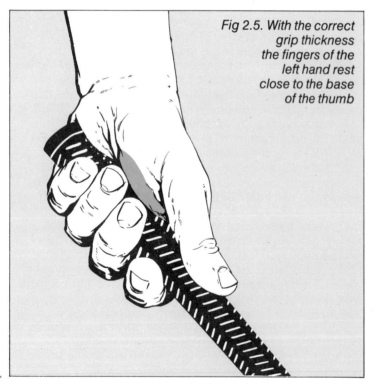

Fig 2.5. With the correct grip thickness the fingers of the left hand rest close to the base of the thumb

CHAPTER THREE

The importance of the correct grip

If you look at the best players in the world, it is obvious that they do not all grip the club in exactly the same way. Their different styles of playing are best suited by the grip that they use. However, among the vast majority of these golfers, both men and women, certain fundamentals are common. In other words, although their grips may vary slightly, they do conform within certain boundaries. Take a look at a group of club golfers at any driving range or practice ground, and unfortunately I can guarantee that the majority will be gripping the club in such a way that producing consistently good golf shots will be very difficult.

So often, when people start to play golf, they grip the club in a manner that feels most comfortable, but which, in most cases, will not produce powerful shots. Sound foundations are necessary in order to achieve your maximum potential in golf and build a powerful, reliable swing. The grip is mainly responsible for the clubface alignment and, as I have already stated, when using the driver, if you do not have the clubface square at impact, the ball is going to curve more violently than with any other club. Unfortunately, changing the grip can be the most uncomfortable experience in golf, and there is often the temptation to stick with what *felt* right, but which in fact was wrong. But a sound grip is worth taking time over, as it contributes so much to your swing's shape and also to clubface alignment.

This chapter will teach you a grip of which you can be proud – one that will stand you in good stead as you gradually build the swing. The main purpose of the grip is to return the clubface squarely to the ball, without any unnecessary manipulation by the hands, and to allow the hands to work in harmony throughout the swing. The left hand and arm are very much the guiding and pulling force, while the right provide the extra speed and power.

Consequently, each hand is placed on the grip to allow it to work effectively. It is important to place the left hand on the grip correctly first, then apply the right, and do make sure that the leading edge of the club is square to the target.

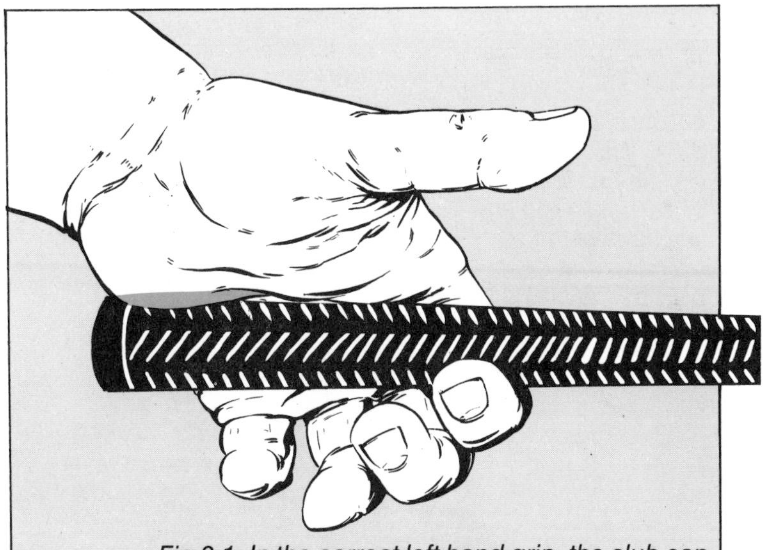

The left hand

The club sits very much in the palm and fingers of the left hand, thus giving a more solid grip for its guiding role than if it were held only in the fingers. The club rests across the index finger and under the fleshy pad at the heel of your hand, so that it could actually be balanced in the air without the support of the last three fingers of this hand (Fig 3.1). However, these last three fingers provide the main pressure, and they should fit round the grip in such a manner that the club feels quite snug and firm. When you look down you should be able to see about two to two-and-a-half knuckles of the hand, and the 'V' formed by the thumb and forefinger should point towards your right ear, with the thumb sitting just to the right of centre of the top of the grip (Fig 3.2). Try not to let a large gap develop between the thumb and forefinger, since they need to provide a solid support at the top of the backswing. It is also a common mistake to stretch the thumb too far down the shaft. This action tenses the front of the arm and prevents the muscles from working efficiently. If you stand with your arms relaxed beside you, the end of the thumb and the knuckle of the forefinger are relatively level, and that is how you should grip the club: with the knuckle of the forefinger and the end of the thumb about level on the grip. When applying the left hand to the grip, do so with your hand opposite the inside of

Fig 3.1. In the correct left hand grip, the club can balance without the support of the last three fingers

13

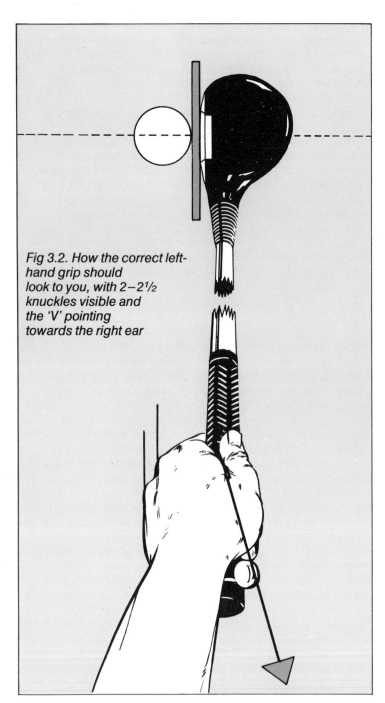

Fig 3.2. How the correct left-hand grip should look to you, with 2–2½ knuckles visible and the 'V' pointing towards the right ear

your left thigh. This will help to ensure that the shaft and clubhead are in the correct relationship to the hand and arm, i.e. virtually forming a straight line. Ensure that the back of the left hand does not become too concave, and that the shoulders are set with the left one higher than the right.

Incidentally, I do believe that it is a great help to practise taking your grip looking in a mirror, and five minutes' practice a day will quickly develop a good, comfortable grip.

The right hand

The club is gripped more in the fingers of the right hand, to encourage it to create a lively and slinging action through impact. The hollow of the palm should fit over the left thumb (Fig 3.3), so that when viewed in the mirror you can see very little of the left thumb. The 'V' formed by the thumb and forefinger, which again should not have a large gap between them, should point between the right ear and shoulder. The thumb will sit just to the left of centre on the grip, and the forefinger will be triggered at the side of the shaft (Fig 3.4). Again, as with the left hand, do not stretch the thumb down the shaft. The middle two fingers supply the main pressure, which should be sufficiently firm to control the clubhead, but not so tight that the muscles become tense.

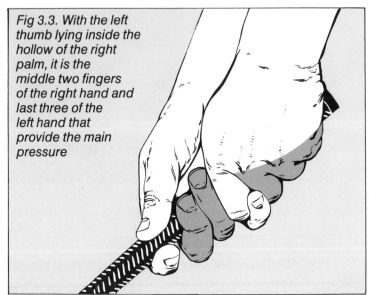

Fig 3.3. With the left thumb lying inside the hollow of the right palm, it is the middle two fingers of the right hand and last three of the left hand that provide the main pressure

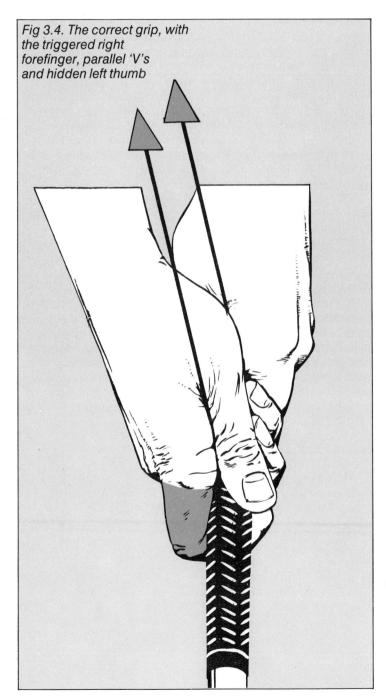

Fig 3.4. The correct grip, with the triggered right forefinger, parallel 'V's and hidden left thumb

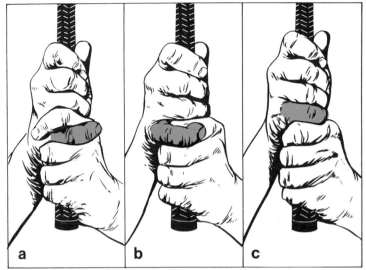

Fig 3.5. Placement of right little finger, showing: (a) interlocking; (b) overlapping or Vardon; (c) baseball or two-handed grips

What to do with the little finger

In order to make the hands work together as one unit, the right little finger is taken off the grip and either interlocked with, or allowed to overlap, the left forefinger. Most top-class players choose to overlap, and I tend to favour this, since it allows the whole of the important guiding left hand to remain on the grip. However, many players interlock, most notably Jack Nicklaus, and it does not appear to have done him any harm! He favours this grip as he has smallish hands, but many people with even smaller hands overlap, so I suggest that you adopt whichever method is most comfortable to you. Some ladies may find a two-handed grip, where all 10 fingers are on the grip, even better, but make sure that there is no gap between the two hands.

How the two hands should look

Having taken your grip, when you look in the mirror, most of your left thumb should be covered and therefore hidden from view, and the two 'V's formed by the thumb and forefinger should be parallel. If they are parallel so your hands will be also; so take your grip, then just uncurl your fingers and see if this is true. If the hands are parallel they will work in harmony – otherwise they fight each other.

Grip pressure

It is difficult to be precise about this aspect of the grip. A golfer with naturally strong hands will not need to grip the club with as much force as another player with weak hands. However, the last three fingers of the left hand and the middle two of the right provide the main support, and should only grip the club hard enough to control it. If you grip with too much pressure, the muscles in the hands and forearms will become hard and tight, and in this state they do not work efficiently. The grip will also be inclined to tighten slightly as backswing pressure is felt. Thus if you start with too tight a grip, by the time you have reached impact, your grip will be vice-like. To check the pressure, grip the club, then ask a friend to take hold of the clubhead and gently turn it from left to right. The pressure should be sufficiently tight to resist any turning of the grip in your hands. But a word of warning: I tell many more people to grip lighter, than tighter, so do not strangle the club.

Bad grips to avoid

The most common bad grip among beginners is one in which the left hand is turned too much to the left, and the right hand too much to the right (Fig 3.6a). This way, both hands are too much under the grip and will prevent the wrists from working correctly throughout the swing. To correct this fault the player must move both hands more on top of the grip, and follow the guide lines in this chapter. Some players place both hands too much to the right on the grip (Fig 3.6b), and will usually hook the ball or completely block their wrist action, neither of which is acceptable in driving long distances. Again follow the guidelines in this chapter, making sure that the palms face more towards the target. As an aid, ensure that the right forefinger triggers correctly at the *side* of the shaft. The player who has both hands turned too much to the left is less common (Fig 3.6c) and is more likely to slice, and swing too upright. Neither is conducive to length. Reconstruct your grip as detailed earlier in the chapter, noting the new position of the 'V's.

What is the correct position on the grip?

As you develop good hand and arm action, so you may need to adjust your grip. The beginner is better served by a grip on the strong side of neutral, i.e. the 'V's point more towards the right shoulder, thus helping to square the clubface. Once a good action is achieved and the ball starts to draw too much, then the position can be changed slightly to a more neutral grip, where the 'V's are in the standard position described earlier.

Fig 3.6. Three incorrect grips to be avoided

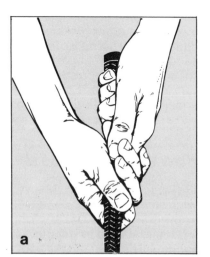
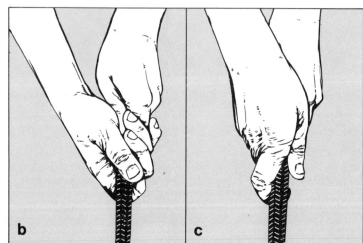

CHAPTER FOUR

How to aim and set up correctly

Nothing is more annoying than to strike the ball well, only to see it shoot off in the wrong direction. Since the driver is going to produce the longest shots in golf, it is all the more important that you aim correctly, since being out, say, 10 to 15 degrees at address, can cause a ball that travels about 200 yards to be as much as 30 to 40 yards off-line. Unfortunately, it is easy to get into bad habits and aim the shot too casually, convinced, of course, that you are firing in the correct direction. What generally happens is that to compensate for bad aiming, a swing fault is incorporated to bring the whole thing back on track. One of the most common mistakes is seeing someone who has aimed too far right, throwing the right shoulder at the ball from the top of the swing in an effort to straighten the shot. This will only prevent the correct sequence of movements from taking place in the swing, with consequent loss of power.

You must aim in the correct direction if you are trying to build sound foundations. In many sports you face your target, but in golf you are standing sideways on to your's, and several feet to the left of the intended line of flight. Also, your target may be hundreds of yards ahead, so it is easy to see why aiming the shot correctly can be such a difficult task with a combination of these factors. However, by following a set routine, you can improve this department of your game quite easily.

The intermediate target

Watch most of the best players and they adopt a routine in which instead of aiming vaguely into the distance, they select an intermediate target over which to aim, to assure them of a more precise result. Adopting this method will help to rule out sloppy and careless aiming.

Therefore you should stand behind the ball, looking towards the target, and pick out something to aim over, perhaps an old divot, or a leaf, about one yard ahead of the ball, on the ball-to-target line. Then, standing opposite the ball, feet together, with the inside of the left heel level with the back of the ball, place the clubhead at right angles to an imaginary line drawn from the ball to the intermediate target (Fig 4.1a). It is much easier to aim over something one

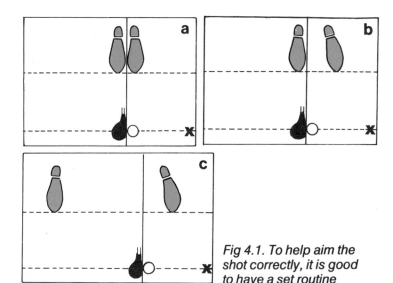

Fig 4.1. To help aim the shot correctly, it is good to have a set routine

yard away rather than 250, and with a little practice you will not find this too difficult. So having aimed the clubface correctly, now move your left foot about two inches to the left (Fig 4.1b) and the right foot a suitable distance to the right, so that the width of your stance provides a solid base on which to swing, but not one that will stifle leg action (Fig 4.1c). A line drawn across your toes should be parallel to the ball and the intermediate target line. Now make sure that your knees, hips, eyes and, most importantly, your shoulders are also parallel to this same line. The shoulders are most influential in directing the line of the swing, so do pay special attention to them.

The railway track

It will help you to aim correctly if you imagine a set of railway lines (Fig 4.2). The ball and clubhead are on the far track, and you will stand on the nearer one. That way your whole body will be parallel to the intended line of flight. So many people think that the body aims *at* the target, but if it did, the ball would start right of target. Remember that the body is aligned parallel left of the target, so that a club placed across your shoulders would point *not* at the target, but parallel left.

The best way to practise this is with two clubs on the ground to represent the railway lines. It is also useful if a

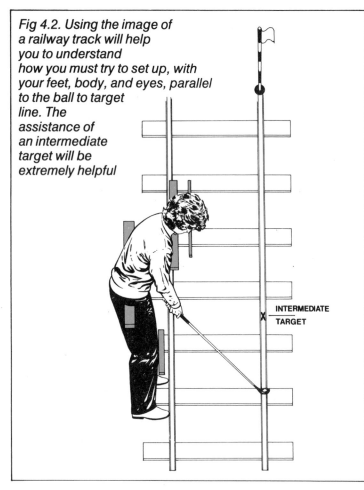

Fig 4.2. Using the image of a railway track will help you to understand how you must try to set up, with your feet, body, and eyes, parallel to the ball to target line. The assistance of an intermediate target will be extremely helpful

INTERMEDIATE
TARGET

play normal iron shots with the ball about two balls' widths inside my left heel. Therefore with the driver, the back of the ball is about one ball's width, or approximately two inches, inside my left heel. You may need to experiment to find the best position, as this will vary from player to player, but bear these facts in mind. If the ball is too far forward, it will tend to aim the shoulders left at address and will cause a weak out-to-in swing (Fig 4.3). If the ball is too far back, the shoulders will tend to point right, and you will possibly hit it while the clubhead is descending, losing distance, and will also hit it to the right (Fig 4.4). You can check the ball position by putting tee pegs in the ground to mark your toes, and one at the left heel (Fig 4.5). Place a club across the toe line, and one behind the ball. Then walk round to the other side of the ball, and see from face on just where it is. So often it appears to be in one position at address, when, in reality, it is in another. It is also extremely useful to check your set up in a mirror in which you can see the ball position easily.

Beware of the shoulder line

For powerful driving, you should play the ball nearer the left foot than for any other normal shot, and in order to

friend places a club across your shoulders to ensure that they are parallel, since if your aim has been wayward, the new set up will feel strange, and consequently you may interpret this as being incorrect. Any changes made in golf will often feel awkward and wrong, but this is why you must persevere and practise – otherwise, you will never improve.

The ball position

For powerful driving, you need to strike the ball when the clubhead is at the bottom of the arc or just on the way up. Position it a little nearer the left foot than for iron shots. I

Fig 4.3. With the ball positioned too far forward, the shoulders are pulled open, i.e. aiming to the left, and the ball starts left of target

Fig 4.4. With the ball positioned too far back, the shoulders become closed, i.e. aiming too far to the right, and the ball starts right of target

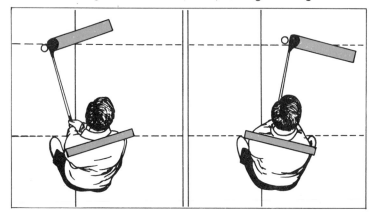

accommodate this position, it is all too easy to allow the right shoulder to be pulled forward. Instead, it should feel very much back and low, with the left shoulder feeling quite high (Fig 4.6). In the correct position, although the left arm is straight, the right elbow should be slightly bent and pointing towards the right hip bone. The left arm and shaft should form a straight line, with the back of the left hand almost level with the front of the ball.

Tailoring the stance

When driving, you use a wider stance than for any other golf shot. It is difficult to be exact about the width: too narrow,

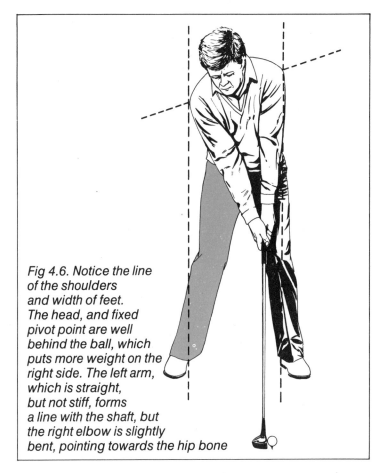

Fig 4.6. Notice the line of the shoulders and width of feet. The head, and fixed pivot point are well behind the ball, which puts more weight on the right side. The left arm, which is straight, but not stiff, forms a line with the shaft, but the right elbow is slightly bent, pointing towards the hip bone

TEE

TEE

Fig. 4.5. By placing the tees and clubs as shown, you can check the ball position

and you will not have enough stability; too wide, and you will inhibit good leg action. It is suggested often that the inside of the heels should be shoulder width apart (Fig 4.6) but this will not work in practice if you have short legs and wide shoulders, or vice versa. However, try to leave the left foot about two inches left of the ball, and vary the width by moving the right foot until you find the best position.

As you move your right foot to the right, you must allow your weight to move in that direction, so that it is distributed about 60:40 in favour of the right side (Fig 4.6). This will help you to take the clubhead back on a shallow arc, and to strike the ball slightly on the upswing. To help set your weight correctly, you may find it helpful to flex your right knee a little more than usual, which also helps to position your head behind the ball, just where it should be at impact. Your experience now should be of looking at the back of the ball.

Most professionals position their feet so that the right is at right angles to the line of flight and the left turned slightly towards the target (Fig 4.7). The principle behind this positioning is that the right foot and leg are required to provide a stable support in the backswing, while a high degree of freedom is needed in the left leg and hip area during the through-swing. However, since we do not all have the same level of flexibility, you may find that by turning your right foot out fractionally, you can make a better backswing turn, with less strain. Certainly the older and not so slim players may find this beneficial. Again, you must experiment and find the best arrangement for support and turn on the backswing, and ease of movement on the through-swing.

The eye line

While placing your body parallel, you must also ensure that your eye line is the same. If your head is set at an angle, you will be inclined to see the line to the target incorrectly, and thus wrong messages may be fed to your brain about where you are trying to hit the ball. By holding a club across the bridge of your nose and under your eyes (Fig 4.8), you will be able to tell if they are set correctly. When looking up at the target before you hit the ball, make sure that you rotate your head in that direction, rather than lift it, which can easily offset the eye line. However, before making your backswing, it is quite in order to rotate your head slightly to the right, so that your left eye is closer to the ground than the right, thus encouraging a full turn. Many world-class players do it, so why shouldn't you?

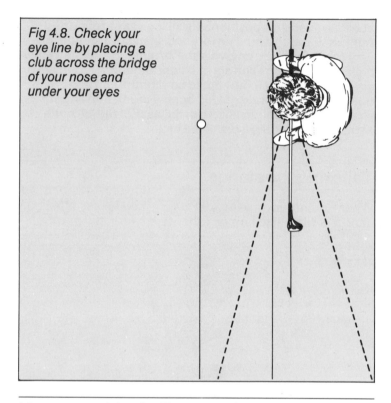

Fig 4.8. Check your eye line by placing a club across the bridge of your nose and under your eyes

How to tee the ball correctly

Since you are trying to hit the ball slightly on the upswing, it is important to guard against teeing it too low. As a good guide, the centre, or equator, of the ball should be approximately level with the top of the clubface (Fig 4.9). Usually the higher the ball is teed the higher it flies, but if you tee it too low, this may well encourage you to hit down on it and create a weak ineffectual shot.

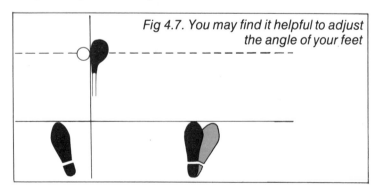

Fig 4.7. You may find it helpful to adjust the angle of your feet

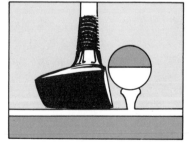

Fig 4.9. If a ball is teed correctly, the top of the club face should be about level with the equator of the ball

CHAPTER FIVE

Why good posture is essential

Aiming in the correct direction is essential for powerful accuracy, but it is no use aiming correctly if your posture is wrong. Many golfers are not sufficiently aware of the important role that their posture plays in the swing, and consequently how to distinguish good from bad. So let me try to enlighten you on the subject. If I had carried out all the instructions in the last chapter regarding aiming, it would be of no benefit to me if the position in which I had allowed my body and legs to settle (although parallel to the target line) prevented me from making a free swinging arm action. In a good golf swing, it is essential that the body is not in the way of the arms, and that it turns throughout the swing. The legs also play a vital and somewhat athletic role and must be positioned accordingly at address. So posture really means the way in which you angle your body and legs, and is best viewed from behind the line of flight.

The correct sequence

The correct way to gain good posture, is to stand opposite the ball with your legs straight, and then lower the clubhead to the ground behind the ball by bending from your hip bones and lowering the arms, slightly flexing your knees (Fig 5.1a). In this position, you will have a space in front of you in which your arms can swing. In fact, by bending in this fashion, the arms will hang quite freely from the shoulder joints, without the body getting in the way (Fig 5.1b). To check whether you have done this correctly, maintain your address position, take the driver in your right hand only, and hold it against your left shoulder so that the shaft hangs vertically. The clubhead should be just outside a line across your toes, although the exact amount will depend on your build. As you bend from the hips, your seat will be pushed backwards as a counter balance, so that the pelvis is pushed back and up rather than forward and under. This is essential to allow the hips to turn correctly out of the way in the backswing.

If your posture is good, the weight will be more towards the balls of your feet rather than the heels, and should be more towards the inside of each foot, with the knees slightly

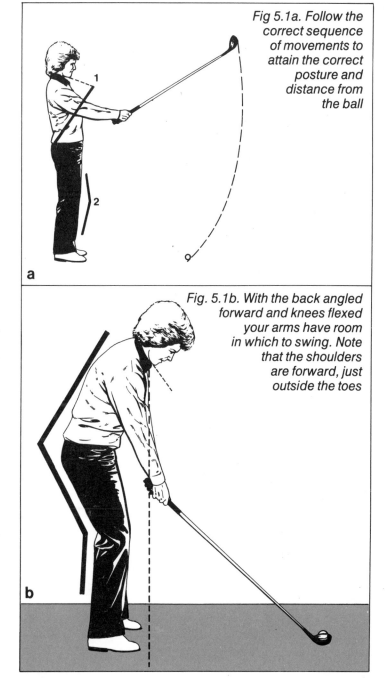

Fig 5.1a. Follow the correct sequence of movements to attain the correct posture and distance from the ball

Fig. 5.1b. With the back angled forward and knees flexed your arms have room in which to swing. Note that the shoulders are forward, just outside the toes

knocked towards each other, and the right marginally more flexed than the left. At this stage, the legs should feel in a 'lively' position, ready to support the swing. There is a theory regarding posture that you should feel as though you are just about to sit on a shooting stick. I have to disagree with this since most of your weight would be on your heels, and this is not what you require in good posture.

You also need to position your head correctly – you should hold it as an extension of the spine, in the same way as when you are standing upright. You may find, like many other golfers, that your chin is resting on your chest, often as a result of that other well misunderstood phrase: 'Keep your head down'. As you stand opposite the ball, before lowering the clubhead to the ground, fix your eyes on the horizon. Then, when taking your position, keep your head in the same relationship to your spine, just allowing your eyes to look down at the ball. Remember, head up, eyes down.

Bad faults

One of the most common bad address positions is when the player's back becomes rounded and slouched, too much weight is on the heels, and the arms and hands are too close to the body (Fig 5.2a). This type of golfer would have to feel that his spine is very much straighter but angled forward at address, thus creating the desired space in which to swing. I have to admit that more women than men have bad posture, and I believe that this is partly because we are taught from an early age to try to walk erect with our backs straight and seat tucked in. Thus many women are often loath to bend sufficiently from the hips and to push their seat out. Instead, they compensate and create space in which to swing by raising their wrists (Fig 5.2b) but in so doing they prevent good hand action, so again we see one

Fig 5.2a. Bad posture and ball position will inhibit a free arm swing and reduce power

Fig 5.2b. This posture, with the spine too erect and the wrists arched, is often adopted by ladies but should be avoided

to standing too close to, and too far away from, the ball. So the distance you place between you and the ball, and your posture are inter-related. It is not possible to say exactly how far you should be from the ball, as this depends on your size, and the club length, but if your posture is correct and you take your stance as advised, you should adjust the ball position to suit this stance. One further aspect to consider is the distance between the end of the grip and your thighs. With the driver it is at its greatest (in my own case about six inches) and this helps to guarantee enough space in which to swing your arms freely. Again, it is difficult to be exact about this distance, but as a general guideline, two to three inches would be too close, and nine inches too far. It really depends on your height: taller people tending to stand closer than shorter ones. One way I have found of retaining my correct distance is to 'sight' my left forefinger knuckle against an imaginary line across my toes (Fig 5.3). In my case it appears about three inches outside this line and thus it is easy for me to see if I get too close or too far away – just by checking this measurement now and again.

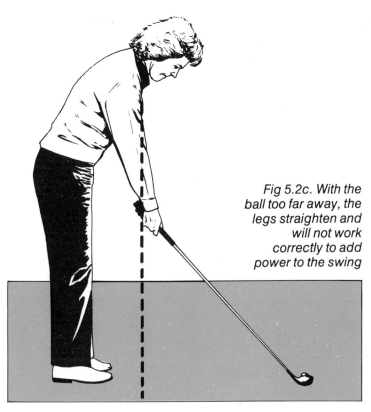

Fig 5.2c. With the ball too far away, the legs straighten and will not work correctly to add power to the swing

fault leading to another. A woman's anatomy makes it imperative that she has her pelvis tipped back and up, since this allows the hips to turn out of the way in the backswing. In the all too familiar tucked under position, the hips get stuck in the way, and this usually results in an incorrect swaying, rather than a turning, action.

Distance from the ball

Figs 5.2a and 5.2c illustrate bad posture, allied respectively

Summary

Remember that the important points in good posture are to bend first from the hips, keeping the spine fairly straight and not rounded, and then flex the legs. Feel that more weight is towards the balls of the feet, and keep your head *up,* and eyes *down.*

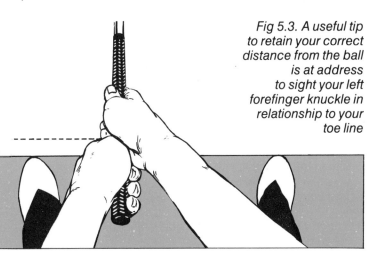

Fig 5.3. A useful tip to retain your correct distance from the ball is at address to sight your left forefinger knuckle in relationship to your toe line

CHAPTER SIX

The essential address points

The last three chapters have dealt in some depth with the most important points to consider in developing a good address position. I cannot emphasise too much the degree to which your game will improve even if you just start to look like a professional. However, do not be lulled into thinking that a good set up will happen simply by reading this book – you must practise the advice given here. The beauty of practising the address is that so much can be done at home indoors, using a mirror as your guide, or outdoors using a mirror or a long window in which you can see your reflection. It is also helpful if you have square tiles or patio slabs; otherwise, just use clubs laid down, and perhaps another golf ball as your intermediate target. By practising without the opportunity to actually hit the ball, you will concentrate better on the new position in which you will find yourself without the usual thoughts that accompany such changes: that you will never be able to hit a shot from this set up. This is a natural reaction, since anything new in golf always feels so uncomfortable, but with as little as 10 minutes' practice a day, I assure you that very soon the new set up will start to feel right, and then you will be able to concentrate on swinging the club.

So to summarize the last three chapters, and to make your mirror practice a little easier I will highlight the essential points to note.

Fig 6.1. Compare your set up with the illustration shown here, going through the check lists provided in this chapter

Face on (Fig 6.1)

1 The clubface must be square to the target.
2 The two 'V's formed by the thumb and forefinger of each hand, must be parallel and pointing between the right ear and right shoulder.
3 The left thumb should be totally, or almost totally, hidden by the right hand.
4 The back of the ball should be positioned about two inches inside the left heel.
5 The inside of the heels should be *about* shoulder width apart.
6 Your weight should be distributed approximately 60:40 in favour of the right foot.
7 The weight should favour the inside of each foot.
8 The knees should be flexed slightly towards each other, with the right a little more flexed than the left.
9 The left arm and shaft should form a straight line.
10 The left shoulder is higher than the right.
11 Your head is behind the back of the ball.

Down the target line, with the mirror to your right (Fig 6.2)

1 Your feet, knees, hips and shoulders should be parallel to the target line.
2 Although the shoulders must be parallel, because of your eye position, you should be just able to see the left shoulder.

*Fig 6.2. Again, compare
your set up with
the position shown
and refer back
to the highlighted
points on page 38*

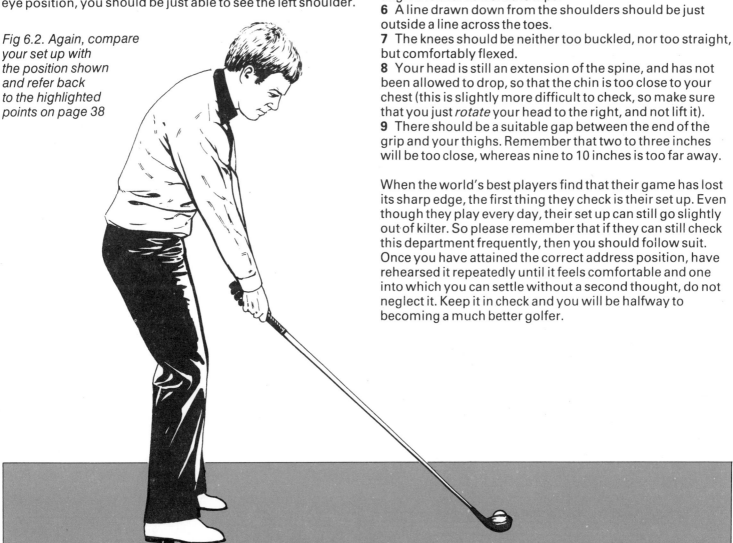

3 Provided that you do not alter your shoulder line, hold the club across your shoulders with your right hand, and check that the club points directly away from the mirror.
4 The right elbow should be bent a little, with the elbow joint pointing towards the hip bone so that the left arm is just visible.
5 The back should be fairly straight, not rounded, and angled forwards from the hips.
6 A line drawn down from the shoulders should be just outside a line across the toes.
7 The knees should be neither too buckled, nor too straight, but comfortably flexed.
8 Your head is still an extension of the spine, and has not been allowed to drop, so that the chin is too close to your chest (this is slightly more difficult to check, so make sure that you just *rotate* your head to the right, and not lift it).
9 There should be a suitable gap between the end of the grip and your thighs. Remember that two to three inches will be too close, whereas nine to 10 inches is too far away.

When the world's best players find that their game has lost its sharp edge, the first thing they check is their set up. Even though they play every day, their set up can still go slightly out of kilter. So please remember that if they can still check this department frequently, then you should follow suit. Once you have attained the correct address position, have rehearsed it repeatedly until it feels comfortable and one into which you can settle without a second thought, do not neglect it. Keep it in check and you will be halfway to becoming a much better golfer.

CHAPTER SEVEN

The unified swing

In Chapter 1, I stated how and where the clubhead should swing in order to produce your best drive. Now let us consider how you must move in order for this to happen. I plan to dissect the swing in order that you can have a comprehensive knowledge of its working parts. However, and I cannot emphasise this enough, golf is not a series of positions but one continuous movement, and in order to improve you have to work on specific parts of the swing in a logical order and then incorporate them into the whole movement.

It would also be fair to say that the better you become, the more finely tuned each component part of the swing has to be. You could compare it to a motor car – the average family-owned car will function even if the engine is not highly tuned, but try to drive a racing car that is not tuned correctly and you will be lucky to get out of the pit lane. The club golfer will have an enjoyable game, even with some imperfections in his swing, but he will not become a champion until they are so minute as not to cause high scores. Thus the better the component parts of the swing, the better the whole swing will become. However, do not forget that no matter how much you practise the component parts and attain different positions throughout the swing, you must work to incorporate the component parts into the whole swing – when you play and during your practice time.

As I stated earlier, golf is not a series of positions, but in teaching we have to isolate certain parts of the swing in order to highlight them, and to give you reference points. You are trying to swing the club on a certain route and if, in any part of its journey, it goes wrong, you need to be able to identify where. For example, if I was planning to travel between two places, I would pass through certain cities and towns *en route*. If I suddenly found myself in a town not mentioned on my schedule, I would know that I had gone the wrong way – this reference point would indeed warn me of my error.

So now let us take a look at the swing: first as a whole; and then in parts.

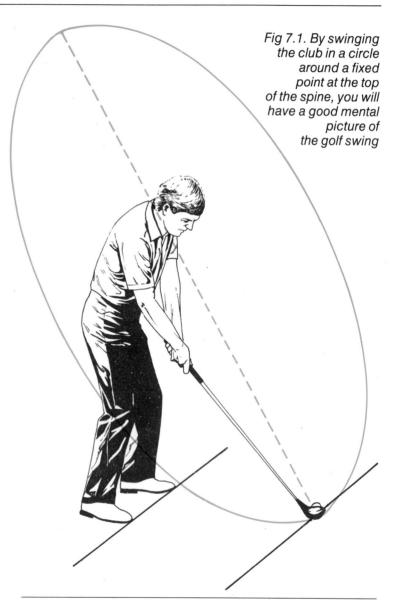

Fig 7.1. By swinging the club in a circle around a fixed point at the top of the spine, you will have a good mental picture of the golf swing

The swing image

As you stand at address, imagine swinging the clubhead on an inclined circle around a fixed point in the body, i.e. the large bone at the top of your spine and the base of your neck and you will then have a good mental picture of what happens in the correct swing (Fig 7.1). The arms will swing

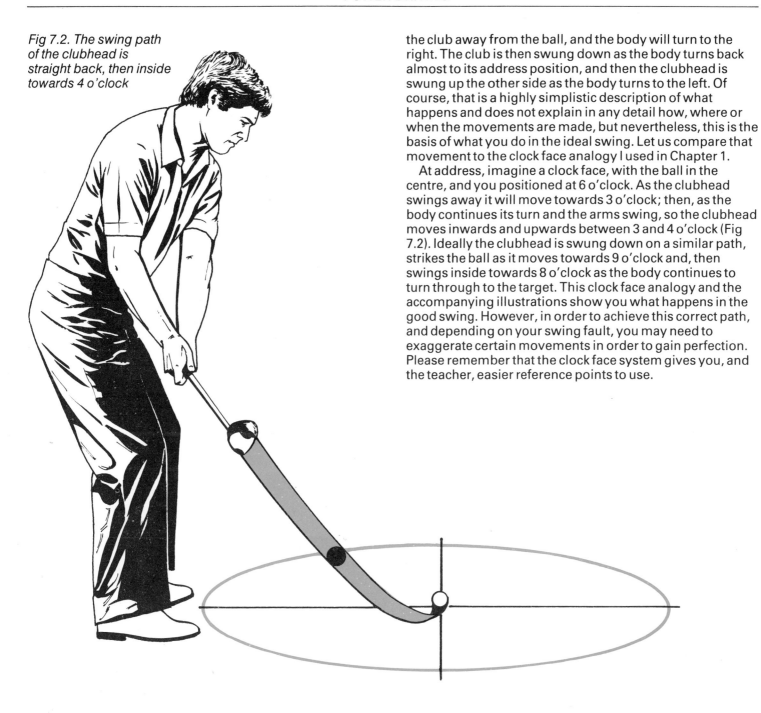

Fig 7.2. The swing path of the clubhead is straight back, then inside towards 4 o'clock

the club away from the ball, and the body will turn to the right. The club is then swung down as the body turns back almost to its address position, and then the clubhead is swung up the other side as the body turns to the left. Of course, that is a highly simplistic description of what happens and does not explain in any detail how, where or when the movements are made, but nevertheless, this is the basis of what you do in the ideal swing. Let us compare that movement to the clock face analogy I used in Chapter 1.

At address, imagine a clock face, with the ball in the centre, and you positioned at 6 o'clock. As the clubhead swings away it will move towards 3 o'clock; then, as the body continues its turn and the arms swing, so the clubhead moves inwards and upwards between 3 and 4 o'clock (Fig 7.2). Ideally the clubhead is swung down on a similar path, strikes the ball as it moves towards 9 o'clock and, then swings inside towards 8 o'clock as the body continues to turn through to the target. This clock face analogy and the accompanying illustrations show you what happens in the good swing. However, in order to achieve this correct path, and depending on your swing fault, you may need to exaggerate certain movements in order to gain perfection. Please remember that the clock face system gives you, and the teacher, easier reference points to use.

The correct way to start the backswing

So let us return to the address. As you stand there, your arms and shoulders form a triangle, with the left arm and shaft in a straight line (Fig 7.3a). As the backswing starts, you must keep that triangular relationship intact. You should feel that you are swinging the clubhead, left arm and shoulder away together, thus swinging that triangle to the right (Fig 7.3b). Since the pressure is applied with the last three fingers of the left hand, the muscles at the back of the left arm are brought into action as are those in the shoulder. Focus on your left side at this stage, and this will help to make sure that your body turns as your arms move, thus

Figs 7.3a. and 7.3b. By initiating the backswing with the left shoulder, arm and clubhead, you will maintain the triangle formed by the arms and shoulders at address

creating a unified start to the swing. If the right hand and arm are used too actively at this point, they tend to pick the club up too abruptly, short-circuiting most of the turn required in the swing. By swinging the clubhead away with the whole of the left side, from shoulder joint to clubhead, the triangle will remain intact, and the clubhead will stay close to the ground. To the good golfer, this is a natural movement; he probably feels that if he swings his arms, then his body will respond correctly. But the high-handicap golfer and the beginner have to concentrate on ensuring that arms and body move together, so what is a conscious action for them has become ingrained and natural for the better player.

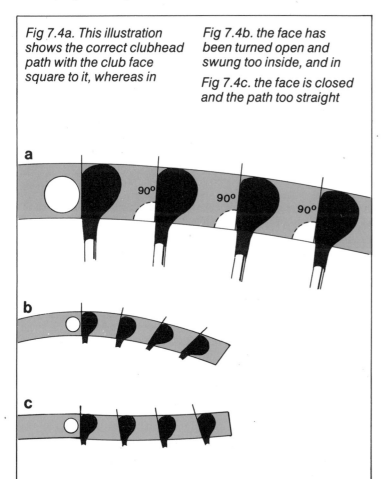

Fig 7.4a. This illustration shows the correct clubhead path with the club face square to it, whereas in

Fig 7.4b. the face has been turned open and swung too inside, and in

Fig 7.4c. the face is closed and the path too straight

a

b

c

The clubface

During these early stages of the backswing, there must be no manipulation of the clubhead by unwanted hand action. Indeed, the hands must feel passive at this stage, or the clubhead will be turned out of its correct path, and you will fail to achieve a shallow arc at the start of the swing. A good takeaway will see the club face remain square to the swing path, although in doing so (Fig 7.4a) it gradually starts to look right of the target. If the hands and arms turn too much to the right, the path becomes too inside, and the face rolls open (Fig 7.4b). If you interpret the takeaway as too much of a straight line, then the face may close (Fig 7.4c).

How wide should you swing the clubhead?

It is often said that width in the backswing is essential – and that is correct. However, do not imagine that if you stretch your arms away from your body as you start your backswing, that this will give you the desired width to your swing. In fact, this just puts another unwanted movement into the swing. The correct width is gained by turning your body as your arms swing. The player who fails to do this will find his body is in the way, and the arms will be forced into a steep and narrow upward swing. He may get away with this imperfection to some extent with the short irons, but not with the longer clubs, especially the driver. So to give your swing the correct width, a unified turn of the body and swing of the arms, without any undue stretching away by the arms, will provide the answer.

Leg action

Even at this early stage, the legs begin to play their part, with the left knee starting to point a little more behind the ball. Some additional pressure will be felt on the right leg, which must retain its original address position.

CHAPTER EIGHT

Checkpoints halfway back

As the swing continues from its correct start, by the time your hands reach hip height, there will be a number of points to check. Ideally, the toe of the club should point to the sky and the face should be at right angles to the horizon (Fig 8.1). Providing your grip is correct and you do not

Fig 8.2. Note that the triangular relationship of the hands and arms still exists; the toe of the club points to the sky, and added pressure is being felt by the right foot and leg

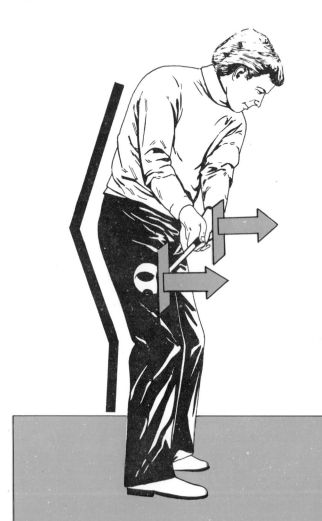

manipulate your hands independently, your arms will rotate slightly to the right, and the back of your left hand will face forwards. The wrists will start to cock because of the swinging weight of the clubhead, but the hands must not turn the club face open or closed. The triangle formation of the arms and shoulders should still be intact, and the right elbow will start to fold inwards and downwards. The right hip will begin to turn out of the way, the left knee will point more behind the ball, and there will be considerable pressure on the right knee and inside of the leg (Fig 8.2). While retaining the spinal angle set at address, the clubhead

Fig 8.1. The correct halfway back position shows that the club face is at right angles to the horizon, and the back of the left hand faces forward. The flex of the right knee and angle of the spine have remained unchanged

Fig 8.3. If the hands incorrectly roll the club face open, the club face points towards the sky, and the swing path will be too much on the inside

into an early upward movement, outside the desired swing path, leading to a chopping action which is exactly what you are trying to avoid. The triangular relationship of the arms and shoulders no longer exists, and therefore you have lost some of the required coordination in the swing.

The hands can work incorrectly either by turning the clubface open or closing it. If the face has been rolled open (Fig 8.3), then your hands and arms have rotated too much to the right in the backswing. Thus at hip height, the back of the left hand and clubface will not face forwards, but too much towards the sky, and the clubface will no longer be at right angles to the horizon, as in Fig. 8.1. The clubhead also will have been swung on too much of an inside path. There are two ways of getting the clubface closed on the backswing. If you keep the clubhead swinging back in a straight line for too long, the face becomes closed, as in Fig 7.4c. As the backswing progresses, the face must start to *look* open, i.e., right of the ball-to-target line, but is still square to the swing path (Fig 7.4a).

The second method of getting the club face closed is to make the backswing primarily with the right hand and arm (Fig 8.4). In this instance the club is swung inside very early,

will swing to the inside, and will be more or less in the 4 o'clock position. Remember that you are swinging around a fixed point at the base of your neck, so do not sway off the ball to the right.

If all these points are evident in the backswing, you should be able now to turn to face the club, lower the clubhead to the ground, and be back in the address position.

Positions to avoid

The two main things that can go wrong at this stage:
1 Failure to turn the body.
2 Incorrect hand action.
If these two factors are evident, either singly or combined, then you will be forced to build in compensating errors later in the swing in order to have any chance of a good and consistent strike.

Firstly, let us consider what happens when the body does not turn sufficiently. In this instance, the arms will be forced

Fig 8.4. An overactive right hand and arm have swung the club too much to the inside and have rotated anti-clockwise shutting the club face

and the wrists and arms rotate anti-clockwise. The back of the left hand becomes very *convex*, and the arms soon grind to a halt as they jam up against the right side of the body.

The correct wrist action

Perhaps the easiest way to understand how the wrists work in the swing is to perform the following exercise:
1 With your driver, stand in your address position.
2 Without moving your arms, raise the clubhead off the ground, simply by cocking your wrists straight up in front of

you. Stop when the shaft is just higher than parallel to the ground (Fig 8.5a).

3 As you do so, note that the leading edge of the club does not change its angle.
This is the position the wrists should be in at about hip height. If the clubface has turned open or closed, check that your grip is not too weak nor too strong. Having carried out actions 1–3 as outlined above, turn your feet and legs 90 degrees to your left, leaving your arms and body where they were, and you will be in the correct halfway back position (Fig 8.5b).

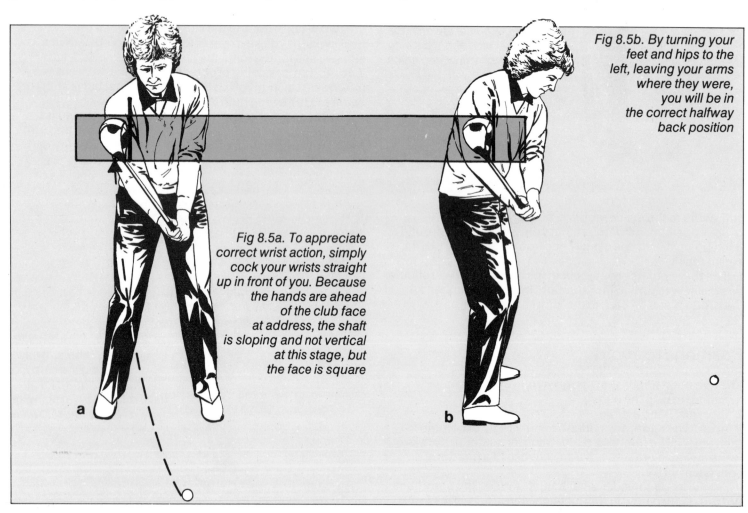

Fig 8.5b. By turning your feet and hips to the left, leaving your arms where they were, you will be in the correct halfway back position

Fig 8.5a. To appreciate correct wrist action, simply cock your wrists straight up in front of you. Because the hands are ahead of the club face at address, the shaft is sloping and not vertical at this stage, but the face is square

a

b

CHAPTER NINE

The best backswing position

Before I examine in detail how you should look at the end of the backswing, I want to emphasise again why teachers place such importance on this point in the swing. Go for any golf lesson and the professional will first check your set up, and then will be most interested not only in the whole swing but also in the position you achieve at the top. This is the launch pad for what is to come, and if you are in a good position, then the downswing movement will become a more natural reaction. If you are way out of position at the top, you will have to make compensating errors along the way if you are to have any chance whatsoever of hitting the ball consistently.

I believe that to play golf well:

1 The better the address and set up you have, the better the backswing you will achieve.

2 The better the backswing you make, the better the downswing you will achieve.

3 The better the downswing you make, the better the strike you will achieve.

The classic position

Ideally at the top of the swing, the club shaft will be virtually parallel to the target line, and also about parallel to the ground. The club face will still be in the square position. So that tells you where the club is, but how should your body have moved to attain that position? From the correct hip height checkpoint, the shoulders *continue* turning, and the arms, dominated by the left arm, continue swinging, until the shoulders are turned approximately 90 degrees, with the hips about 45 degrees. The left shoulder will now be virtually above the right knee, which should retain about the same amount of flex as at address. Most of your weight will be resting on the right leg, with more weight directed towards the heel, but still nearer to the inside than the outside of the foot. There is, at this stage, a lot of downward pressure felt in the right leg. To facilitate this turning, the left heel may be allowed to rise slightly off the ground, but only as a last movement. The left arm, despite what is often quoted, is *not* straight, but neither is it bent into an 'L' shape. Instead it should be *slightly* bowed to prevent any unwanted tension developing. You will also notice from Fig 9.1 that the head has rotated to the right to allow a good shoulder turn, but the fixed point of the swing, near the base of the neck and top of the spine, has remained steady.

The plane of the swing

The plane of the swing is the angle at which it is inclined, and this is predetermined at address, mainly by your

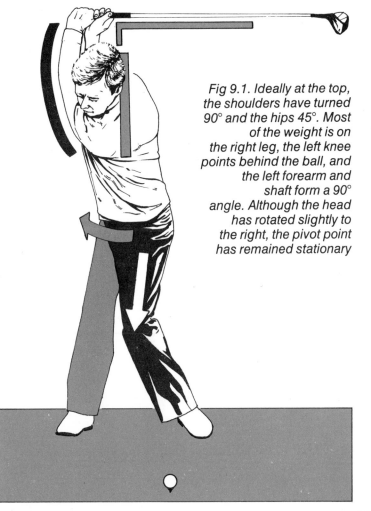

Fig 9.1. Ideally at the top, the shoulders have turned 90° and the hips 45°. Most of the weight is on the right leg, the left knee points behind the ball, and the left forearm and shaft form a 90° angle. Although the head has rotated slightly to the right, the pivot point has remained stationary

Fig 9.2. The spinal angle has been retained, the back of the left hand and forearm, and the club face are in line at right angles to the plane

2 Turn your shoulders at right angles to your spine. If you stand upright and turn first to your right and then to your left, your shoulders should turn at right angles to your spine. This action is duplicated in the golf swing, with the exception that the spine is angled forward.
3 Allow your wrists to cock square to the plane as described in previous chapters.
4 Keep your elbows the same width apart throughout the backswing. If your right elbow rises too high, or gets too close to your right side, the plane will be affected.

However, as a general guideline, if you can swing your left arm into the gap between your right shoulder and your head, your swing plane will not be too far out (Fig 9.2). A short person will naturally swing his or her arms on a slightly lower plane than a tall person, so match your arm swing to your posture and build.

The hands

From the hip height position, the left wrist continues to cock upwards, (in the same direction as in Fig 8.5). Thus, at the top, it forms a 90 degree angle between the shaft and inside of the forearm. The left thumb is underneath the shaft, providing most of the support, and maximum pressure is felt in the last three fingers, which should remain firmly on the grip. The right wrist tends to be hinged back on itself, so that the palm faces half skywards. You will notice from Fig 9.2, that the back of the left hand, the forearm and clubface are in line with each other, i.e. in the same plane. If the hands had worked incorrectly, they would have turned the club face out of this good square position, which would have meant counteracting it on the downswing. That method of playing golf leads to inconsistency, since the whole swing relies too much on the small unpredictable muscles in the hands. Therefore, provided that you have a fairly neutral grip, as described earlier in the book, the clubface will be at right angles to the swing plane.

Fig 9.3a highlights how the correct clubface and wrist position should look. If the clubface is nearer right angles to the horizon (Fig 9.3b), it is open to the swing plane, and the left wrists will be excessively cupped. Fig 9.3c shows the clubface pointing towards the sky, which means it is closed to the swing plane, resulting in the back of the left wrists being convex. Whilst the wrist position in Fig 9.3a is the

posture and distance from the ball. The correct plane is found at address by extending an imaginary line upwards from the ball across the top of the shoulders. At the completion of the backswing, the left arm should lie along this line. Naturally, we cannot all afford the luxury of taking video film or photographs of our swings to check this aspect, but if you adhere to the following principles, then your plane should be acceptable:

1 Having set the spinal angle at address, do not change it – if you do, you will change the plane.

ideal one to achieve, it is possible, although more difficult, to play from the open position as in Fig 9.3b but more independent hand action is needed to square the club, and thus your timing has to be spot on. If you get into the closed position (Fig 9.3c), you will not be able to release the clubhead at maximum speed, thus losing distance, and you may also hook the ball violently. In the correct position, the right elbow will point to the ground. In fact, the elbows, throughout the swing, stay approximately the same width apart as at address.

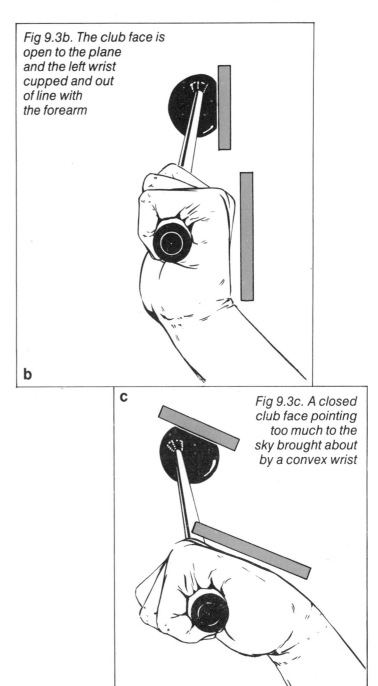

Fig 9.3b. The club face is open to the plane and the left wrist cupped and out of line with the forearm

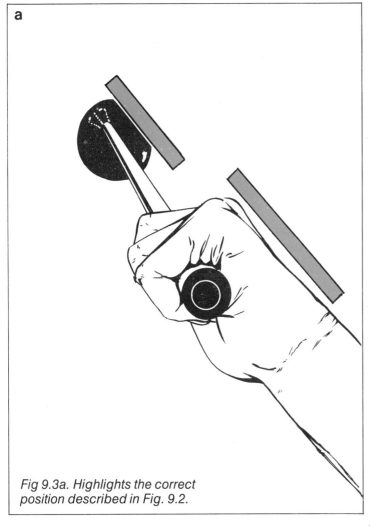

Fig 9.3a. Highlights the correct position described in Fig. 9.2.

Fig 9.3c. A closed club face pointing too much to the sky brought about by a convex wrist

Fig 9.4. Insufficient shoulder turn results in the shaft aimed left of the target, left knee pointing ahead of the ball, and a bent left arm. A weak position – not designed for a powerful drive

If you swing the clubhead too much inside at the start of the swing, i.e. directly towards 4 o'clock right from the start, then you will probably cross the line. By allowing your wrists to collapse at the top of the swing (Fig 9.3b), you will get the same result. If the shaft points left of target at the top, it could be due to taking the clubhead away more towards 2 o'clock at the start, or lack of shoulder turn (Fig 9.4).

Head still

'Keep your head still' is one of golf's favourite sayings, but it is very misleading and misunderstood. The golf club is swung around a fixed point at the top of the spine, so it is quite in order for the head to rotate to the right on the backswing, or even move to the right a *little* when driving. If you strain to keep it anchored to the spot, it may prevent the necessary weight transfer to the right side during the backswing. Thus too much weight is retained on the left side, which during the downswing will then go to the right. This is totally the reverse of what you are trying to achieve, and is called a reverse weight shift. Avoid it!

Also retain your head height, which is often lowered if a player dips the left shoulder, or raised if the same shoulder is lifted during the backswing. Swinging the arms too high can also raise the height of the head. So set your head height and maintain it.

Summary

The most important check points at the top of the backswing are as follows:
► shoulders turned approximately 90 degrees;
► hips turned approximately 45 degrees;
► majority of weight, about 80 per cent, on the right leg;
► weight retained more towards the inside and heel of the right foot;
► right knee still flexed;
► left heel just off the ground;
► arms swung into the slot between your right shoulder and head;
► left arm just slightly bowed, not straight or bent;
► back of the left hand, forearm and blade in line;
► shaft parallel to the target line;
► shaft virtually horizontal.

The line of the shaft

The shaft should be parallel to the target line and, by and large, with most top players this is true. However, since they are often trying for additional length with the driver, due to a *greater shoulder turn* the shaft may point *slightly* right of parallel. This is acceptable, but you should not confuse their method of crossing the line with other ways of reaching the same position.

CHAPTER TEN

The downswing

During the backswing you are creating power that is used to strike the ball. However, to maximize this power, you must endeavour to swing the different parts of your body in the correct sequence in the downswing. In the backswing, your upper body and arms move before the lower half, with the left heel probably being the last part to move. This ensures that you attain a stretched feeling in your left arm and shoulder, and in the muscles down the left side of your back. You also allow the swinging weight of the club head to cock your wrists into a 90 degree angle with the left forearm creating leverage, which again is a source of power. So to swing the clubhead into the back of the ball at maximum speed, having created the power, you must store it and then use it. The best way to do this is to move your body sequentially in the right order.

The correct sequence

You could ask ten top golfers how they feel they start their downswing, and you would possibly get ten different answers. Although photography and high-speed film may well indicate that the left heel is the first part that moves, the player may not be focusing on that as his particular key to get the downswing under way. Indeed, even the top players change their ideas about how to initiate their downswing, but generally the onlooker would do well to spot any changes. Often the player may be more conscious about what a specific part of the body does at this moment in time. What happens is as follows:

▶ the left heel returns to the ground, and as it does so, the leg and hip move laterally left, transferring the weight to the left side;

▶ at the same time the left arm pulls downwards into the space created on the backswing by the right side of the body turning out of the way;

▶ the angle between the left forearm and wrist is retained in this early part of the swing, so that this power source can be used later to strike the ball (Fig 10.1).

However, problems often arise because from the top of the backswing, it is the right shoulder area that feels the more powerful, and consequently many players use that part of their body to initiate the downswing. This results in throwing the clubhead onto an unwanted outside path, from the 2 o'clock direction. You must appreciate that speed on the downswing is best provided by the arms, and then the hands, and to maximize the speed available from these two sources, the legs move in tandem with the arms, preserving that stretched feeling created in the backswing. Swing the arms correctly, and the body will follow.

Personally, I like to change direction, by moving my *left knee* towards the target, and at the *same time* I pull *down* with my *left arm,* feeling that the last three fingers of this hand are doing most of the work. This gives me a smooth change of direction, where my left hip moves laterally, my weight starts to move back to the left, and my lower and upper body move in a co-ordinated manner. It automatically enables me to retain the angle between my left forearm and the shaft, and it also keeps the club head

Fig 10.1. By pulling down with the left arm and moving the left knee towards the target, your weight moves onto the left side and you will retain the important angle of the wrists

Fig 10.2. By swinging your arms into the space created by turning the right side out of the way in the backswing, you will swing the club on the correct inside path

(Fig 10.3). Whilst the backswing and change of direction are made very much with the left arm in control, the left and right hands and arms must accelerate the clubhead into the ball to get maximum speed. This is best achieved by making sure that you swing *through* the ball and not at it. So many golfers lack clubhead speed simply because they do not concentrate on swinging through the shot, and at impact the clubhead is slowing down. So as you approach impact your arms will rotate to the left, and your hands will uncock provided that you allow a free-wheeling action of the clubhead through the ball. This happens quite naturally for the better player, who allows the centrifugal force of the swing to unleash the leverage, i.e. power created between the hands and arms in the backswing. The beginner and high-handicap golfer may consciously have to think of their right hand and arm rotating towards the left, i.e. anti-clockwise, through impact, in order to square the club face (Fig 10.4).

However, the back of the left hand must not fold back on itself (Fig 10.5). It should be as it was at address, i.e. in line with the forearm, and the rotation should take place from elbow to hand.

While the arms are swinging, the legs are providing support, so that by impact you should be pushing off the instep and ball of the right foot and the heel will be starting to leave the ground. Most of the weight will be felt towards the outside of the left foot. The head and fixed point at the top of the spine, are still very steady, with the eyes focused on the back of the ball. The original spinal angle is still the same (Fig 10.2) and will continue to be so well into the follow-through. You set up with a triangular relationship between the arms and shoulders, and at impact you achieve almost exactly the same arrangement.

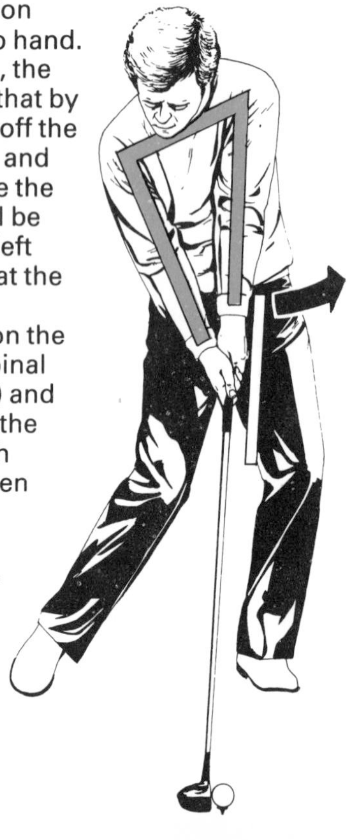

Fig 10.3. Impact is almost a mirror image of address. The left wrist has not buckled under the power of the right side

swinging on an inside path from the 4 o'clock direction (Fig 10.2).

You may see strong men golfers employing fairly exaggerated leg action at the start of their downswing, but they match this with equally as strong hand and arm action. Do not think that by copying them you will achieve similar results. You must match leg, arm and hand action to your own particular strength. The best advice for the majority of golfers is to swing their arms down at the same time as they move their legs.

Impact zone

As the downswing progresses, the hips continue to turn back to the left, so that by impact they are slightly open, i.e. facing left of target and left of their original address position. The forearms start to rotate to the left, the right arm begins to straighten and the angle between the shaft and forearm will widen, until at impact the arms have returned back to the ball virtually as they were at address

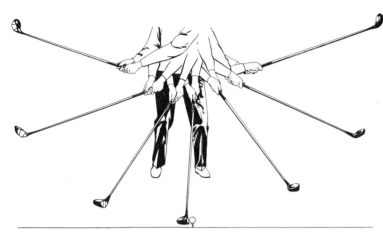

Fig 10.4. This highlights how the hands and forearms rotate anti-clockwise as they approach impact, by which time the angle between arm and shaft has straightened

The extra few yards

I think it only right to add at this point that the top-class player often chooses to draw the ball, i.e. move it from right to left for extra distance. In this instance the clubhead would be travelling more in the 4 to 10 o'clock direction, but with the club face square to the target. To draw the ball in a controlled manner, the player must have well trained hand action, and be able to swing the club on the required path. As your game develops, you can start to consider drawing the ball, but this will be when you can *consistently* swing the club down on the correct inside path, and release the clubhead at impact. Until such time as this is evident in your game, your aim should be to hit the ball consistently out of the middle of the club face, as straight as possible, at *your* maximum speed. Strive to hit it better, and you will hit it further.

The follow through

The follow through is very much a result of what has gone before in the swing, and to the trained professional eye can indicate what has happened to the shot. You will seldom see top-class players finish off balance, but go to any local club and you will notice many golfers finishing in the most bizarre fashion, totally out of control.

As the clubhead accelerates through impact, the left side, i.e. hips and body, turn out of the way to allow the hands and arms to swing through and square the club face. The right arm straightens soon after impact, and the left elbow begins to fold downwards, much as the right elbow did on the backswing. By the time the hands have reached hip height, they will be starting to cock upwards again, the back of the right hand will be facing forwards, and the toe of the club will be in the air. Whilst you may not be able to feel this happening at full pace, it is worth checking it in slow motion, and you will find that it mirrors the hip height position on the backswing. The right side of the body is pulled through so that the triangle of the arms and shoulders remains intact (Fig 10.6). Many players retard the swing by stopping the body at this point, but you should finish with your stomach either facing the target, or just to the left of it.

While the body turns, you should have the feeling of swinging your arms towards the target, in the direction of 9 o'clock. The clubhead will in fact swing back inside towards 8 o'clock because the body is turning. The same spinal angle set at address is retained, but the head starts

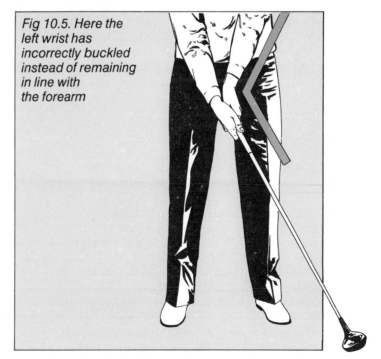

Fig 10.5. Here the left wrist has incorrectly buckled instead of remaining in line with the forearm

Fig 10.6. This halfway through position sees the toe of the club in the air and the back of the right hand facing forward, almost the reverse position to halfway back (see Fig 8.2.)

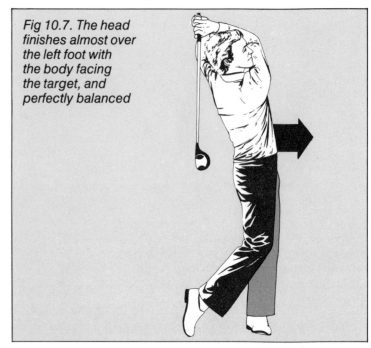

Fig 10.7. The head finishes almost over the left foot with the body facing the target, and perfectly balanced

to *rotate* towards the target in order not to inhibit the follow through. As the swing finishes your arms will be in the slot between your head and left shoulder, body facing the target or left of it, most of your weight on the outside of your left foot, with the right toes being the only part of that foot in contact with the ground. You must also allow the head to move towards the target a little, so that it finishes above the left foot, with the back fairly straight (Fig 10.7) and not arched in a reverse 'C' position.

Many players deny themselves a full follow through simply because they do not release the right heel off the ground. If they felt that at impact the right knee tried to touch the left knee, they would get better leg action through the shot, and would then finish correctly.

While the spinal angle is maintained until after impact, it is permissible to allow it to rise slightly at the completion of the swing. It is also *essential* that you allow your head to rotate to face the target, and this is when you should ignore the saying: 'Keep your head still'. You must keep it steady until and just after impact, at which point it must start to rotate on the original spinal axis towards the target. At the completion of the follow through, it should be turned fully to face the target.

Why the follow through is important

Many players find it hard to understand why the follow through is so important. As I have already said, it results from what has gone before the swing, and helps to guarantee that you accelerate through the ball. The player who becomes too ball-orientated decelerates into the shot, does not achieve maximum distance, and each swing finishes differently. This sloppy action tends to eat its way back into the swing until such time that consistent striking is a thing of the past. However, ask someone to hit the ball and hold his or her finish, and the player will swing further through the shot than before. In fact, having taught my pupils what I consider to be a decent backswing, I ask them to swing through to the finish and hold that position. By doing this, they think of swinging the club with their arms, and their hips and legs have to work more or less correctly to get them to the finish. As a professional tournament player, I prefer to leave complicated thoughts on the practice ground, and have often found that by thinking of swinging to a balanced finish, I have played my best golf.

CHAPTER ELEVEN

Timing and tempo

Once you have developed a swing that more often than not gets the clubhead swinging down the correct 4–9 o'clock track, it will be the timing and tempo of the swing that will improve your distance.

Timing is the relationship of the movements between each part of the body or, in other words, the sequence in which the various parts move.

Tempo is the pace at which the above happens.

These two aspects of the swing are inter-related, and the player who discovers his or her correct tempo will find that timing of the swing will improve, and with it the quality of strike.

Timing

The problem you face in golf is that you are using different sets of muscles that work most efficiently at different paces. During the backswing, many beginners feel that if they swing their arms back and up quickly, then they will be able to do the same on the downswing and thus hit the ball a long way. What they fail to consider or understand is that in order to hit the ball as far as possible, they must give the swing the correct width and direction, and that comes from turning the body. However, the large muscles in the body (mainly those in the back) move slowly, whilst those in the hands and arms move fast. The compromise is to adopt a backswing pace, whereby you give the large back muscles time to turn. This inevitably means slowing down the pace of the arm swing and thinking about turning the body.

The same problem is experienced on the downswing. When you want to move the lower half, i.e. the legs, at the same time as, or a little before, the arms swing down. The large muscles in the thighs again move more slowly than those in the hands and arms, and therefore must be given time to contribute to the swing. Unfortunately, all too often, from the top of the swing the player cannot wait to 'have a go' at the ball, and throws the clubhead onto an out-to-in, i.e. 2 to 8 o'clock, path with the hands and shoulders before any other part of the anatomy has a

Fig 11.1. Rushing the swing from the top throws the club head on to a steep out-to-in path, resulting in a pull, slice, hook, topped or skied shot

chance to respond (Fig 11.1). Whereas from the top of the backswing you want to accelerate the clubhead into the back of the ball, you must never hurry the swing at this crucial 'change of direction' stage. I always want to start the downswing at the same pace I finished the backswing, and then allow myself to accelerate the clubhead through to the finish position. In this way, I give my legs time to get the downswing under way in partnership with my arms.

The other essential timing factor involves the release of the hands. Ladies, due to possessing less innate strength than men, tend to be more guilty of throwing the clubhead with their hands from the top of the swing, thus widening that angle between the shaft and forearm too early (Fig 11.2). Before I explain how you should use your arms and hands to their greatest benefit, I must stress that I am *not* talking about hitting *late*, but about hitting at the *right* time, so that the clubhead is travelling at maximum speed at impact. During the backswing, you create power by turning your body, swinging the arms and allowing your wrists to cock under the swinging weight of the clubhead. If you start the downswing by *pulling* smoothly with the left arm

Fig 11.2. By using the hands too early, the angle between the shaft and forearms is widened, preventing this power source being used to hit the ball. The weight also remains, quite incorrectly, on the right leg

at the same time as you move the left knee towards the target, then you will retain that angle between shaft and forearm, and will be able to use that power later in the swing (Fig 10.1). By the time you strike the ball, the wrists will have fully uncocked into much the same position as at address. The problem usually results from a player thinking mainly of the hands, and not the arms swinging down.

Change direction more slowly and think of the arms swinging. Provided that you do not grip too *tightly*, the swinging weight of the clubhead will help to uncock the wrists. Beginners may have to consciously feel that the right hand and arm rotate to the left through impact, expecially if their shots are slicing. However, players who hook the ball too much usually need to speed up their leg action and check their grip.

Perfect timing is achieved on the downswing when you have co-ordinated the lower body unwinding, with:
► a free and uninhibited arm swing, leading to
► partial rotation to the left of the forearms, combined with
► the wrists uncocking, resulting in
► the clubhead swinging towards the target with a square club face at impact.

Although this may sound complicated, it will start to happen naturally once you have a reasonable idea and a picture in your mind of what should happen during the swing. Remember that in the golf swing, you create power, save power and then use power.

Tempo

You probably now realise how tempo and timing are inter-related, but sadly tempo is a much neglected part of the game. The average male beginner thinks that the faster he swings, the better the shot will be. The average female beginner tends to let herself down, not so much by swinging too fast overall because she does not have the strength, but by lacking co-ordination and timing in the downswing, and so the overall tempo is uneven.

Watch the top-class players and their swings appear to be very smooth. Some may swing faster than others, and it is always easy to appreciate the smoothness of the slower swingers, but each has found the best tempo for his or her own particular swing and stature. One way of finding your best tempo is to hit say twenty 6 irons at your usual pace, and note their average distance and spread. Then hit twenty more shots at a faster tempo, and see how these compare not only in length but also in accuracy with the original twenty. Repeat this exercise using a slower than normal pace, and again note the length and accuracy. You should be able to assess your best pace for maximum distance and accuracy. I generally tell more people to slow down rather than speed up their swing, but sometimes women have benefited by speeding up their backswing a little. This advice applies only to the woman who takes the club away so slowly that she builds no momentum or rhythm into her swing and then just lurches at the ball with the top half of her body.

I want to highlight an instance that is familiar to most golfers. On the course, you are faced with a shot from the fairway that requires your best strike with a 3 wood to carry a bunker or ditch. You decide to lay up with an iron and make a smooth, leisurely swing that sends the ball into the distance like a rocket, sometimes landing in the hazard. In that swing, your tempo and timing were perfectly matched, and yet you probably felt that you did nothing. Try using this scenario to encourage and promote good rhythm, timing and tempo.

CHAPTER TWELVE

The feel of the swing

It is difficult to be precise about how your swing should feel. Whereas 20 pupils may all be executing the same movement, each may feel the movement in a different way. I want to highlight some advice that I have found useful both as a teacher and as a professional tournament player.

1 At address, try to make your upper body as relaxed as possible, although your legs should feel a little more lively. One good way to encourage as relaxed an attitude as possible is to have a set pre-shot routine. This should start by standing behind the ball and finding your intermediate target. Address the ball and then if you usually look at the target twice, keep to that routine whatever the situation. You might like to incorporate a few waggles of the clubhead, as this action serves two purposes: it stops the muscles from getting tense; and it also programmes the initial move of the clubhead. Many players also build in some sort of trigger movement so that the swing does not start from a stationary position. Some forward press their hands, others move the right knee slightly towards the target, or maybe rotate the head a little to the right. It does not really matter what you do, but if it helps you make a smooth takeaway, then develop a trigger action. You will also find that it helps to take a deep breath and then exhale prior to making your swing.

2 The art of golf is *swinging* the golf club in a controlled manner. If you lose that control, you will also lose the opportunity of making consistently powerful golf shots. If your backswing is too fast, thereby ruining your control of the club, then you should feel that in the backswing, you are positioning the club at the top. In this way, you will become more aware of where the backswing ends and the downswing begins, and you will consequently swing in a slower and more controlled manner.

3 Make the start of the swing smooth, and it is more likely to be smooth throughout. Jerk the club away from the ball, and you will never achieve the smooth powerful swing that is necessary for long drives. It is well known that players like Jack Nicklaus and Sam Torrance hold the club just above the ground at address, as this helps them to start the backswing smoothly – give it a try.

4 As the downswing progresses, feel that your arms swing close to your right hip, and away from your left hip. This helps to encourage the correct inside swing path.

5 In golf we are trying to propel an object forward in much the same way as a javelin or a discus thrower. In each pursuit, the weight moves to the back foot as the arm is taken back and then transfers to the front foot, and the arm throws the object forwards. Golfers are often too timid to make a decent weight transference to the right side on the backswing, as they fear moving the head. What happens instead is that they do not move any weight at all and consequently hit weak shots. If you want powerful drives, then you must feel a good weight transference without getting over-concerned about slight head movement, provided that you swing round that fixed point. Pick up a stone, throw it over-arm and just note where your weight moves and where your head finishes. Now I am not saying that there is anywhere near as much movement of the head and body in the golf swing, but you must feel your weight move to the back foot, even if your head moves a *little* – it will probably rotate, rather than move, to the right. Then as you finish the swing, allow your weight to shift forwards so that your head finishes over your left foot.

6 As I have said, the change of direction from back to downswing is one of the most crucial parts of the swing, and one that is usually rushed. To help in this area, imagine a roller coaster ride as it climbs the steep track. By the time it reaches the top it has almost come to a standstill. When it moves over the summit, it starts to descend the other side quite slowly, but gradually increases in speed until, at the bottom of the slope, it is travelling at full speed. The golf swing should be considered in the same way. Then you will have the power when it matters – at impact (Fig 12.1).

7 In an effort to get distance, many golfers move themselves laterally too far to the left, and by impact are ahead of the ball. The result is often a skied shot or loss of power because they cannot release the clubhead sufficiently. From the top of the swing, try to imagine that you are hitting the ball *away* from yourself. The fixed point at the top of your spine and base of your neck will be more likely to remain still, and you will get maximum clubhead acceleration.

THE FEEL OF THE SWING

8 I have used the clock face as a guide to the clubhead path. You may need to tailor the 'hours' that I have used to suit your swing. In the ideal swing the club approaches the ball from between 3.30 and 4 o'clock, and moves towards 9, but since more golfers hit from out-to-in, i.e. in a 2 to 8 o'clock direction, I find that most people get the club on a better track by *feeling* that they are swinging from either 4 to 9, or even from 4 to 10. If you still start the ball left and slice it back onto the fairway, you are losing distance, so

you may need to *feel* that you are swinging from 5 to 10 o'clock, ensuring that your grip is sufficiently strong, i.e. hands positioned far enough to the right on the grip, and that your arms and hands work through impact as described in Chapter 10. If you swing too much from in-to-out, then use the reverse procedure. The beauty of this clock face analogy is that you can adapt it specifically to suit your needs.

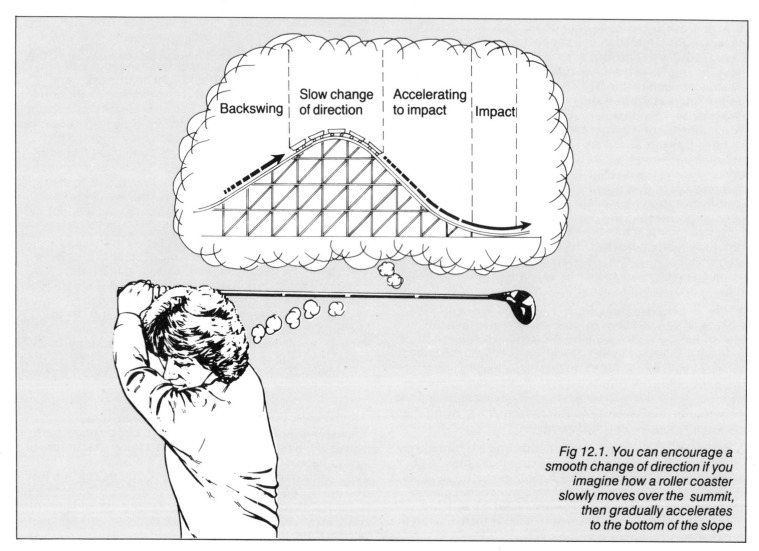

Fig 12.1. You can encourage a smooth change of direction if you imagine how a roller coaster slowly moves over the summit, then gradually accelerates to the bottom of the slope

CHAPTER THIRTEEN

Exercises for power

To develop your golfing muscles need not take hours each day, but if you can regularly devote just 15 minutes a day to this, then you will soon see improvements. Here are some exercises that will help to create a powerful swing.

Exercises to develop strength

1 Place a club behind your back and under your arms, and bend forwards from the hips as at address. Rotate to the right and left so that the back muscles are exercised, making a good turn easier.
2 Attach a light weight – maybe 2lbs initially – to the end of a rope attached to a piece of broom handle or something similar. Sit, with your elbows resting on your thighs, or over the back of a chair, and wind the weight up and down. This is a marvellous exercise for strengthening your forearms and hands.
3 Sit with your elbows and forearms resting on your thighs and a weight in each hand. Raise the weights up and down keeping your elbows and forearms still. Do this with your hands above and below the weights. Again, this is good for the forearm muscles.
4 Skipping is a good way to improve your hand and leg speed and will also develop your oxygen intake. However, this should be carried out only by those whose doctors would approve!
5 To improve the strength of your thigh muscles, stand with your feet apart and hands by your sides. Bend your knees, lowering yourself to the ground. Keep your weight on your toes, and your back as straight as possible. Stronger leg muscles will mean you will not tire so much towards the end of a round, and will add power to your swing more effortlessly.
6 To develop your left side, which is usually less powerful than the right, grip down the shaft of a 5 iron with just your left hand, and practise half swings. Ladies may need to support the left arm by placing the right hand, thumb uppermost, on the forearm. You must make sure that you swing as correctly as possible, so that you are ingraining the correct muscle messages. So check that halfway back the toe of the club is in the air, and the back of the left hand faces forward. Similarly, check the finish. In addition to strengthening your muscles, the feeling of how your left hand works through impact will be heightened. You can expand on this exercise until you feel able to make a full swing; then grip at the end of the club and do it.
7 To develop all parts of the body gently, swing a weighted club, perhaps an old wood that has either had lead added inside the head (your professional will do this for you), or lead tape or something similar stuck onto the outside of the head.
8 Swinging an iron through rough is also a good exercise for strengthening hands and arms.
9 Simply by hitting golf balls each day, you will be exercising the right muscles.

A word of warning

Do not try to do too much too soon. Start with light weights, and low repetitions. Keep a note of what you have done, and gradually build up. You will injure yourself in some way if you overdo it, and you may have to rest until the injury heals.

Exercises for technique

1 To improve hand action, using a 7 iron, make a backswing where your arms move no higher than your waist, but your wrists are almost fully cocked. Now strike the ball, creating as much clubhead speed as possible. To do this your hands have to work hard, with the right hand and forearm crossing over the left. In the backswing the end of the grip should point at the ball, and to where it was in the abbreviated follow through.
2 Insert a row of tee pegs in the ground just outside the correct backswing and downswing path, and just beyond where the ball would lie. Then practise swinging, trying not to hit the pegs. Do this without a ball and later with one.
3 Make 10 swings without the ball, concentrating on holding a balanced finish position. Then hit five shots doing exactly the same thing, and try not to let the ball inhibit you. Hold the finish to the count of five. This will develop your balance and leg action.
4 Hit twenty 6 irons, concentrating on your rhythm, and then hit 10 drives without letting the urge to 'have a go' ruin that rhythm. This will help you to appreciate that you do not have to throw everything at the ball to hit a drive a long way, but you must maintain your rhythm and balance.

CHAPTER ONE

Putting—so easy yet so hard

I can remember that during one family holiday, we went to the putting green on the seafront and proceeded to have a competition. I had been playing golf for some three or four years, and had a fairly good idea of what I was supposed to be doing. But did I win? Beaten by non-golfers, I don't think I even came a poor third. I was so overcome by the inadequate conditions and equipment with which I was playing that I completely forgot what I was trying to achieve.

So what are you aiming to achieve when you are putting? Ideally, you are setting the ball rolling on a predetermined line, which will result in the ball going in the hole. Obviously, there are times when you know that you will be lucky just to get the ball near to the hole, but even then, you must concentrate on making the best stroke possible. In my seafront disaster, I took one look at the surface of the putting green, and the putter in my hand, decided that there was no way to ever get the ball near the hole, and then proceeded to confirm my negative ideas by putting appallingly. I had lived up to my own expectations of what I thought was or was not possible, and in that one instance learnt that confidence was so important.

Of course, confidence is always essential in golf, but when it comes to putting—the simplest of movements that even the rawest beginner can develop a halfway decent putting stroke very quickly—is of the utmost importance if you are to capitalize on your ability.

I have given many putting clinics during golf tuition weeks, and I know that most pupils feel that their time would be better spent on perfecting their driving skills. However, they often come back to me later in the week having played under their handicap, simply because, for the first time in their lives, they had a good idea of what they were trying to do on the putting green, and had therefore eliminated three and four putting to a large degree.

Nothing is more galling than to outplay an opponent from tee to green, only to see him or her, time and again, slot the most impossible of putts. You may regard this as an injustice, and so often your frustration at being beaten by a superior putter, rather than a superior golfer, detracts from your concentration on the game, and thus you go from bad to worse.

Since there is so little movement involved in a putt, we are quite capable of incorporating unwanted adjustments at any time throughout the stroke. Unlike the full swing, in which, once you have started the downswing, the sheer momentum takes over to a great extent, in a putt you have little momentum and consequently can turn the putter blade out of line quite easily.

Good putters only see and feel positive things, and on good days they know that they will hole many putts. However, confidence alone will not overcome poor technique, so first you must learn the correct basic fundamentals, such as grip and set up, before you even consider the stroke.

CHAPTER TWO

The grip

I have seen a wide range of weird and wonderful ways of gripping the putter, which seem to work for their owners, but as a teacher I would never recommend them to anyone. Today's best putters all tend to grip the club in a similar fashion, which has evolved over the years, so among professionals you are less likely to see many grips that vary significantly from the norm.

When putting, try to place your hands on the grip so that the palm of the right, and back of the left are parallel to the club face. This enables you to relate very easily to the position of the club face during the stroke and, more importantly, at impact. With your hands in this position, both thumbs will sit on top of the grip. Incidentally, I would recommend that you have a putter grip on the club, rather than just an ordinary golf grip. The putter grip has a flattened front, which assists considerably in obtaining the correct grip every time, and also helps to line up the club

face squarely. I believe that the most successful way to putt is with firm, passive wrists, especially through the impact zone, and one of the best ways to ensure this is to adopt the reverse overlap grip. This is where the left forefinger is taken off the grip, and allowed to overlap the fingers of the right hand. The normal overlap and interlocking grips that most people use for hitting other shots fail to give the additional firmness at the back of the left wrist that the reverse overlap grip provides. So to adopt the correct grip you should do the following:

1 Stand with the putter face square to the target, palms either side of the grip and parallel to the club face, with the thumbs at the front of the grip (Fig 2.1a).
2 Grip the putter with both hands completely on the grip, i.e. ten fingers, then remove the left forefinger from the grip (Fig 2.1b).

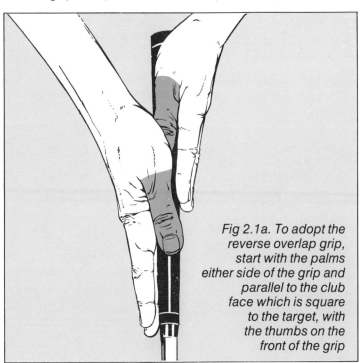

Fig 2.1a. To adopt the reverse overlap grip, start with the palms either side of the grip and parallel to the club face which is square to the target, with the thumbs on the front of the grip

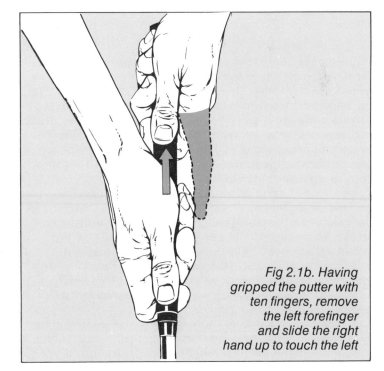

Fig 2.1b. Having gripped the putter with ten fingers, remove the left forefinger and slide the right hand up to touch the left

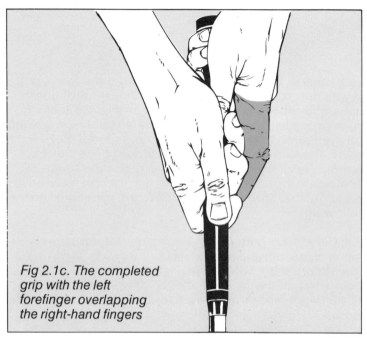

Fig 2.1c. The completed grip with the left forefinger overlapping the right-hand fingers

3 Slide the right hand up to butt against the left, then place the left forefinger over the fingers of the right hand (Fig 2.1c).

You should find that the grip of the putter passes more through the middle of the left palm, than it does when gripping other clubs. This is because you stand further over the ball than for any other shot, and therefore grip the club in a more upright manner. I have changed many golfers' grips to the reverse overlap, which may feel strange initially, but like any other aspect of golf, if you practise it, even for five or ten minutes before you go out to play, it will soon become comfortable and automatic.

This is the putting grip that I and many hundreds of professional golfers use, and it helps to ensure that the back of the left wrist does not collapse inwards through the stroke. Some professionals use adaptations of this grip — you may have seen Seve Ballesteros placing his right forefinger slightly down the shaft, whereas Nancy Lopez places hers completely down the right side. This has the effect of firming up the right wrist, and you may find it helpful.

In order to create even more firmness and control in the left hand and wrist, some golfers place their hands on the grip, with the left below the right (Fig 2.2). Try it, and you

will instantly see how you can sustain more rigidity in the left wrist area. However, this may seem too extreme and lacking in feel for many golfers, so I would suggest that you persevere with the reverse overlap.

Grip pressure

One hears and reads many different ideas on grip pressure, and it is probably a personal preference as much as anything. However, since we are trying to eliminate unwanted independent hand action, I like to grip the club firmly, rather than lightly. I work on the principle that, as in the golf swing, the tighter we grip, the less the hands are inclined to work, and apply that theory to my putting. However, I would add a proviso that I do not grip the putter in a vice-like fashion which tenses my hands or forearms. Instead, I would describe my grip as firm, and equal in both hands rather than light, and it works for me. However, you should experiment with different grip pressures, and find the one that suits you best. Certainly, on very long putts your grip should be firmer, since you are using considerably more force than for a three foot putt, and you must ensure that you have total control of the putter head.

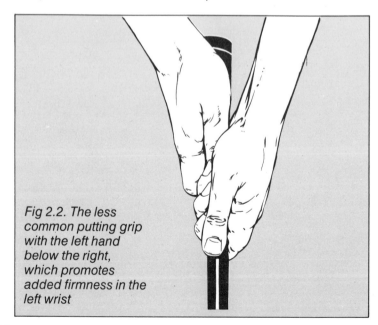

Fig 2.2. The less common putting grip with the left hand below the right, which promotes added firmness in the left wrist

CHAPTER THREE

The address position

Like all shots in golf, how you stand to the ball will affect how the club is swung. In putting, you stand closer to the ball than for any other shot, and this gives you the opportunity to swing the clubhead on a straighter line than for other shots. However, it is important to understand that the clubhead moves away from the ball in a straight line, and the further back it travels, the more inside the ball to target line it moves. It is only on the shortest of putts that it will move in a straight line.

Posture

In the long game, you bend from the hips in order to create space in which your arms can swing – you must do likewise in putting. The extent to which you bend over will vary from player to player depending on your build, but make sure you bend sufficiently to allow your arms to hang freely from the shoulder joints. Some of the best putters in the world have adopted a very low position over the ball, whereas others choose to stand more upright. So you can experiment as to which feels more suitable. If you choose to stand fairly upright, your arms will be almost straight when you putt, much like Ben Crenshaw; but should you crouch lower over the ball, you will have to bend your arms at the elbow, or grip further down the putter.

However, another important aspect to consider in bending forward, is where your eyes are in relation to the ball to target line. In putting, you have the best chance of setting your eyes directly over the line the ball will travel, which must help with the direction (Fig 3.1). So, having taken your address position, you can easily check this by

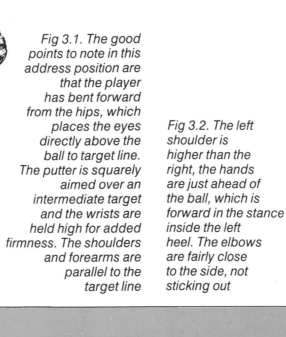

Fig 3.1. The good points to note in this address position are that the player has bent forward from the hips, which places the eyes directly above the ball to target line. The putter is squarely aimed over an intermediate target and the wrists are held high for added firmness. The shoulders and forearms are parallel to the target line

Fig 3.2. The left shoulder is higher than the right, the hands are just ahead of the ball, which is forward in the stance inside the left heel. The elbows are fairly close to the side, not sticking out

49

dropping a ball from under your left eye, and seeing where it hits the ground. Ideally it should either hit the ball you are putting, or drop just inside it. If it is way outside or inside, you need to adjust either the ball position or your posture until you meet the necessary requirement.

Lining up

As with my long shots, I find it useful to have an intermediate target, about two feet ahead of the ball, over which I want to set the ball rolling. I therefore line up the putter square to that spot.

I would always recommend that you try to set your shoulders and forearms parallel to the ball to target line, since this will make it much easier to swing the clubhead in the correct direction. Also ensure that your left shoulder is higher than the right (Fig 3.2). This should happen naturally, since the right hand is lower than the left on the grip, but it is easy to allow the left shoulder to drop, and the right to come forward. This action also tends to kink the back of the left hand too much – just what you want to avoid!

How you place your feet and hips is a more personal choice. I tend to have mine open, i.e. a line drawn across my feet and hips would point left of parallel, since I find this gives me a clearer path for my arms and club on the through swing. The width of stance is dependent on your build, and is also a matter of preference, but do not be too extreme. Few top-class golfers putt with their feet either together or very wide apart.

It is also vital that your eyes are parallel to the target line, and you can check this by taking your address position. Now without moving your head, in both hands hold the shaft of the putter across the bridge of your nose, and under your eyes (Fig 3.3). If the shaft is not parallel to your target, then neither are your eyes.

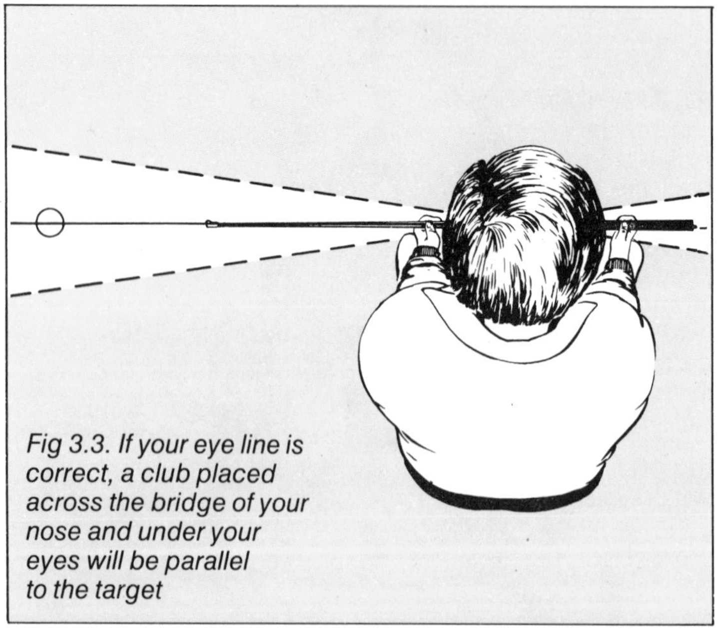

Weight distribution

In putting, you should try to hit the ball at the bottom of the putter's arc, or just on the way up. Therefore I feel that your weight should be evenly distributed. It will be more towards the balls of your feet than the heels, and for added stability some people like to have more weight on the inside of each foot. It is essential that you feel balanced, since the head must remain still throughout the putting stroke.

Ball and hand position

As I have already said, you are trying to contact the ball at the bottom or slightly on the upswing, so it must be placed fairly forward in the stance near the left foot. This may be inside the heel for some golfers, or opposite the left toe for others, depending on your stance. I also like the putter shaft to be sloping slightly towards the target, rather than vertical, since this means that at the start my hands are just ahead of the club face, which will help them to stay that way throughout the putt (Fig 3.2). This point can be checked in a mirror. I hold my wrists quite high rather than low, since high or arched wrists will help eliminate unwanted hand action, and make the swing path straighter, thus improving accuracy.

The address position for putting is a more personal one than for any other shot. If you putt well, and yet do none of the things that I believe are important, far be it for me to change a winning formula. But when I teach someone to putt, the grip and address position detailed in the last two chapters are the fundamental points I instil in a pupil.

Fig 3.3. If your eye line is correct, a club placed across the bridge of your nose and under your eyes will be parallel to the target

CHAPTER FOUR

How to strike putts consistently

To putt well the clubhead must be swung on a very shallow arc, so that there is no suggestion of hitting down on the ball. Instead, it is *rolled* forwards as the putter approaches from very close to the ground. On short putts the putter will swing back and through on almost a straight line, whereas on longer putts, the clubhead must start to move inside on the backswing, strike the ball while it is moving directly towards the target and will then tend to swing back to the inside (Fig 4.1).

To guarantee a shallow arc, keep the clubhead close to the ground by moving the arms and hands away together. Any hint of the hands moving and the arms staying still, will see the clubhead leave the ground quite sharply, and you will tend to hit down too much on the putt. Instead, the whole action should feel firm. In fact, I like to use my forearms, rather than my hands, to swing the putter, thus keeping my hands out of the action on all but the very longest of putts. Some people like to feel that the left hand and arm push the clubhead back, while the right hand and arm swing the putter forward, and I have to admit that there have been times when this method has worked for me. You may like to work on keeping the whole of the grip on the putter, or the back of the left hand moving towards the hole, both of which again promote the very action required. The method you select is a personal choice, and one that may change from day to day or from week to week, but those golfers whose hands work independently, will need to concentrate on their forearms moving.

Throughout the stroke you should try to preserve the angle set between the hands and forearms at address since, if you can do this, the unit of your hands and arms will be moving together (Fig 4.2 a, b and c). It is a good idea to check

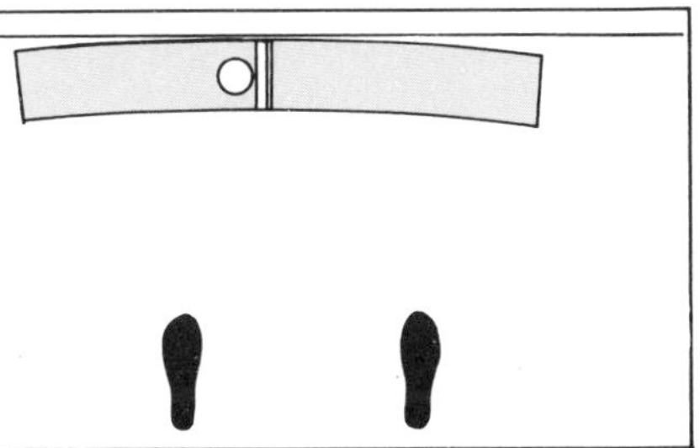

Fig 4.1. On all but the shortest putts, the club head moves back in a straight line, then inside the ball to target line

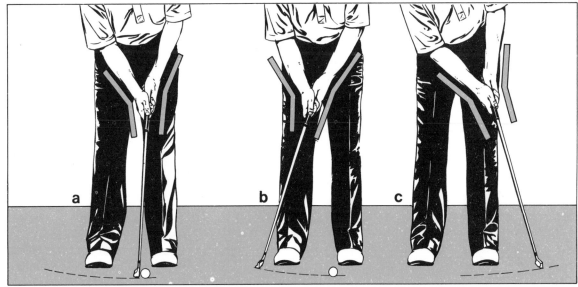

Fig 4.2 a, b and c. In a good putting action the angle at the back of the hands and arms remains the same throughout the stroke, keeping the club head low to the ground. In Fig 4.2c. you will see that the whole of the putter grip has been kept moving towards the target after impact

a   b   c

the swing path of the putter by laying a club on the ground just outside the putter head. In the backswing the clubhead should not touch the shaft, and should move inside on the longer putts. The whole stroke must be made smoothly and in an unhurried manner, much like a pendulum. As you complete each putt, check that the back of your left hand has not collapsed inwards but has retained the original angle. You should start with short straight putts of about three feet, making certain that the club face is square to the target, then try to hit each one from the middle of the putter to the middle of the hole. You should feel that the putter head moves directly towards the hole after the ball has been struck, since this gives a better chance of hitting the ball down the desired track.

Incidentally, most putters these days have a mark to indicate the middle of the putter, but you can check this is in the correct spot, by holding the club between your thumb and forefinger and letting the shaft hang vertically. Take a coin and tap along the face until you hit the spot where the putter swings straight back

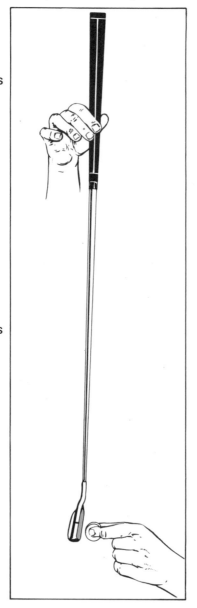

Fig 4.3. You can find the sweet spot of your putter by using a coin to tap the face. When it swings straight back without the heel or toe twisting, you have found the spot, which you should mark

without the toe or heel twisting (Fig 4.3). This is the middle, or sweet spot as it is known, and you should always address the ball lined up with this spot.

Judging distance

You must accelerate through a putt, so it is essential to have the correct length of backswing; one that is too long encourages you to decelerate into the ball, whereas one that is too short will make you use your hands to flick at it at the last minute. It is also important that you learn to strike the ball from the middle of the putter if you are to become adept at judging distance. For example, you are on the first green with a fifteen foot putt; you hit it out of the heel and it pulls up well short of the hole. On the second green you have a similar length putt. Having been short on the first green you hit it a bit harder, but this time you strike it out of the middle of the putter and it goes six feet past. So you go to the third green knowing no more about the pace of the greens than when you started, and are thoroughly confused.

Therefore, it is important to work on a good strike in developing your putting, rather than becoming too concerned initially about holing the putts. In fact, you might strike the putt well but read it wrong – this tends to improve with experience. When I have a long putt, I always try to view it from the side, since this gives a better sense of the true distance. I stand with the ball on my right, halfway along the line and try to imagine the pace at which the ball will leave the putter in order to finish in or near the hole. I stand beside the ball and have a couple of practice putts looking at the hole, and imagining the ball rolling along the line into it. I then use the same strength putt to hit the ball. You may think that this routine is rather time consuming, but you can look at the putt while others are putting, or whilst you are walking onto the green – it need not take too long.

Obviously, the longer you play, the easier it becomes to compute quickly how the pace and slope of the green, together with the length of the putt, determine how hard you should hit the ball, but this can only be calculated if you strike the ball well. In fact, I tell my pupils that if they wish to test how purely they strike a putt, they should hit long putts, where such imperfections are highlighted. On a three foot putt, you may well get away with a putt not hit right out of the middle, since it has not far to travel, but a 30 footer out of the heel or toe will pull up well short of the target.

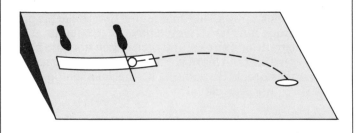

Fig 4.4a. On a putt breaking from left to right, play the ball further forward in the stance than normal to guard against pushing the putt

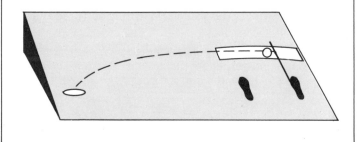

Fig 4.4b. On a putt breaking from right to left, play the ball further back in the stance than normal to guard against pulling the putt

Head still

It is essential that on all putts you keep your head and, for that matter, your whole frame as still as possible. Any movement of the head or swaying of the body before the ball is struck will only be detrimental to the result. So having addressed the ball, try to allow your hands and arms only to swing the putter. You will find that your shoulders will move as well in response to your arms, but you should not try to move them consciously as this can lead to swaying off the ball. Look at the back of the ball until it is struck, and then keep your head still and eyes focused on the spot where the ball was placed until it is well on its way. Some golfers favour listening for the ball to drop in the hole, which is a good idea. I like to ask people to keep the head and eyes still and guess where the ball has gone. They may not always guess correctly, but it does have the desired effect of stopping them looking up too soon.

How to practise your putting

As I have said, you should practise striking the putt well, perhaps giving yourself marks out of ten for each putt based on the quality of strike and direction, rather than getting too concerned about always holing out. Few greens are absolutely smooth, and even machines set up to hole putts in laboratory conditions do not succeed every time. So your practice should be to set up correctly, with the club face square to the target, and to make a smooth putt along the correct swing path. Use a club laid down just outside the putter head and parallel to the target to help or, if you practise indoors, you can use the skirting board to check the line of your swing. Remember that it should be straight back on only the shortest of putts, and then the putter head must swing to the inside.

Some time should be spent practising one-handed, using each hand in turn – you will then appreciate better how each hand works through the stroke. Practise also with the left hand below the right, and then switch back to your usual grip. This highlights how the left hand should feel throughout the stroke, and promotes the necessary firmness. Putting with your eyes shut will increase your sense of feel, and focus your attention on your action. To develop a positive action and attitude, practise a straight, slightly uphill putt, from about three to four feet. This needs to be struck authoritatively, which is a good asset in putting. However, you must not neglect putts from any angle, so after the uphill putts, you should practise the same putt downhill and then across the slope. On right to left putts, you will find it useful to play the ball a little nearer the middle of the stance, as this helps to ensure that you do not pull the putt, while with a left to right borrow, play the ball more forward to guard against pushing it (Fig. 4.4).

It always helps to compete against someone on the putting green, so do this as often as possible; failing that, putt just one ball and count your score.

CHAPTER FIVE

How to read greens

Having played in hundreds of Pro-Ams, I know that all club golfers could improve their putting statistics if they could read the greens better. I try to read most of my partner's putts, providing they wish me to do so, as a result of which they then seem to putt with greater confidence, and in the right direction. Much of the information needed to read a putt can be gleaned before you are on the green just by observing the lie of the surrounding land. So as you walk towards the green, if the land on the right is higher than that on the left, the chances are that the whole of the putting green will slope in that direction. The same applies if you are walking up a slope towards the green: it is likely that the green will slope upwards from front to back. It does not take a genius to work out these facts – you just need to be observant. However, these generalities do not apply every time, and you must always check the line of your putt.

Developing a routine

Over the years I have developed a routine: I walk to a spot behind the cup and look back to my ball trying to judge the line. I found that I could always estimate my partner's line reasonably accurately while I attended the pin and thus I started to read my putts from the same position. You may wish only to look from behind the ball, and if that works for you, then stay with that method. While I walk back to my ball I view the putt from the side, also checking that there are no stones or pitch marks on my line. Then I have a quick glance from behind the ball to confirm my first observations on the line, and I also select an intermediate target about two or three feet ahead on the line of the putt over which I can aim. It is not always possible to find something identifiable on the line, but if I can do so, it helps me enormously to line up correctly. I personally can learn a lot by walking between my ball and the hole, since I can often feel through my feet any slope that may be there. This all takes time, and when playing professionally we take longer than the average club golfer to get round, so far be it from me to encourage slow play!

However, do try to adopt a routine that you repeat for

each putt, bar the very short ones, and one that does *not* take too much time. It is always a good idea to watch your playing partner's putts. I like to imagine that I have his putt and try to judge how hard I would have hit it, check that against my partner's stroke, and then watch how the putt breaks. From this I can learn something about the pace and borrow on the green. So again, it is a matter of being observant rather than clever!

How pace affects borrow

The pace of the green, apart from any slopes, is affected by the length of the grass and whether it is wet or dry. Obviously, a wet green with long grass is going to be slower than one that has just been cut and is dry, so allow for these variables.

Having read the line, have a couple of practice putts to judge how hard to hit the ball. I tend to see the ball dying into the hole, or at most going a foot past, in which case I have to

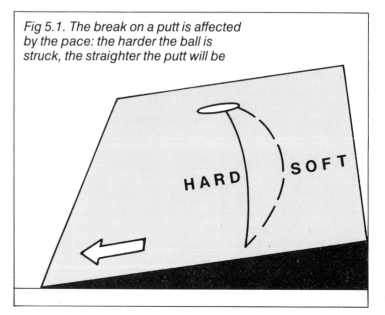

Fig 5.1. The break on a putt is affected by the pace: the harder the ball is struck, the straighter the putt will be

HARD   SOFT

allow the maximum borrow for any putt. If you like to putt more aggressively, then the line will be straighter, but bear in mind that if you miss the hole, the putt may be longer than you would have liked (Fig 5.1). It is fine to be aggressive on uphill putts, but be careful with the downhill ones when it is probably better to trickle them allowing for plenty of break. Remember that uphill putts never break as much as downhill (Fig 5.2). If your putt has more than one break, it is the one nearest the hole that will be most influential on your choice of line. The early breaks will not affect the ball so much since it will be rolling more quickly than when it is near the hole. If you are unlucky enough to have a putt, say of ten feet, with two different breaks, then you will have to make allowances for the ball to break in two different directions (Fig 5.3). Sometimes one break can offset the other, and the line becomes almost straight, but I think that your perception of the situation would be improved on this occasion by looking at the putt from more than one direction.

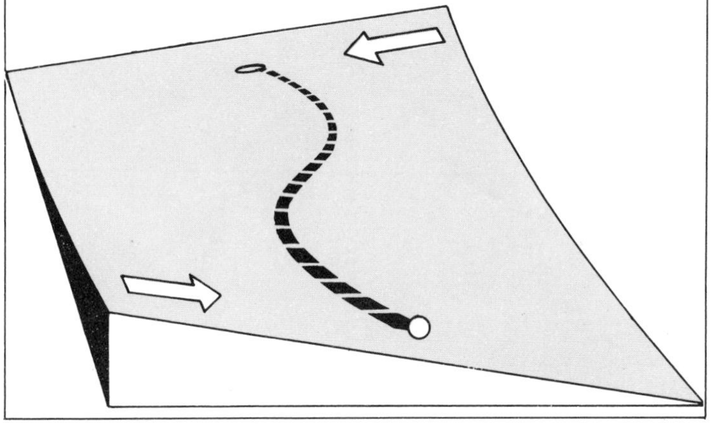

Two-tier greens

Two-tier greens can also be tricky, not only from the reading point of view, but also in determining the pace. Not all

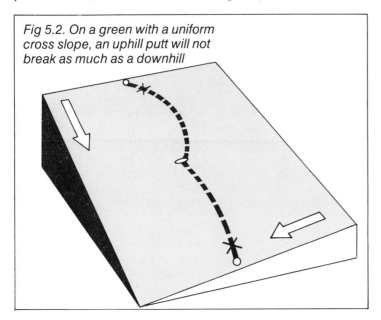

Fig 5.2. On a green with a uniform cross slope, an uphill putt will not break as much as a downhill

Fig 5.3. On a putt with two opposing breaks, it is the one nearer the hole that will affect the putt most

courses have distinct two-tier greens, and thus many golfers are not accustomed to putting on them, and their judgement of line and length is affected greatly. You must decide first to what extent the slope will make the ball break, and then choose the pace. If you are putting across the slope, rather than straight up it, remember that the ball will curve towards the lower level as it climbs (Fig 5.4). It may be affected also by any other slopes on the top tier, so you can understand why these are difficult putts. If you have to putt down a two-tier slope, depending on the position of the pin and the pace of the green, you may find that you have only to putt the ball to the edge of the top tier and the slope will do the rest. But remember that when a ball is moving slowly, it takes more borrow.

Grain or nap on the green

In some parts of the world, the grain or nap on the green can affect the putt greatly; so much so that sometimes a ball can appear to be breaking up a hill. You can see which way the grass grows by the change in shading. If the grain is lying with the putt, which means it will roll faster, then the grass will appear light and shiny. However, if it lies against the putt, thus slowing the pace, it looks darker and dull. A putt

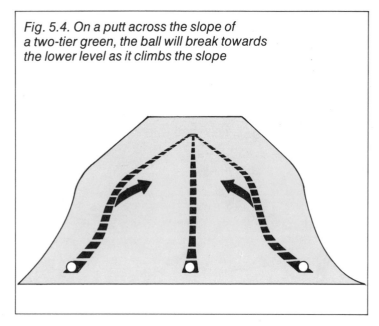

Fig. 5.4. On a putt across the slope of a two-tier green, the ball will break towards the lower level as it climbs the slope

across the grain will tend to move in whichever direction the grain is growing, so that if the grain lies in the opposite direction to the slope, there will be a tendency to straighten the line. In Great Britain there are few courses that have grainy greens, but in parts of Europe, the United States and other hotter climates, there are many courses where the grain must be considered when reading a putt.

Plumb bobbing

This is a method of reading the green, whereby standing behind the ball you hold the putter between finger and thumb so that it hangs vertically (Fig. 5.5). Looking down the line, with your master eye only open, cover the ball with the lower shaft of the putter and then see which side of the hole the grip end is positioned. This will indicate the higher side of the hole and the direction in which the green slopes. It does not necessarily give you the exact amount of borrow to allow, but the further away from the hole the grip appears, the more slope on the green. However, this method works only if you are standing on ground that slopes in the same direction as that near the hole, and you are perpendicular to that ground. So plumb bobbing can be used successfully

only on certain putts, and is of no benefit unless carried out correctly. Some people regard it as a useful system, whereas others never understand it. However, you should try everything, and if it works you keep it: otherwise reject it.

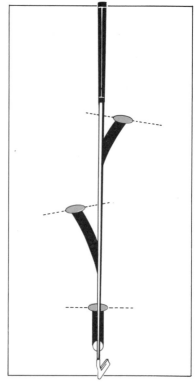

Fig 5.5. With the plumb-bob method, stand behind the ball and hold the club so that it hangs vertically. With the lower end of the shaft covering the ball, note where the grip end is in relation to the hole and this will indicate in which direction the ground slopes

Visualization

You really must develop a great sense of imagination in putting, especially for those more difficult putts. In order to do this, you must be able to visualize how the ball will roll. Many players like to imagine that there is a three foot wide circle around the hole, and that they are putting into that area. If you feel that helps you, then use it, but I always prefer to imagine the ball going into the hole. On long difficult putts I know that it is unlikely that I will hole them, but it gives me a more definite target. With middle range putts I try to get a strong mental picture of the ball going into the hole when I take my couple of practice putts. I visualize the exact line the ball must take, and sense the pace at which it must be moving. You too can develop this ability, which is essential if you are to become a first-class putter. So put a little more thought into your putting, both on the practice green and on the course, and I am sure that you will be pleasantly surprised at the improvement.

CHAPTER SIX

Which putter?

Nowadays there is such a variety of putters available that it is difficult to know which to choose. However, I can give you a few guidelines which would be worth considering regardless of the type of putter you select.

1 The length

Obviously those golfers who are tall, or stand very upright to putt, need a longer putter than a short person or someone who bends over a long way. Find one that does not leave too many inches sticking out from your left hand, since this may catch on your thighs through the stroke.

2 The grip

I would strongly recommend a putter grip that is flat at the front, as this will not only help you to grip the club correctly, but also to line up the face. However, do make sure that the grip has been put on squarely, which, unfortunately, is not always the case.

3 The lie

The lie refers to the angle at which the shaft leaves the putter head, and ideally the bottom of the putter should be flat on the ground at address. However, there are some superb putters, notably Seve Ballesteros, who address the ball with the toe of the putter in the air, but you should aim to find a putter with the correct lie. I would recommend a fairly upright putter, since it will help you to putt on a straighter swing path than a flat one (Fig 6.1). However, personal preference, and what you feel most comfortable and confident with, will have to play a part in your choice.

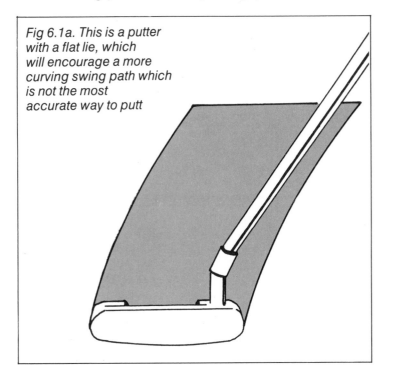

Fig 6.1a. This is a putter with a flat lie, which will encourage a more curving swing path which is not the most accurate way to putt

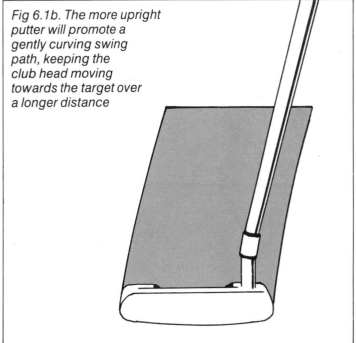

Fig 6.1b. The more upright putter will promote a gently curving swing path, keeping the club head moving towards the target over a longer distance

4 The weight

There are many different weights of putter, and again it really is a matter for personal preference. Heavy putters are harder for you to twitch off-line, their weight making a pendulum action slightly easier, but you may find that you get more feel from a light putter. Some professionals like to vary the weight according to the pace of the greens, but keeping the same model putter. Experiment with a variety of weights, perhaps even putting some lead tape on the back of yours to increase the weight.

5 Style of putter

There are many different styles, such as mallet-headed, centre-shafted, blade, or Ping type, and again it is a matter of what you like best (Fig 6.2.). However, it is a scientific fact that the Ping or a Ping-type putter, which has more weight at the heel and toe, creates a bigger sweet spot, and therefore a larger area of strike. Probably more top professionals currently use this type than any other putter, so it must have some special qualities.

Consider all these aspects before you buy your next putter, and try a few out in the professional's shop, or borrow a friend's before you make a final decision. If you find the right one, you will probably never part with it.

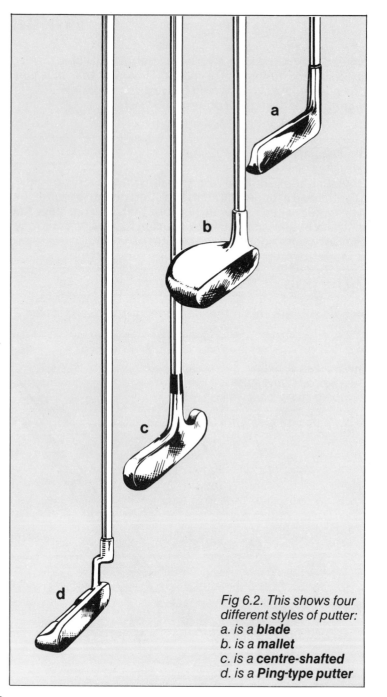

Fig 6.2. This shows four different styles of putter:
*a. is a **blade***
*b. is a **mallet***
*c. is a **centre-shafted***
*d. is a **Ping-type putter***

CHAPTER SEVEN

To putt or not

You do not have to restrict your use of the putter to the green alone, but there are a few factors to consider before you decide where else to use it. If you just miss the green, and the ball is sitting up nicely on a short cut fringe, there is no reason why you cannot putt it. In this instance you just have to hit the ball harder than usual to allow for its journey through the slightly longer fringe grass. Links courses in Great Britain have fairways that usually have very short grass, and so you often find that the putter is the best club even from a considerable distance off the green, especially if the alternative is a formidable chip shot. Always remember that more often than not, a poorly hit putt will give a better result than a poorly hit chip, so if you miss the green always check first whether you can putt the ball. The instances where you should steer away from using a putter are as follows:

1 If the fringe grass is quite long, so that the ball is sitting down in it (Fig 7.1a).

2 If the fringe grass is very wet (Fig 7.1b).

3 If the fringe grass has grown, or has been cut so that the ball will be rolling significantly against the way the grass lies (Fig 7.1c).

4 If the ball is in a divot (Fig 7.1d).

5 If there is uneven ground between your ball and the hole (Fig 7.1e).

In any of these circumstances, it will be difficult to know just how the ball is going to react, and so it would be more prudent to chip the ball. It is easy to shy away from chipping, especially if your technique is suspect, but if you stand over the ball preparing to putt it, but some nagging doubt at the back of your mind is telling you that you should be chipping, the indecision can lead to a lack of concentration and, inevitably, a poor result. So always try to be 100 per cent certain that you are playing the right shot.

Fig 7.1. If you miss the green, do not putt the ball if:

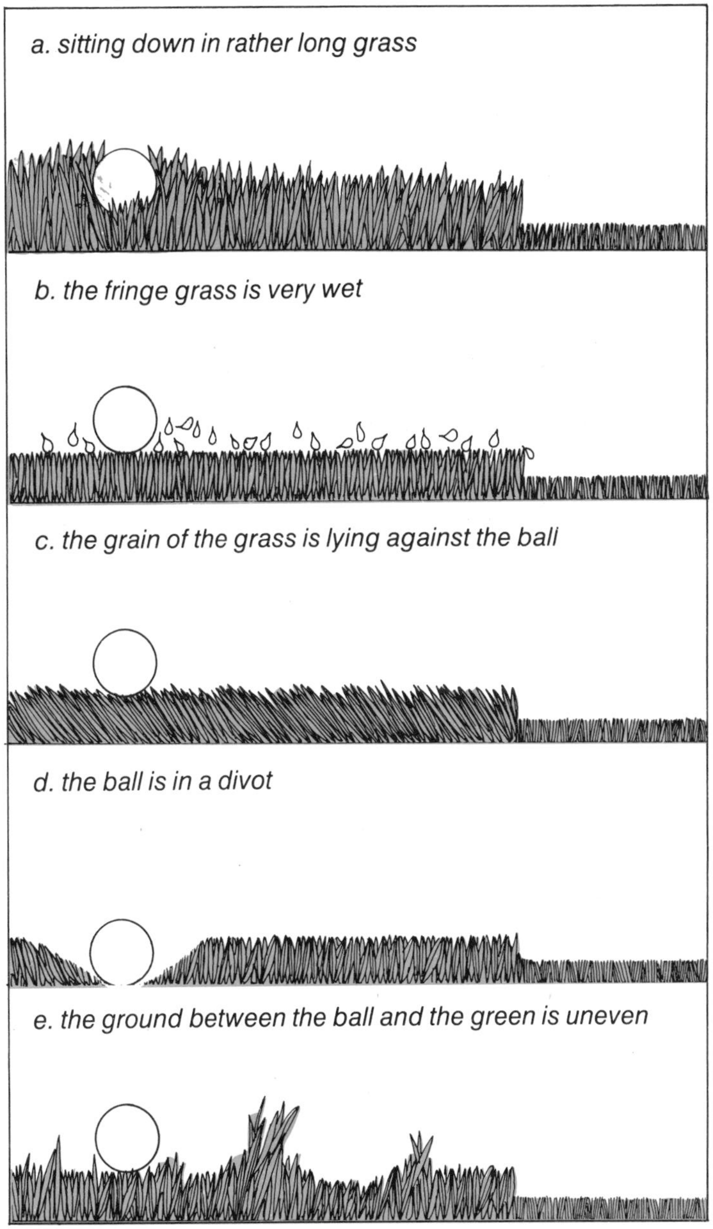

a. sitting down in rather long grass

b. the fringe grass is very wet

c. the grain of the grass is lying against the ball

d. the ball is in a divot

e. the ground between the ball and the green is uneven

CHAPTER EIGHT

The art of chipping

Chipping is essentially a very simple part of golf, and one that can save you many shots. If you could guarantee getting down in two nearly every time you just missed the green, your handicap would drop considerably, so do not neglect this department. The main point to remember is that you are trying to hit slightly down on the ball, which will loft it in the air sufficiently to land *just* on the green and roll up to the pin (Fig 8.1).

The set up

Because chipping involves very little movement or leg action, you set up with your feet close together, and feet and hips slightly open to the target. This allows the arms to swing through the ball unimpeded and gives you a better aspect of the shot. However, I would recommend that you keep your shoulders parallel to the ball to target line, since

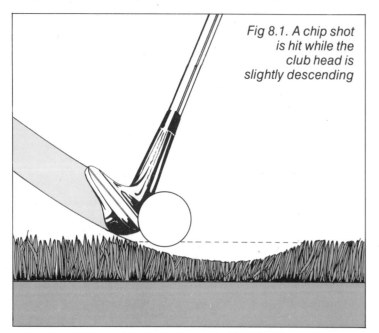

Fig 8.1. A chip shot is hit while the club head is slightly descending

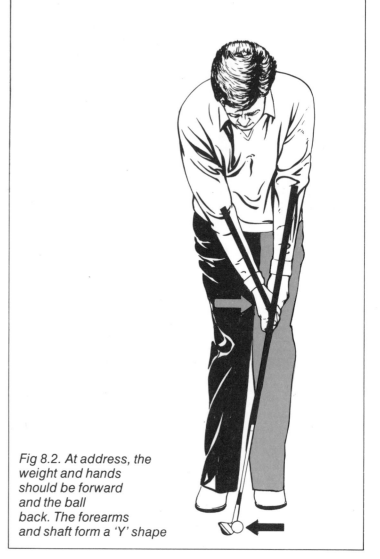

Fig 8.2. At address, the weight and hands should be forward and the ball back. The forearms and shaft form a 'Y' shape

this will ensure that the club is swung in the correct direction. You must bend forwards from the hips, so that your arms have room in which to swing, and this will bring your weight forwards onto the balls of your feet. About sixty to seventy per cent of your weight is placed on the left foot, and the ball is positioned well back in the stance, so that it is quite close to the right foot (Fig 8.2). Many players make the mistake of playing the ball too far forward in the stance, so check the ball position by taking your set up, then place a club behind the ball and just withdraw your right foot backwards. This will enable you to see where the ball is in relation to your left foot – it should be inside the left heel. The exact amount will depend on the lie, which I will explain later, but it is better to err by having the ball too far back since this will encourage the slightly descending strike that you require.

It is also essential that your hands are well ahead of the ball at address so that your left arm and the shaft form at least a straight line. You can best check this and the ball position by looking in the mirror. This address position does tend to de-loft the club a little so that a 7 iron will become more like a 6 iron. One of the best ways I have found to help my pupils adopt the correct address position is to remember it as two forward and one back. The two forward

are: the weight and the hands; and the one back is: the ball position. It is advisable to grip down on the club, since this gives you additional control and feel. Most people use their normal golf grip for chipping, but if you putt using the reverse overlap grip (as I hope you do after reading the first part of this book) you might like to experiment with that grip, since it does give extra firmness in the left hand – an important feature of a good chipping action.

The stroke

As you address the ball, your forearms form a letter 'Y', and you should chip the ball, simply by swinging the 'Y' shape (Fig 8.3a). In this way, your hands will play only a small role in the shot, while the forearms are the major contributors. Ideally the left hand and arm swing the club back and

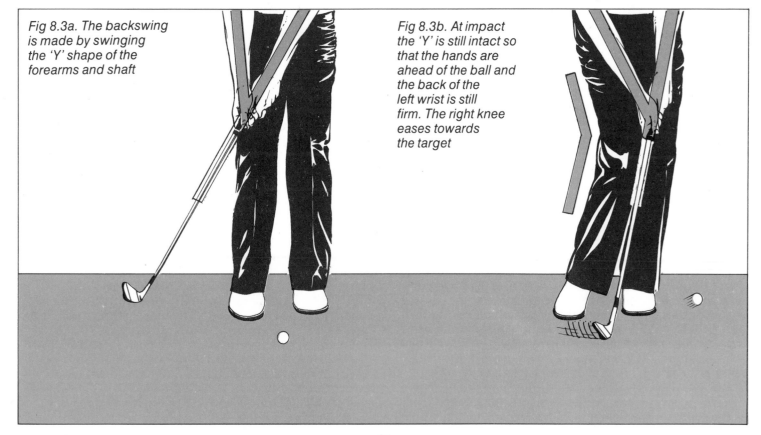

Fig 8.3a. The backswing is made by swinging the 'Y' shape of the forearms and shaft

Fig 8.3b. At impact the 'Y' is still intact so that the hands are ahead of the ball and the back of the left wrist is still firm. The right knee eases towards the target

Fig 8.4. If the left hand does not keep moving towards the target, it collapses and the ball is hit off the wrong part of the club

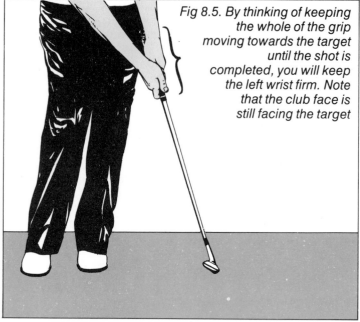

Fig 8.5. By thinking of keeping the whole of the grip moving towards the target until the shot is completed, you will keep the left wrist firm. Note that the club face is still facing the target

through the ball, with the most important point being that at impact the hands are ahead of the ball (Fig 8.3b) and the left arm continues moving through the shot. If it stops, the right hand carries on, the back of the left wrist collapses (Fig 8.4) and the bottom edge of the club usually hits the ball, resulting in a very poor shot, which more often than not shoots across the green and off the other side. The address position advocated will encourage the club to be swung back on a gently ascending arc, thus permitting the slightly descending strike that you need. Any attempt to help the ball in the air by trying to scoop it will defeat the whole object, so hit down slightly on the ball and allow the loft of the club to do the work. To improve the contact, you will find it helpful to keep the whole of the grip moving towards the target (Fig 8.5). When the left hand stops, usually in an effort to scoop the ball in the air with the right hand, the end of the grip stops too, but by keeping the whole of the grip moving towards the target, the back of the left hand remains firm.

I like to feel that my left hand and, more importantly, my left forearm swing the club, but if you can obtain a better feel for the shot by using your right hand and arm, then so be it.

But remember that the angle at the back of the right hand must remain constant, especially through impact. On longer chip shots the wrists do give a little on the backswing, but the same firm left wrist position at impact is essential. The length of the swing will obviously depend on which club you use and the length of the shot, but you should always take a couple of practice swings, visualizing where the shot should land. Do not make the backswing too long so that you decelerate at impact, but neither should you make it too short, or the hands will tend to flick at the ball at the last minute, causing a mis-hit. Make sure that you accelerate smoothly, and try to make the backswing and throughswing the same length. There is virtually no weight transference on the backswing, but you will find it helpful to ease the right knee towards the target as the ball is struck. This will prevent the hands from closing the club face, and also keep the swing on line. Keep your head still and eyes down until well after the ball is struck – any temptation to look up too quickly will affect the quality of strike. The stroke itself should be smooth and unhurried; it is accuracy, not power, that is essential.

Which club for which shot?

When deciding on the club for a chip shot, you should select one that will land the ball on the edge of the green and then run up to the hole. It is therefore useful to know how the ball will react with different clubs, i.e. what proportion of its journey the ball will spend in the air and on the ground. It is not essential to know initially how each club reacts, but by understanding the flight characteristics of a few clubs, you can work from there. So the following should be treated as a suitable guideline:

Fig 8.6. This shows the proportion of air to ground time with different clubs

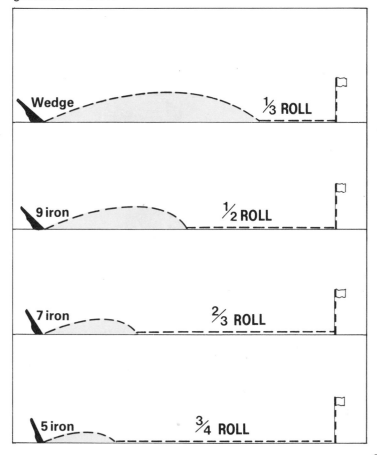

Wedge – two-thirds in the air, one-third on the ground.

9 iron – half the time in the air, half on the ground.

7 iron – one-third in the air, two-thirds on the ground.

5 iron – a quarter in the air, three-quarters on the ground.

All shown in Fig 8.6

By remembering how these four clubs work, you will be prepared for most situations, and experience will enable you to appreciate how all the clubs work and which you prefer using. Obviously when using those with more loft, i.e. the higher numbered clubs, the ball spends more time in the air than on the ground, whereas with the straight faced clubs, like a 3 or 4 iron, the ball spends less time in the air than on the ground. However, choice of club is often a personal preference, and some professionals may use one club, usually a wedge or sand wedge, for all their chipping and pitching, but they have plenty of experience in adapting how the club face sits and where to position the ball to vary the height and roll of the shot. You should try to keep to the principle of using the most appropriate club for the shot.

One way to appreciate how different clubs affect the ball's height and roll, is to hit shots with various clubs from one spot onto a green, but using the same strength swing. You will see how the ball travels varying distances – the shots with the low numbered clubs going the furthest. Choice of club is related to how hard you hit the shot, and so there are many combinations that can be used. Practise with the clubs I have suggested and get a working knowledge of them. You can then expand on this groundwork, but always try to land the ball just on the green and let it roll up to the pin.

Bad lies

If the ball is lying in a divot, or well down in the grass, you must make sure that it is well back in the stance, even opposite the right toe, and that the hands and weight are well ahead of the ball. Swing the clubhead back on a slightly steeper path than usual, allowing the right wrist to cock a little, and be certain to hit down on the ball. The throughswing may be curtailed somewhat, and the ball will come out low and run. If you have only a short distance to cover, it may be best to use a sand iron for this shot, as its extra loft will offset the loft lost by this particular address position.

CHAPTER NINE

The long chip and run

When the ball lands only a few yards off the green, it is usual to play a chip and run shot, or putt the ball. It is only when a ball is perhaps fifteen or twenty yards off the putting surface that you may be torn between a chip and run, or a pitch shot.

A pitch is an elevated shot that applies backspin to the ball, preventing it from running too much on landing. It is the more difficult of the two shots to play, requiring additional hand action, which, if not timed correctly, can create the more destructive shot. So often club golfers feel that at any time they are off the green they should be pitching the ball, but instead you can extend the action of the chip shot, simply by making a longer backswing and increasing the leg action. You should adopt a similar set up but use a slightly wider stance; position the ball about three to four inches inside the left heel and grip nearer the end of the club. The choice of club is dictated by the situation, but generally you will be using the higher numbered clubs, since you still want the ball to land on the green. As your arms swing the clubhead away, with the left arm in command, do not make any conscious effort to use your hands. Your wrists will naturally cock in response the weight of the club head (Fig 9.1). Your weight will transfer a little onto your right leg and then, as your arms swing down and through, your weight must move back to the left side. It is not a steep angle of attack on the ball, more of a 'U' shaped swing, and providing you do not grip too tightly, the little amount of wrist break developed in the backswing will naturally unwind at impact. The left arm should be

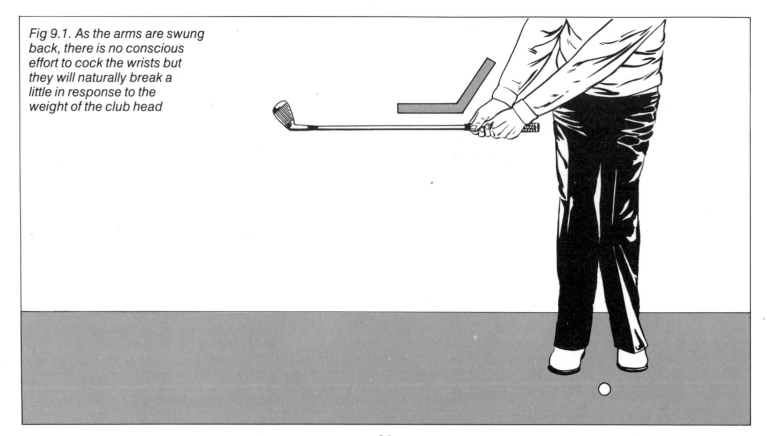

Fig 9.1. As the arms are swung back, there is no conscious effort to cock the wrists but they will naturally break a little in response to the weight of the club head

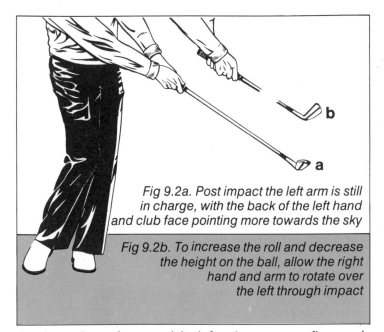

Fig 9.2a. Post impact the left arm is still in charge, with the back of the left hand and club face pointing more towards the sky

Fig 9.2b. To increase the roll and decrease the height on the ball, allow the right hand and arm to rotate over the left through impact

dominant throughout, and the left wrist must stay firm, and ahead of the club head through impact.

For normal shots the right hand and arm should not cross over the left, so that the club face points more towards the sky at the completion of the shot, (Fig 9.2a). However, if you are playing into a strong headwind, or the pin is at the back of a very long green, allowing the right hand and arm to cross a little over the left (Fig 9.2b), will have the effect of de-lofting the club, and making the ball fly lower and run more on landing.

The swing path

Since the club head is now being swung back further than for the short chip shot from the fringe, you must allow it to swing to the inside, so that it returns from the inside and strikes the ball while moving directly towards the target. I like to teach people using the clock face as an analogy. Imagine that the ball is in the middle of a clock face and you are standing at 6 o'clock, with your shoulders parallel to the ball to target line; 3 o'clock is on the right and 9 o'clock is on the left (Fig 9.3). Initially the club head swings straight back and then, as the body starts to turn, it is swung inwards and upwards between 3 and 4 o'clock. Ideally it is swung back

down on the same path, the ball is struck while the club is moving straight towards 9 and then, as the body turns through the shot, the club moves back inside towards 8 o'clock.

So having progressed far enough off the green to demand a fuller swing, you must let the club head swing inside a little on the backswing as the body turns. Admittedly, with the shorter irons the club head will not swing as much to the inside as for the longer clubs, but by having it in mind that you are trying to swing from between 3 and 4 o'clock to 9 o'clock, it will help you to improve the direction of your shots.

If the ball is sitting badly, i.e. in a divot or in short rough, you will need to position it further back in the stance and swing the club back more steeply, creating more of a 'V' shaped swing.

Too many club golfers try to play a high pitch shot whenever they miss the green. Instead, you should think about playing the long chip and run, as it is the safer percentage shot, and one that is easy to execute. But like any shot in golf, you will have to practise and experiment a little to appreciate just how the ball will react.

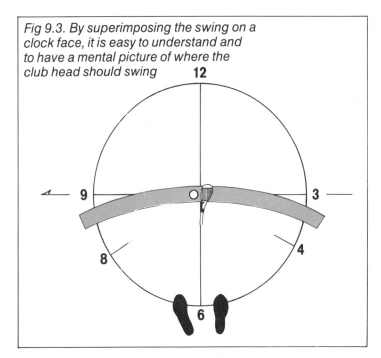

Fig 9.3. By superimposing the swing on a clock face, it is easy to understand and to have a mental picture of where the club head should swing

CHAPTER TEN

The short pitch

When you have to get maximum height and minimum roll on a shot, then you should use a pitch shot. In this chapter I will deal with the short pitch that you will have to play from just around the green, maybe over a bunker. It has to be admitted that this is not one of the easiest shots in golf, requiring as it does, well-timed hand action, a reasonable lie and confidence.

Many players are so afraid of this shot that they rush to complete it and lack any sense of discipline in how they should approach it, so try not to quicken your actions. However, since this is one of those shots that, if not executed correctly, can ruin your score, I feel that the beginner, the higher handicap player, and any golfers who are not totally confident, might do better by using a wedge or sand wedge and employing an action similar to that used in the rather more passive handed long chip and run shot. This is not admitting defeat, but rather a matter of being sensible and realistic about your ability; it is also the shot that, under pressure, the better golfer could choose.

The set up

With the ball sitting well, i.e. with a cushion of grass beneath it, use a sand wedge and set up with the club face square,

Fig 10.1a. Set up with a narrow, open stance, with the weight favouring the left leg. The hands are just ahead of the ball which is inside the left heel. The left arm and shaft form a straight line

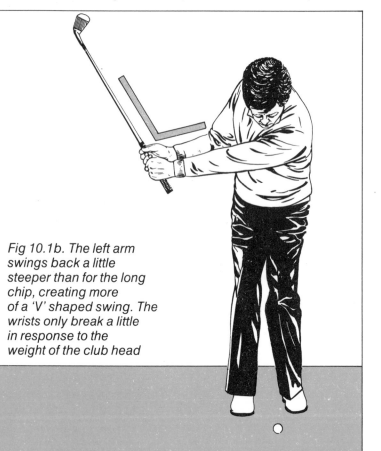

Fig 10.1b. The left arm swings back a little steeper than for the long chip, creating more of a 'V' shaped swing. The wrists only break a little in response to the weight of the club head

gripping nearer the end of the club than for the chip shot. The stance should be narrow and open, i.e. aimed left of the target, but the shoulders parallel to the target. Ensure that you bend forward from the hips so that your arms have room in which to swing, and your weight is towards the balls of your feet. The back of the ball should be positioned just inside the left heel, with the hands ahead of the ball so that the shaft and left arm form a straight line. The ball is not as far back in the stance as for the chip shot, and so more effective loft faced on the club will be used. The weight should slightly favour the left side (Fig 10.1a).

The swing

Swing the left arm away more steeply than for the chip shot, and you will find that the wrists will cock naturally a little under the swinging weight of the club head, but do not make any conscious effort to break them (Fig 10.1b). Some of your weight will transfer to the right leg, and then as the left arm swings the club *down* and through, just feel that you are pulling the club head through the ball with no conscious strike. At the same time, the weight transfers

Fig 10.3. In the more advanced short pitch shot, the wrists actively cock early in the backswing so that the angle between the shaft and arms is greater than for the easier pitching method. This creates a steep narrow arc with little shoulder turn, and the club shaft is almost vertical

Fig 10.2. In order to prevent the club head closing the arms are pulled across the body at the end of the swing so that the club face still points more towards the sky than the ground

back to the left leg, which not only gives some rhythm to the shot, but enables you to swing through without closing the club face. It is important to keep the back of the left hand firm. When you finish, the face of the club and the back of the left hand should be looking more towards the sky than the ground, and your hands and arms will have been pulled across your body (Fig 10.2). The swing is not dissimilar to that of the long chip, although the shape of it is more of a 'V' than a 'U'. The club head swings slightly to the inside on the backswing, so that it can approach the ball from the inside and swing straight through to the target.

Although this particular pitching action does not provide the steepest attack or maximum height on the ball, none the less, it is a good way to play those delicate shots around the green, especially when under pressure. If you have to carry a bunker with little green to work with, you may not get as close as you would like, but at least you will be on the green. So if you have trouble pitching, no matter what your handicap, use a firmer and more passive handed action, and your consistency will improve.

The more advanced short pitch

For this example, we will assume that the ball is sitting reasonably well on a cushion of grass. This will enable you to use a sand wedge, the most lofted club in the bag, and ideal for the shot. With the same set up as above, in the backswing, you should swing your arms up steeply, feeling that your wrists cock quite early, creating a steep narrow arc. Where many people go wrong is that they initiate the backswing with their hands alone. Instead, you must swing the arms up, and cock the wrists as well, creating a 'V' shaped swing where the shaft is almost vertical at the top of the swing (Fig 10.3). There is minimal shoulder turn and not much weight transference, with the head remaining quite still. From the top of the swing, the left arm pulls down, and the club head slides under the ball as the knees move towards the target. In this method of pitching, you will feel that your hands are more active through impact, with the right hand working under the left, and never crossing over it. You will also cut across the ball a little from out to in, due to

the extra wrist action and lack of shoulder turn. The finish is the same as for the more passive handed shot, with the arms drawn very much across the body. When the ball is not sitting on a good cushion of grass, you will have to think of hitting down more, rather than sliding the club under the ball, and perhaps playing it marginally further back in the stance.

In each of these methods, the left arm must swing through the ball, not just at it, and the head must remain anchored until the ball is on its way, as any temptation to look up too soon can be disastrous.

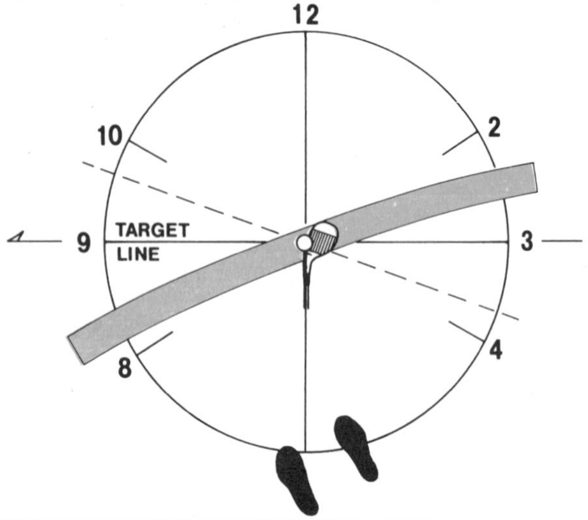

How to vary the shot

There are many combinations that can be applied to this shot, whether you use the passive or active handed technique, and each situation may demand something different. Practise first as described above with a square club face and shoulders parallel to the target so that you can learn how high your particular action and sand wedge will hit the ball.

Then open the club face, i.e. turn it to the right before gripping it, thus adding loft to the club, and aim yourself left of target. In doing this, you align your body and thus the swing line more in the 2 to 8 o'clock direction, so that you create a slicing action across the ball in relation to the target (Fig 10.4). The actual swing is just the same, but because you have set up left of target it thereby creates a steep out to in swing which, combined with the open clubface, will send the ball much higher and it will not roll very far on landing. However, a word of warning about this shot: when you open the sand iron, you bring the flange into play which tends to bounce off the ground. So really you can open the club face only when you have enough grass under the ball, thereby allowing the flange to slide beneath it. You can always open the wedge, which has no flange, and play the same shot, but the ball will not fly so high. The amount that you open the club face and your body will alter the height and length of the shot, so you do need to be aware of the effect of these adjustments in order that the power of your swing is correct.

Spend some time practising from bad lies as well as good, so that when faced with the same shot on the course, you will know what to expect and approach the whole situation in a calm manner.

Fig 10.4. To alter the height of the shot, experiment by opening the club face and the body by varying amounts, creating an out to in swing

CHAPTER ELEVEN

The long pitch

This is the shot that sometimes draws gasps of admiration from the galleries as the ball lands and then spins backwards. However, many golfers fail to appreciate that you can only make the ball behave in such a fashion under certain circumstances. First, the ball must be lying well with no grass behind it, so that the face of the club can contact the ball cleanly; secondly, the shot must be hit quite hard, and therefore you must be an adequate distance from the green; thirdly, the green must be receptive, i.e. fairly soft, or sloping towards the player. In Great Britain, the greens tend to be on the firm side in summer, and so to be able to spin the ball backwards is quite difficult, if not impossible.

Fig 11.1a. The stance should be open and reasonably narrow, with the feet just angled towards the target and the weight on the outside of the left and inside of the right foot. The hands are ahead of the ball with the left arm and shaft in a straight line

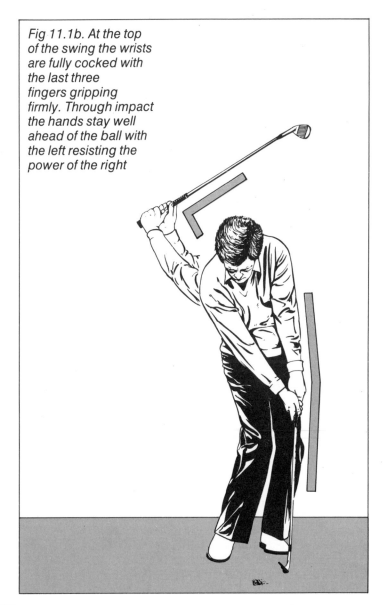

Fig 11.1b. At the top of the swing the wrists are fully cocked with the last three fingers gripping firmly. Through impact the hands stay well ahead of the ball with the left resisting the power of the right

However, it would be wrong to let the spectacular element of the shot overshadow its real purpose, i.e. to send the ball to the green, mainly through the air, so that when it lands it runs a minimum distance.

The set up

Although we use a full backswing for a long pitch, it is still a fairly narrow arc so that the club head descends quite steeply onto the ball. To get the correct amount of resistance in the backswing, the feet are set open to the target, i.e. aimed left, are not too wide apart and are angled slightly towards the target with the weight favouring the outside of the left, and the inside of the right, foot (Fig 11.1a). The shoulders are parallel to the target line so that the line of the swing is inside-straight-inside. The ball is about three inches inside the left heel, hands ahead of the ball, with the shaft and left arm forming a straight line.

The swing

The left arm swings the clubhead away on a relatively steep arc, and quite early in the backswing the wrists will be fully cocked. Since this is a long shot, you are not so likely to fall into the trap of starting the backswing with the hands, but do make certain that it is your arms that get the club head moving initially. At the top of the swing, your shoulders will turn, although not as much as for a drive; the weight will transfer to the inside of the right foot, but the left heel should not leave the ground, since you want to build up a resistance between your legs and the top half of the body (Fig 11.1b). The last three fingers of your left hand should grip the end of the club firmly, as there is considerable pressure at this point with the wrists fully cocked.

As the downswing starts, the weight transfers back to the left leg, and the left arm *pulls* the club head *down* towards the ball. At impact the wrists straighten but the hands are ahead of the ball, just as they were at address. There is a definite strike with the hands to give added crispness and to help create the backspin. Do *not* let the left wrist buckle under the power of the right hand, but keep the back of the hand moving towards the target (Fig 11.1b). The follow through is somewhat curtailed so that the shot is punched away with a good divot being taken after striking the ball.

How to vary the height of the shot

If you want to play a pitch shot with less height, position the ball further back in the stance towards the right foot, thus the club hooding at address, and therefore subtracting effective loft from it. Keep a little more weight on the left leg

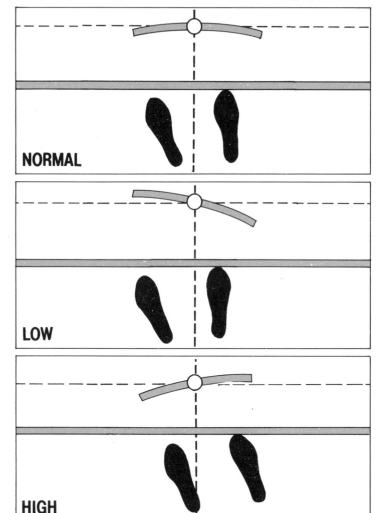

Fig 11.2. This shows the feet and ball position, and swing path for the normal, low and high pitch shots

NORMAL

LOW

HIGH

than for the standard pitch shot, with the hands well ahead of the ball. As the ball is played back in the stance, contact is made whilst the clubhead is still swinging from inside the target line, rather than straight towards the target. Therefore, there is a tendency for this shot to fly a little right of target (Fig 11.2). Allow for this either by aiming just left of target, or closing the clubface – the second option will take more loft off the club and hit the ball lower. As with the standard pitch, swing the arms steeply in the backswing, then hit down on the ball, with a good release of the hands at impact. Keep the left wrist very firm – to promote the punch element in the shot and abbreviate the follow through.

If you have a tall tree to play over, you may need extra height to the shot, and in this instance you should play the ball a little further forward in the stance, i.e. nearer the left foot than normal (Fig 11.2). I should add that if the lie is awful, you will find this shot very difficult and may have to consider another route to the hole. Ideally, you do need some grass under the ball. So with the ball forward, open your stance and your shoulder line so that they aim left of target, creating a steep out to in swing path (Fig 10.4). Depending on how high the ball needs to go, you can open the blade of your wedge, or sand wedge, so that it aims right of target. Keep your hands about level with the ball so that the shaft is vertical rather than sloping towards the target and your weight evenly distributed or, if you have a very good lie, slightly favouring the right side. This set up will enable you to swing the club back with the hands and arms, cocking the wrists early in the backswing. You must not allow the club face to close through impact, and so the knees must move towards the target as the arms swing down and you finish with the club face pointing more towards the sky. What you must remember with this shot is that most of the force will be sending the ball upwards, and not forwards, so it is good practice to find out how far the ball goes when you hit it as high as you can. You need to be able to carry the depth of a large tree as well as its highest branches.

How far should you hit a pitch shot?

When you are using the higher numbered clubs, you should be concentrating mainly on accuracy, and not length from the club. It is no use thrashing your wedge an extra ten yards if 50 per cent of the time you miss the green. You can play a pitch shot best with the 8 iron to sand wedge, so find out how far you hit each club, and also how far the ball goes before it lands. Your 9 iron may cover a total distance of 120 yards, but it may only carry 110 yards. As you will probably wish to carry bunkers with short shots, it is therefore vital to know the carry with each club. On the practice ground, hit about fifteen shots with each club, note the average distance, and for safety's sake assume that the carry is ten yards less with each club. Your accuracy will improve when you hit the short irons at about 80 per cent of your maximum effort. It is far better to learn how to hit a three-quarter 9 iron than to slog away with the wedge. You can always grip down on a less lofted club and make your normal swing, more in control of yourself and the ball.

Fig 11.3. By trying to force a wedge shot you can easily mis-hit it. Better to play a controlled 9 iron that easily carries the bunker. If you hit your 9 iron comfortably 120 yards, for safety's sake, assume that the ball will land about 10 yards short of the total distance and roll the rest. Do not be afraid to hit beyond the pin; the ball will stand a chance of going in, and 5 or 10 yards past is just as near as 5 or 10 yards short. The only time to be less aggressive is if you wish to leave yourself an uphill putt, or the hole is cut very close to the back of the green

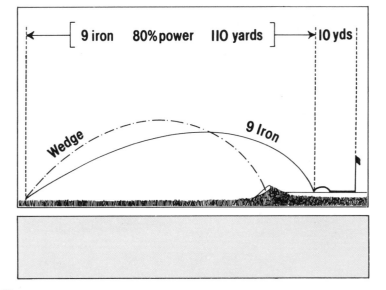

CHAPTER TWELVE

Bunkers need not become a hazard

Despite what many golfers think, to get out of the average bunker is not the most difficult shot in golf. The technique for escaping from these sand hazards – the splash shot – has to be learnt. Once mastered, the fear of bunkers that haunts the golfer who lacks the correct technique, will disappear and his/her results will improve dramatically. There is a tendency to rush the shots you fear, and I see so many players who dart into a bunker, take a short sharp jab at the ball and have to repeat this action three or four times before they manage to get the ball out. It is not difficult to get out of most bunkers. Admittedly, some are easier than others, but becoming accurate with bunker shots takes time and practice, which few club golfers ever devote to bunker play. Unfortunately, many clubs do not have a practice bunker, but you can usually hit a couple of extra shots at some point on the course when it is quiet. Before discussing technique, I would like to explain briefly about sand wedges.

The right equipment

To make bunker shots easier, the sand wedge is the best club to use. Apart from being the most lofted club in the bag,

it has what is called a flange on its sole, which is lower than the leading edge of the club and is designed to bounce on the sand and stop the club head digging in too deeply. When the blade is turned open, this flange comes more into play and the leading edge sits further off the ground. If you do not own a sand wedge, you can use the pitching wedge, which is more inclined to dig into the sand and is not as lofted as a sand wedge. The size and depth of the flange varies from club to club and, depending on the type of sand your bunkers possess, one type of club will be more suitable. If there is not much sand, you want a club with a shallow flange that will not bounce off the harder surface, whereas for bunkers with deep powdery sand, a deeper flange will prevent the club going too far under the ball (Fig 12.1). Many professionals carry a selection of clubs so that they can use the one that best suits the conditions at each course. You cannot go to that extreme, but ask your professional whether the club in your set is best for you and your course.

The grip and set up for the splash shot

The first thing to do is to turn the club face open a little so

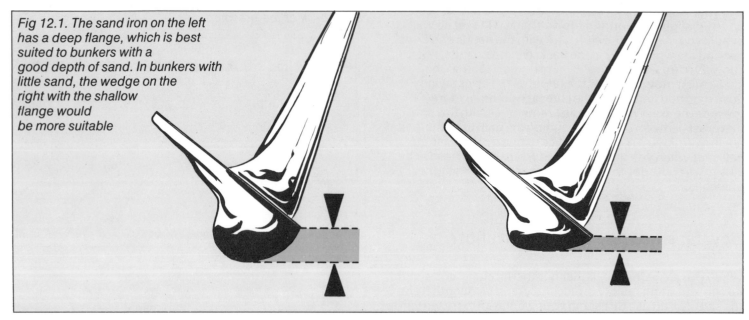

Fig 12.1. The sand iron on the left has a deep flange, which is best suited to bunkers with a good depth of sand. In bunkers with little sand, the wedge on the right with the shallow flange would be more suitable

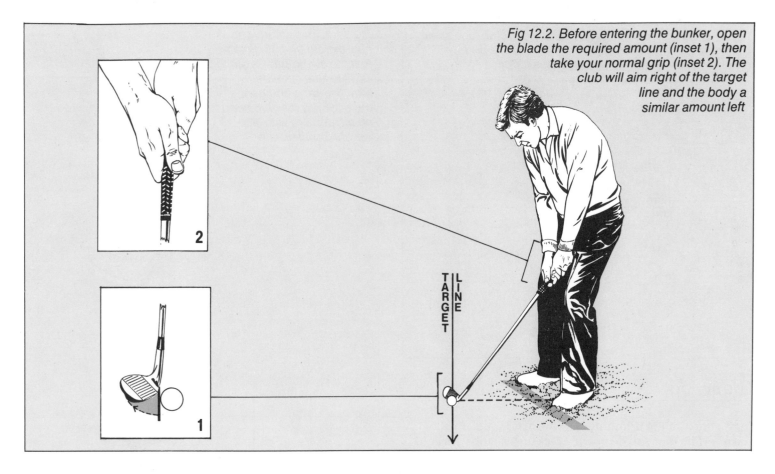

Fig 12.2. Before entering the bunker, open the blade the required amount (inset 1), then take your normal grip (inset 2). The club will aim right of the target line and the body a similar amount left

TARGET LINE

that it faces right of the target, which makes the flange more effective and also adds loft to the club. What you must do, however, is to spin the club open and then take your grip, so that it will remain in this position when you strike the ball (Fig 12.2). It is a good idea to grip down on the club for added control, and since you will incur a penalty if the club head touches the sand prior to impact, you may find it prudent to take your grip outside the bunker. Your normal grip is perfectly suitable, although someone with a strong grip might get better results either by opening the club quite a lot, or turning the hands a little more to the left on the grip.

To offset the open club face, and to promote a steep out to in swing, you must now align yourself left of the target so that a club placed across your shoulders would not be parallel to the target, but aimed possibly three or four yards left, depending on the particular shot in hand (Fig 12.2). So using the clock face analogy, with the target still at 9 o'clock, your shoulders and body will be lined up more towards the 2 to 8 o'clock line with your feet a little open to that, and consequently your swing will also be more in the 2 to 8 o'clock direction (Fig 12.3). The stance is fairly narrow with the weight favouring the left foot. When taking your stance you must wriggle your feet into the sand so that your stance is secure, and in doing this you can, quite legitimately, learn something about the texture of the sand and how deep it is. The ball is played opposite the left instep, but since you are not trying to hit the ball, but the sand behind it, look at a spot about two inches behind the ball, and hold the club just above this point. Remember that you must not let the club head touch the sand until impact.

Fig 12.3. Using the clock face analogy, the club face aims between 9 and 10 o'clock, whilst the body line and swing line will be more on the 2 to 8 o'clock line

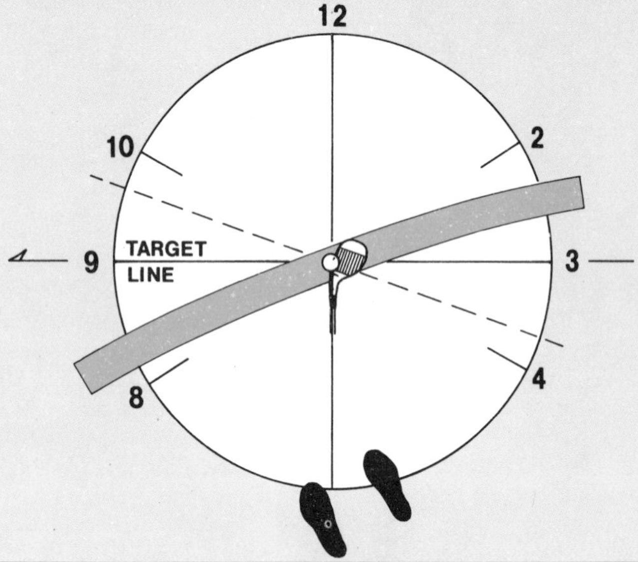

Fig 12.4. This clearly shows how the set up has dictated that the swing path is out to in. With little shoulder turn, the arms and hands have swung the club head on a steep arc with little weight transference

The swing

The swing is made primarily with the hands and arms, but make certain that you do not just pick up the club with your hands and chop at the ball. In an effort to swing from out to in, some golfers feel that they should quickly raise their hands and swing their arms significantly away from the body on the backswing. By setting up as I have just described so that your body is open to the target, you have pre-selected the line of the swing, which is automatically out to in (Fig 12.4). So just swing your arms up in the backswing allowing your wrists to cock, but do not push your arms away from your body. There is little shoulder turn or weight transference. Swing your arms down and, with your hands leading the club head, enter the sand at the predetermined spot behind the ball. At the same time, just as in the short pitch shot, your legs must be active. Transfer the weight more onto the left side ensuring that your knees slide towards the target. Hit right through the sand so that the club head removes a shallow divot of sand about six inches long, on which the ball is sitting. The club face must

not close through impact and should be facing more towards the sky at the completion of the shot (Fig 12.5). Again, as with most shots in the short game, the left hand must not be overpowered by the right, but must stay firmly in control throughout. In the follow through, the arms are drawn very much across the body.

Through and just after impact, you must keep your eye firmly fixed on the sand, resisting any temptation to see the results of your efforts too soon. Just because you are not hitting the ball very far, do not imagine that you should take a very short backswing. Sand provides a great resistance to

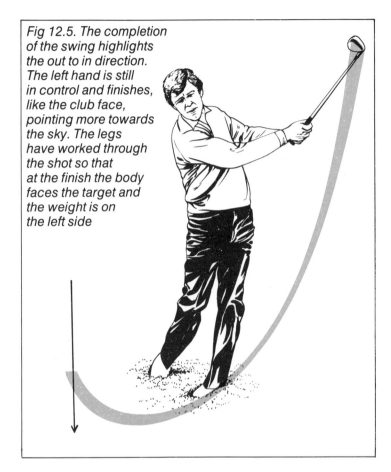

Fig 12.5. The completion of the swing highlights the out to in direction. The left hand is still in control and finishes, like the club face, pointing more towards the sky. The legs have worked through the shot so that at the finish the body faces the target and the weight is on the left side

Remember that you are trying to remove the sand around and under the ball from the bunker, and the ball will go with it (Fig 12.6). At first, you should consider success as being able to get the ball out of the bunker each time with your first shot, not worrying too much about the length but concentrating on making a rhythmical swing right through the ball so that it goes virtually towards the pin, even if it finishes short or runs past it.

Bunker practice

Like all shots in golf, you need club head control, and to test this, and indeed to improve it, draw a straight line in the sand representing the spot at which you want the club head to enter it. Then swing without the ball, trying to hit that line. Until you can do this reasonably efficiently, your bunker play will be inconsistent.

To help you appreciate how to align both yourself and the club face at address, draw a line through your ball towards the pin. This represents the 3 to 9 o'clock line in the clock face analogy, and it will enable you to see that the open clubface will point between 9 and 10 o'clock, whilst your body and swing line are along 2 to 8 o'clock.

To give you a mental picture of what you are trying to do, imagine that the ball is sitting on a five pound note or a dollar bill. You are trying to remove all the sand beneath the note from the bunker, and inevitably the ball will go with it.

the club head, and it must be travelling sufficiently fast when it enters it to create enough momentum to move through the sand. Women golfers often have more problems with bunkers, simply because they will not take a long enough backswing; the club just dies in the sand and the ball goes nowhere. So take a full backswing, just using your arms and hands, and be certain to swing right through so that at the finish you are facing your target, much as you would be on a shot from the fairway. In fact, the splash shot resembles a short pitch shot, but it is aimed left of the pin, hitting the sand and not the ball.

The best bunker players give the impression that the whole swing is rather lazy and languid, almost as though it was in slow motion. Try to imitate them, and make your swing long and lazy rather than short and stabbing.

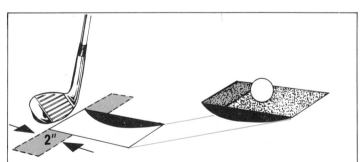

Fig 12.6. To successfully hit bunker shots, you must remove from the bunker the sand on which the ball is sitting. The club head enters about two inches behind the ball and removes a shallow divot about six inches long in the middle of which is the ball

CHAPTER THIRTEEN

Varying the length of a bunker shot

Having practised the basic bunker shot so that you can at least get the ball out of the bunker, you will want to refine this skill in order to vary the length for accuracy. There are a number of ways of doing this and I will outline three different systems.

System 1

In the previous chapter I suggested that the clubhead should enter the sand two inches behind the ball. If you retain the same set up but vary this distance, keeping the same strength swing, you are altering the amount of sand between the club face and ball, and thus altering the power of the shot. The weakness of this system is that you must be well in control of the club head so that you can hit the sand at exactly the right spot. You must also take care that on the really short shots where you are entering the sand perhaps four inches behind the ball, you can still swing through the sand (Fig 13.1).

System 2

By keeping the strength of swing and point of entry the same, but varying the amount that the club face is opened and with it the amount you aim to the left, the power is altered. With the blade opened, so that it is aimed about 45 degrees right of target and your body the same amount left, you will produce a pronounced out to in slicing action across the ball with a very lofted club. In this instance, the ball will go high and not very far; therefore, by varying these two elements of the shot, you can alter the length and height achieved. One of the weaknesses of this system is that a very open club face on firm sand is not easy to use, and the player may find it difficult to get the angles right (Fig 13.2).

System 3

By keeping the amount the club face and body are turned open and the point of entry the same, you can vary the

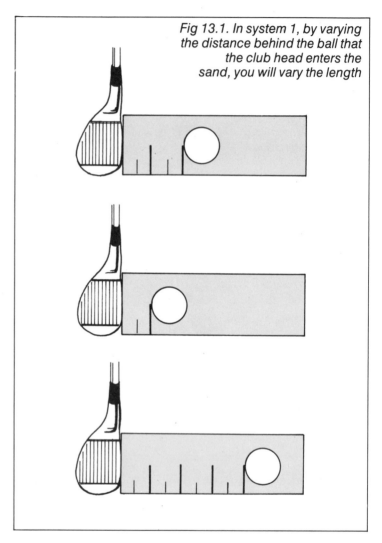

Fig 13.1. In system 1, by varying the distance behind the ball that the club head enters the sand, you will vary the length

distance by how hard you hit the shot. This means that there is only one variable, and it would seem therefore to be the easier system to use, since you just have to work on how far back to swing the club, much as you would with a short pitch shot. The weakness of this system is that on very short shots there is a possibility that you could not swing the club head slowly enough for the correct distance, and still keep it moving through the sand. There is also a limit to how far you could hit the ball. However, once you have mastered the idea that you have to swing through the ball, and not just

three. You must choose the system with which you feel happiest and most confident, and spend as much time as possible practising different shots.

It was one of the best bunker players in the world, Gary Player, who said, 'The more I practise, the luckier I get'.

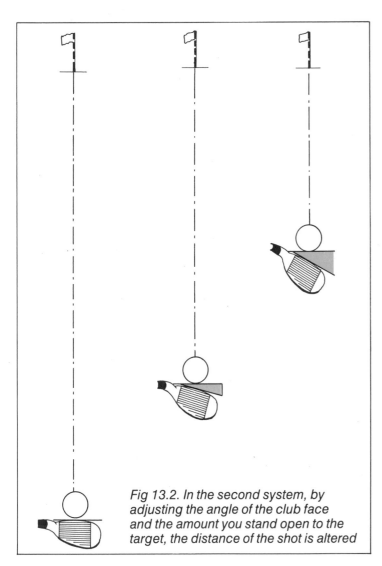

Fig 13.2. In the second system, by adjusting the angle of the club face and the amount you stand open to the target, the distance of the shot is altered

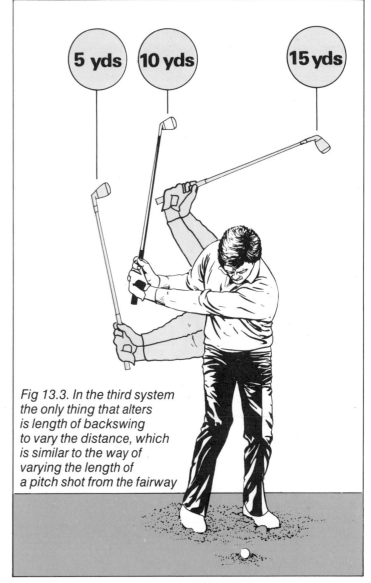

5 yds 10 yds 15 yds

Fig 13.3. In the third system the only thing that alters is length of backswing to vary the distance, which is similar to the way of varying the length of a pitch shot from the fairway

bury the club head in the sand, I think this system is the best because it has only one variable, i.e. the amount of effort in the swing. When its limits have been reached, you have to adjust the club face and body line accordingly, but for the majority of shots, a constant set up and entry point can be maintained (Fig 13.3).

Each system has its weaknesses and strengths, and the best bunker players are able to use a combination of all

CHAPTER FOURTEEN

Imperfect lies

The plugged ball

Playing a plugged ball out of a bunker is not as difficult as it may seem. The main problem with the shot is trying to control the ball, which will run much more than a shot from a decent lie. In the splash shot from the bunker, the club face was opened to increase the effectiveness of the flange, thus preventing the club head from going too deep into the sand. However, when a ball is plugged, it sits lower in the sand, and your challenge is to hit deep enough to get the club head below it. Consequently, by opening the club face, you would make the shot more difficult. Therefore, keep it square or a little closed at address. You also square up the shoulder line, but keep the stance narrow and a little open and wriggle your feet deeper into the sand than normal. The ball is played back in the stance near the right foot, and there is more weight on the left leg than the right.

From this set up, you can easily create a steep angle of attack on the ball, which will remove it readily from the bunker. Swing your arms almost straight up from the ball and concentrate on hitting the sand about one inch behind it. Most of your effort will be downward, and although you must not quit on the shot, the follow through will be curtailed. The ball will come out lower than usual and run, and therefore you should take this into account when deciding on how and where to play the shot (Fig 14.1).

Hard sand

If the ball sits on hard, or firmly packed, wet sand, it will be more difficult for the club head to penetrate the sand, and the flange can be inclined to bounce off it, making it easy to thin the shot. To offset this, play the ball nearer the middle of the stance and aim to hit the sand about one inch behind the ball, concentrating on hitting down through the shot. I would recommend that in very firm sand you keep the club face square, as in the plugged ball shot, so that the flange does not really come into play. Alternatively, you could consider using a wedge, which has a sharper leading edge and will penetrate the sand more easily (Fig 14.2).

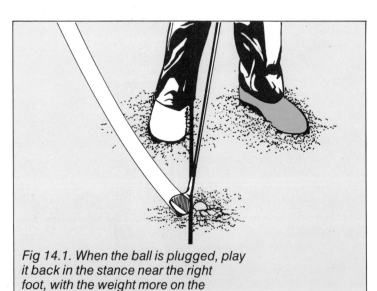

Fig 14.1. When the ball is plugged, play it back in the stance near the right foot, with the weight more on the left foot. Keep the blade square, then swing your arms up steeply, hitting the sand about an inch behind the ball

Fig 14.2. In hard packed sand, play the ball nearer the centre of the stance than for the normal splash shot. If the sand is very firm, also square the blade. Try to hit the sand closer to the ball than normal, concentrating on hitting down through the shot

CHAPTER FIFTEEN

Long bunker shots

The over-riding point to consider with these shots is the angle at which the ball will leave the bunker. It is easy to be over-ambitious and take too much club, resulting in the ball not clearing the bunker face. I would recommend that you position the ball a little nearer the centre of your stance to give yourself a better chance of hitting the ball first, but bear in mind that this will reduce the effective loft on the club. It would be better always to err on the side of caution, and take one less club, i.e. a 7 instead of a 6, and have the knowledge and confidence that you have enough loft to get the ball out of the bunker safely. I always like to open the club face just a touch so that I have some extra loft on my side.

Take your normal stance and set up for the iron in question, and only just wriggle your feet into the sand so that you have a firm base (Fig 15.1). You can align your body parallel to the target, and make a normal inside-straight 4 to 9 o'clock swing. Grip down the club a little with firm rather than light pressure, which will help to eliminate excessive wrist action. Do not transfer too much weight in the backswing; feel that just your arms and hands swing the club back. The downswing should be like a normal shot from the fairway, where the legs just lead the arms. If your legs do not play their part, the club will probably hit the sand first. When the ball is sitting on top of the sand, you will be able to sweep it away, just taking a shallow divot of sand after the ball, and in this instance it is helpful to look at the top, rather than the back, of the ball as this will encourage you to hit it cleanly. Should the ball be lying down even slightly, then you must make a steeper attack on it, trying to hit as close to it as possible. You could set up a little open so that you create an out to in swing (Fig 15.2). The shot will be dampened to some extent by the sand behind the ball, but providing you have not been too ambitious with club selection, it should still come out a reasonable distance. Always swing easily on these shots as any sudden movements can cause you to lose your footing and balance.

Those shots around the green of about 40–50 yards are perhaps the hardest to judge, even for the best players in the world. If you have decided to hit the ball cleanly, then even a few grains of sand can ruin your plans. In firm sand from this distance, it may be worth playing a wedge or a 9 iron and

Fig 15.1. *For long shots from bunkers, take your normal stance for the club being used and grip more firmly, and further down the club than usual, to help eliminate excessive wrist action. Play the ball nearer the centre of the stance, and looking at the top of the ball, try to sweep it off the top, taking a shallow divot of sand after the ball*

hitting just behind the ball, allowing for the sand the take power from the shot.

For the really long shot, providing the bunker is shallow, you will find that a fairway wood, such as a 5 or 7 wood, is the best to play. These clubs have more loft than a 3 or 4 iron and have a tendency to bounce across the sand rather than dig in. Grip down the club as before, and place the ball nearer the centre of the stance than normal. Position the body parallel to the target so that the line of the swing is from inside to straight, i.e. 4 to 9 o'clock, and then try to sweep the ball off the top of the sand. The swing may feel wooden, since there will be little wrist action, but keep it smooth and unhurried and the ball will go a long way. Do not be tempted to thrash it; instead, play it like a three-quarter shot.

As with any shot in golf, this must be practised so that you know how much club you can risk. Unfortunately, if long bunker shots are not successful, they can prove rather costly and then you will wish that you had been more cautious.

Fig 15.2. If the ball sits down a little in the sand, set up with an open stance and club face. This will give you a steeper out to in swing which will fade the ball out of the bunker

CHAPTER SIXTEEN

Putting it to work

The previous chapters in this section have detailed at length a variety of shots played from about 100 yards in. However, no amount of words or tuition will improve your short game to its maximum standard, unless *you* work on this department yourself. Once you have played golf for some time, it will be relatively easy to hit the ball, say, 140 yards; you simply take the appropriate club for the shot. To teach someone to hit the ball 30 or 40 yards for instance, either as a putt, chip, pitch or from a bunker, is more difficult. You do not have a club that is designed by the manufacturers to hit the ball 30 yards, and so you must create a swing that will hit the ball the required distance. Your task is further complicated by the fact that you may need to hit the ball high or low, which means using different clubs for each shot, and consequently differing amounts of power in the swing.

A professional can give you the correct technique for any of the short game shots and, as I have done, explain how to develop a knowledge of how the ball reacts with different clubs. But only by practising will you be able to recall readily which is the correct club and correct strength swing for the different situations that you will encounter during your golfing life. Over a period of time you will build up a casebook history of shots that you can instantly call on, based upon experience and practice. In each of the four main departments of the short game, i.e. putting, chipping, pitching and bunkers, you will seldom use your full power to play any shot. Instead, a combination of club selection and distance must dictate how hard to hit the ball. You should view the development and improvement of your short game in five sections.

1 Perfecting the strike

Until such time as you can strike the ball out of the middle of your club, whether it is your putter, wedge or sand iron, you will not be able to advance as quickly as you could. The beauty about the short game, however, is that you can practise it in very little space, both indoors and outside. You can putt and chip indoors on the carpet, although it may be best to chip off a spare piece of carpet if you have one. You

can also chip and pitch from a coconut mat in your garden, which will save taking divots from the lawn (Fig 16.1). The fact that the ball is not landing on a green will not prevent you from improving your strike, or developing a sense of distance for shots. You can try to land the ball at specific targets, perhaps five yards apart. Most clubs have an area where you can practise these shorter shots, even if they do not have a large practice ground.

Fig 16.1. By practising in your garden hitting balls from a coconut mat to specific targets, you can quickly improve the quality of strike and your judgement of distance

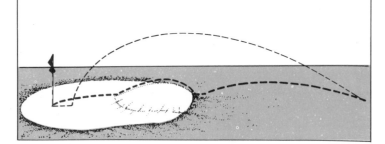

Fig 16.2. There may be more than one way of playing a shot, and you must select the easier and more natural one for you to play

2 Visualization

I am sure that this is an aspect of golf that is most under-used by the majority of club golfers. Instead of developing this sense, so often they take any club from the bag and knock the ball forwards towards the hole without any real preconceived idea of where to land the ball, or how hard to swing. Professionals visualize every shot before they play it, and no department of golf demands this ability more than the short game, where often several alternative shots are possible. You should always try to imagine where the ball must land, how it will roll and then 'see' it going into the hole. You may like to play some shots, allowing the ball to run over contours in the green, or, alternatively, you may prefer to fly the ball over any slight undulations to be assured of a more predictable bounce (Fig 16.2). Start to think about holing shots around the green, even if in reality it may seem an unlikely outcome. By being more positive, you may be pleasantly surprised at just how close you can get to holing shots, leaving yourself the shortest of putts. Always try to visualize your playing partners' shots as well, judging how high or low the ball will go, and where it should land and roll if you were playing it. Not only will this advance your progress, but it will help you also to learn about how the course is playing. If you have spent some time practising successfully hitting balls to an umbrella or ball bag, try to imagine yourself back in that situation and transpose your movements to the shot you have to play.

3 Club selection

Having visualized the shot you want to play, you must then select the right club for the shot. If you have a pitch over a bunker without much green between the bunker and the hole, it would be foolish to use a 9 iron. Make life simple and play a wedge or sand wedge (Fig 16.3). Similarly, from just off the green with no hazards between you and the pin some 25 yards away, your sand iron would not be ideal. It would be safer and easier to use a less lofted club, such as a 6 or 7 iron, so that the ball will roll most of the way to the hole. In time you may develop a liking for certain clubs, or get days when you feel happier using one club rather than another, but try to experiment and practise with several different clubs so that your knowledge and repertoire can improve.

Fig 16.3. Always select the correct club for the shot. For a shot that spends more time on the ground than in the air, use a less lofted club.
For a shot that requires height, always choose a more lofted club. Make full use of your set

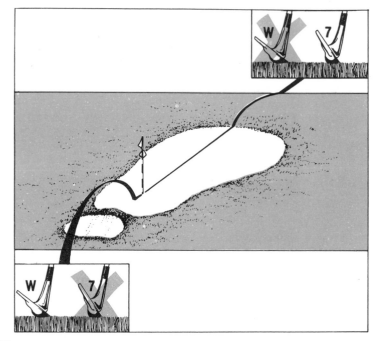

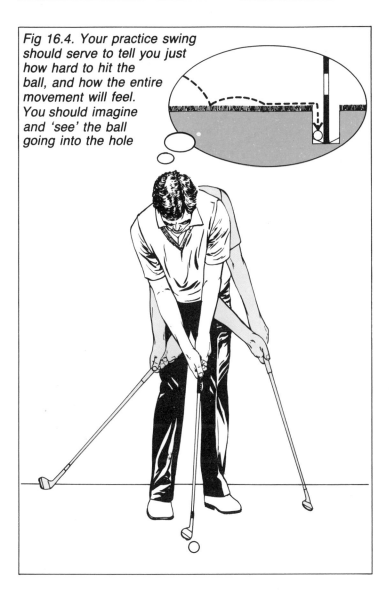

Fig 16.4. Your practice swing should serve to tell you just how hard to hit the ball, and how the entire movement will feel. You should imagine and 'see' the ball going into the hole

to the muscles and brain how much force to put into the shot and how their arms, hands, legs and body must feel. At the same time, they will envisage the ball's reaction and 'see' it running up to or into the hole (Fig 16.4). If professionals need this rehearsal, then so do you.

5 Execution

Having prepared properly for the shot, you must now have the courage to go ahead with what you have decided on. It is usually disastrous to change your mind halfway through the shot on how hard to hit it. If you feel that you are under-hitting the shot, the hands suddenly try to add extra power, which more often than not causes a fat or thin shot. Alternatively, if you feel that you are going to hit the ball too far, you will usually decelerate and quit on the spot. So when it comes to the execution of the stroke, aim the clubhead in the correct direction, using an intermediate target about a yard ahead to help you. Take your stance and then just try to repeat your practice swing in an uninhibited and confident manner.

Short game benefits

For the beginner and higher handicap player, short game improvement will radically reduce your scores. Correct technique is relatively simple to understand and to put into operation. It is also easy to practise; you can hit 100 chips, putts or pitches without feeling too exhausted. I have also found that if you are trying to change your grip, the fact that you can hit a lot of shots with little effort will help to make the new grip more familiar and feel more comfortable. You will also develop the correct aim, set up and posture, and eventually clubhead control far quicker, and thus reap the benefit in your long game. Your progress and improvement will ultimately depend on your ability to perfect each of the five sections I have detailed. By becoming more conscious of trying to hole these shorter shots, you will become a more aggressive player. Always try to make a putt finish just past the hole if it does not go in. Better a foot past than an inch short. Do the same with chip shots so that if you do not hole them, the ball finishes two or three feet past the hole rather than short of it. The only time to be more conservative is if going past the hole will leave you an impossible putt back.

4 Rehearsal

Whilst the professionals may have only the briefest of waggles or swings prior to a full shot, for shots that require less than maximum power, they will always have one or two practice swings. This is a serious rehearsal that will convey

83

CHAPTER ONE

CURING HOOKS AND SLICES

Hitting curving shots is easy

Of all the sports so far invented, golf has to be one of the most exacting when it comes to tolerance of error. Looking at it in an objective manner, you expect to hit an object — the golf ball, which has a diameter of under two inches — with another object — the golf club, on which the ideal and most efficient area of strike, the sweet spot, is nearer one inch in diameter. You swing this club something like twenty feet through a backswing and downswing before you strike the ball and, in order to hit a shot that does not deviate from its intended target, the club must be swinging down the correct path, and the club face must be positioned squarely and approaching from the optimum angle. If you are slightly adrift in any of these requirements, you will hit a shot that curves either slightly or violently, depending on your degree of error.

I also believe that it is a far from natural game, and most aspects have to be learnt rather than coming from some marvellous innate sixth sense. Admittedly, there are those people who take to the game in what seems to be a very natural way, but they are few and far between and are the sort who would excel in any sport. They not only have superb hand and eye co-ordination but also the ability to copy the correct action. Therefore, provided that they have seen the best golfers play (and with so much television coverage of the sport these days, that is almost inevitable) they will most likely swing the club in a respectable manner. However, to progress and to make the most of their talent, they too would need lessons in order to be guided along the correct lines so that they do not start to fall into bad habits. For the rest of humanity, their first attempts at golf will result inevitably in plenty of mis-hits and shots that veer from the straight and narrow. This is only to be expected since the good golf shot requires the correct swing path, club face alignment and angle of attack.

I believe that if you have a good idea and mental picture of what you should be doing and how the club should be swinging, then you have a better chance of producing that swing. This section will give you a working knowledge of the geometry of the swing, why certain shots are hit, and what you can do to straighten those shots.

CHAPTER TWO

The geometry of golf shots

Before deciding what your swing problems might be and how best to cure them, it is important that you are armed with the knowledge to analyse your swing. The best aid for this is to examine the flight characteristics of the ball, thereby revealing the two major factors that affect the shot, i.e. the direction of the swing path and club face alignment. Although your shots may not even have a regular pattern to them, it is more than likely that there are some things that you repeat quite often, perhaps at this stage unknown to you. However, by adding to your knowledge of the ball flight laws, you will make some discoveries about your swing that should help you become more consistent.

The in-to-in swing

In order to give you a good picture of what should happen in the swing, I like to use the clock face as a guide. Imagine that the ball is in the centre of a clock and that you are standing at 6 o'clock with 3 o'clock on your right and 9 o'clock on your left. As the club head moves away from the ball, initially it swings towards 3 o'clock. Then, as the body continues turning, it is swung inwards and upwards between 3 and 4 o'clock. It is swung down virtually on the same path, strikes the ball while it is moving towards 9 o'clock and then, as the body continues turning, swings inside towards 8 o'clock (Fig 2.1). This ideal swing path is known as in-to-in, so called because the club head approaches the ball from inside an imaginary line through the ball to the target (in this case represented by 3 to 9 o'clock) and then, having hit the ball, swings back inside this line.

Club face alignment

Even with the correct in-to-in swing path, if the ball is to go straight then the club face must be square to the swing path at impact (Fig 2.2a). The club head can be facing in one of three directions at impact:

Square — facing the same direction as the swing path;
Open — facing right of the swing path;
Closed — facing left of the swing path.

If the swing path is in-to-in but the club face is open at impact, the ball will start straight and then curve to the right near the end of its flight (Fig 2.2b).

If the swing path is in-to-in but the club face is closed at impact, the ball will start straight and then curve to the left near the end of its flight (Fig 2.2c).

The ball's initial direction is governed mainly by the path of the club head; then, as it nears the end of its flight, any sidespin imparted by the club face causes it to curve in the direction of the spin.

If the club face is square at impact, then only backspin affects the ball and it will fly straight throughout its journey. If the club face is open at impact, left to right spin will be imparted on the ball, and that is why it will curve in that direction towards the end of its flight.

If the club face is closed at impact, right to left spin will be imparted on the ball, and that is why it will spin in that direction towards the end of its flight.

The more the club face is open or closed at impact, the

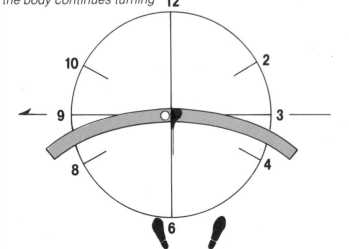

Fig 2.1. This shows the correct in-to-in swing path where the club head swings back between 3 and 4 o'clock, returns on a similar path, striking the ball whilst moving towards 9 o'clock, then swings back inside towards 8 o'clock as the body continues turning

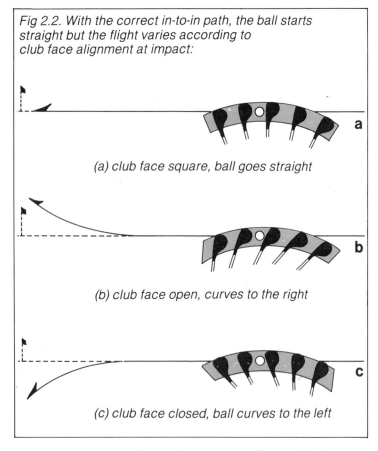

Fig 2.2. With the correct in-to-in path, the ball starts straight but the flight varies according to club face alignment at impact:

(a) club face square, ball goes straight

(b) club face open, curves to the right

(c) club face closed, ball curves to the left

in the same direction but prove to be inconsistent with club face alignment.

It is also indisputable that the more lofted clubs do not impart as much sidespin as the straighter faced clubs. The reason for this is that the less lofted clubs contact the ball nearer to its equator and usually at a shallower angle of attack, thereby imparting more sidespin than backspin, and it is the sidespin that causes the ball to curve in the air (Fig 2.3a). A more lofted club contacts the ball lower

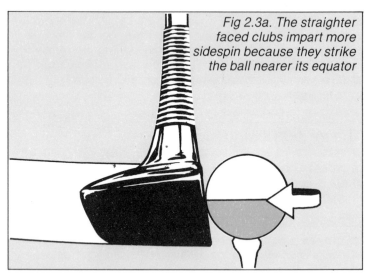

Fig 2.3a. The straighter faced clubs impart more sidespin because they strike the ball nearer its equator

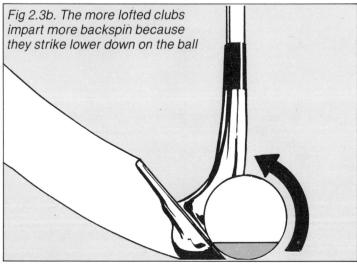

Fig 2.3b. The more lofted clubs impart more backspin because they strike lower down on the ball

greater the curve in flight. Furthermore, if the club face is in either of these extreme positions, it will influence the initial direction of the ball. Usually the beginner who has trouble squaring the club face will be able to produce a great variety of shots from what may appear to be the same swing. What is happening is that the club face may be wide open on one shot, sending the ball immediately to the right on a high trajectory, and then very closed on the next shot, making the ball fly immediately left and very low. Although the club may have been swung in the same direction, the extremely open or closed club face alignment has become the greater influence on the shot so that the ball will start in the direction to which the club face was looking, rather than the direction in which it was swinging. Thus many beginners find it difficult to analyse their shots. However, most players tend to swing the club down, and usually at a fairly steep angle of attack, thus creating maximum backspin and minimum sidespin (Fig 2.3b). In this instance, backspin becomes more influential than sidespin, and the result is a shot that does not curve too much in the air although it may not always be struck in the direction of the target.

The out-to-in swing path

Whenever the club head approaches the ball from outside

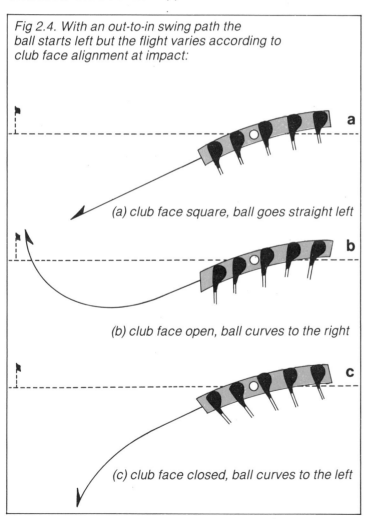

Fig 2.4. With an out-to-in swing path the ball starts left but the flight varies according to club face alignment at impact:

(a) club face square, ball goes straight left

(b) club face open, ball curves to the right

(c) club face closed, ball curves to the left

the imaginary line through the ball to the target, it is called an out-to-in swing path and will cause the ball to start left of the target. To use the clock face analogy, the club head is swinging more along a line in the 2 to 8 o'clock direction although, of course, the out-to-in symptom may not be as extreme as this. However, as with the in-to-in swing, the club face can be in one of three positions at impact — square, open or closed — and each will affect the shot differently.

If the swing path is out-to-in, with the club face square at impact, the ball will start left and continue straight left (Fig 2.4a).

If the swing path is out-to-in, with the club face open at impact, the ball will start left and then curve to the right (Fig 2.4b). The ball will fly higher than normal.

If the swing path is out-to-in, with the club face closed, the ball will start left and then curve left (Fig 2.4c). The ball will fly lower than normal.

The in-to-out swing path

Whenever the club head approaches the ball from inside the ball to target line and then swings to the outside of that line, it is known as an in-to-out swing and will cause the ball to start to the right of the target. Again, using the clock face as a comparison, the club head will be swinging more from the direction of 4 to 10 o'clock, although the swing may not necessarily be as extreme as this. As with the two previous examples, the club face can be square, open or closed.

If the swing path is in-to-out, with the club face square at impact, the ball starts right and continues straight right (Fig 2.5a).

If the swing path is in-to-out, with the club face open at impact, the ball starts right and then curves to the right (Fig 2.5b). The ball will fly higher than normal.

If the swing path is in-to-out, with the club face closed at impact, the ball starts right and then curves to the left (Fig 2.5c). The ball will fly lower than normal.

From these explanations of the geometry of the swing, you can see that three different swing paths are possible as are three different club face alignments. Any combination will give one of the flight characteristics detailed above, and your shots will fall into one or maybe more of these categories. However, there is another factor that affects the ball's flight and that is the angle of attack.

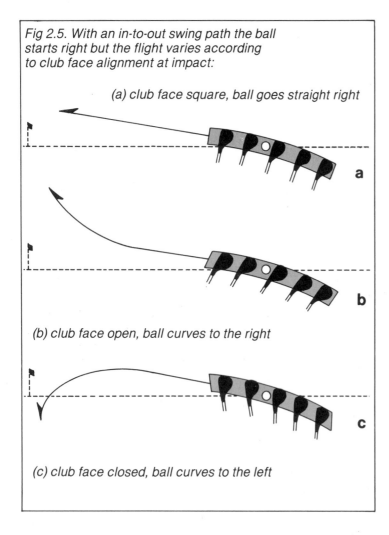

Fig 2.5. With an in-to-out swing path the ball
starts right but the flight varies according
to club face alignment at impact:

(a) club face square, ball goes straight right

a

(b) club face open, ball curves to the right

b

(c) club face closed, ball curves to the left

c

that affects the ball's flight and that is the angle of attack.

Angle of attack

As you address the ball, you stand to the side of it rather
than directly above it, and thus the correct club head path
should be from in-to-in. Because the ball is on the ground
and not sitting on a tee at eye level, you must also have an
up and down element in the swing. In golfing terms, this
is known as the angle of attack. As the club head

approaches impact it swings downward and then parallel
to the ground before starting to swing upwards.
Therefore, you have the opportunity to hit the ball when
the club head is travelling at one of three angles:
downward, level or upward. Different shots call for
different angles of approach.

Different swing paths create and affect the angle of
attack. The correct in-to-in swing path provides an angle
that is the most suitable for all shots, and in order to
create a downward angle for the irons, through to a
slightly upward angle for the driver, adjustment is made to
the ball position, width of stance and weight distribution.
The angle of attack will then become correct automatically
for the type of strike required.

An out-to-in swing will create a steep attack on the ball,
which tends to concentrate too much force downwards
and insufficient forwards and thereby distance is lost. A
player in this category will take quite deep divots which
will point well left of the target (Fig 2.6a) and will be
happier hitting irons, preferably short ones, rather than
woods. The steepness of attack will promote backspin,
sending the ball higher than it should go, and since this
line of swing is more usually accompanied by an open club
face (which adds loft to the club), all shots lack their true
potential in distance. Whereas the steepness of attack can
be tolerated to some degree with the irons, when it comes
to woods, and especially woods teed up, the angle of
attack is a considerable drawback. It is likely that tee shots
will be hit with the top of the face, resulting in a skied shot
(Fig 2.6b) whereas the best result will be a shot lacking in
length.

The in-to-out swing path creates a shallow attack on the
ball and will thus emphasize the forward motion in the
swing, yielding good distance but making a consistent
solid strike with iron shots rather more difficult and
unlikely. Because the angle of attack is shallow, it is easy
to hit behind the ball since the base of the arc often occurs
before the ball is struck (Fig 2.6c). Players in this category
will enjoy hitting a ball teed up or from a very good lie
rather than from a bare lie. Since the swing lacks the
correct downward approach, less backspin is imparted
and so the shots tend to fly lower than normal and can
thereby produce more length.

Summary

These golfing facts will help you to understand how you swing and to appreciate into which category you fit. Most golfers tend to be consistent in the direction in which they swing the club, i.e. the swing path, but less so in getting the club face in the same position at impact, thus leading to shots that go in totally different directions. At first you will not necessarily remember or even understand the explanations of the factors that affect the ball's flight, so take some time to re-read this chapter and refer back to it when necessary.

Try to remember that it is the direction in which the club head is swinging, i.e. the swing path, that is the greatest influence on the initial direction of the ball. Club face alignment will also affect the initial direction of the shot to some extent but will only be of great significance, perhaps over-riding the swing path direction, if extremely open or closed. Club face alignment is responsible for imparting spin which will make the ball curve towards the end of its flight. The angle of attack and club head speed will influence further the height and distance of the shot.

For those of you who have no knowledge of the golf swing and look upon it as one of life's mysteries, I can assure you that by the end of this book you will have learnt a lot, hopefully sufficient to be able to improve considerably.

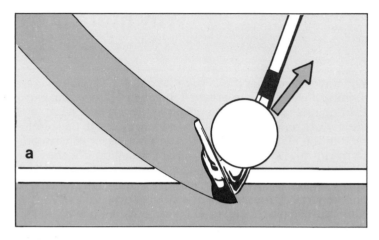

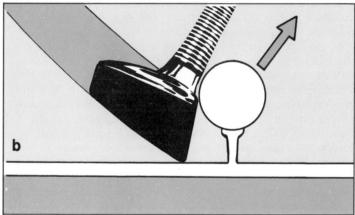

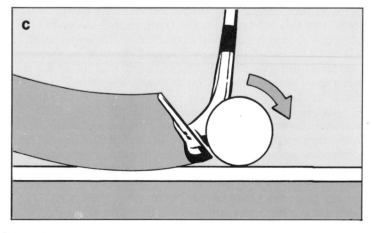

Fig 2.6a. An out-to-in swing path creates a steep angle of attack which means that the player will take deep divots that point left of target

Fig 2.6b. A steep angle of attack can lead to tee shots being struck with the top of the club face

Fig. 2.6c. The shallow angle of attack from an in-to-out swing path can cause the base of the arc to fall before the ball, making it difficult to consistently hit crisp iron shots

CHAPTER THREE

Why more golfers slice than hook

You have learnt that the alignment of the club face at impact is one of the greatest variables in golf, causing the beginner and higher handicap player to hit a wide variety of shots. The correct hand action has to be learnt so that the club face is returned at least reasonably square to the in-to-in swing path at impact, resulting in a shot with little curve to the ball flight. Unfortunately, the correct hand and arm action is not natural to beginners, and generally their version of swinging a club usually returns the club face open at impact, resulting in a shot that curves to the right.

For a start, many people grip the club incorrectly and inevitably have trouble returning the club face squarely to the ball. Many players also grip too tightly, fearing that if they do not do so they will have insufficient control and the club may slip in their hands. Gripping too tightly definitely stifles hand and wrist action so that they lack the freedom of movement necessary if the hands, wrists and arms are to contribute fully to the shot (Fig 3.1). Instead, you are more likely to see a person swinging in a stiff manner — trying to use sheer force to propel the ball forward. In fact, describing a beginner's action as a 'swing' is, in most cases, far from the truth because swing is the one factor that is missing from their action. They lack the freedom to swing their hands and arms which, in turn, will swing the club head, and consequently the clubface is left open at impact sending the ball to the right. Thus it seems only logical to aim to the left to allow for it. But this action aligns the body so that the swing path of the club is out-to-in in relation to the target, and the ball's flight will now be influenced not only by an open clubface but by an out-to-in swing path, both of which will impart slicing sidespin. In this way, the error is compounded.

There is another classic cause of slicing which stems mainly from bad alignment. Aiming the swing and yourself in the correct direction is not the easiest aspect of golf and is often neglected by the beginner. In many instances, a pupil aims a long way right of the target, and then the only way to get the swing back on track is to develop a loop to the outside at the start of the downswing. This action feels quite natural since it involves using the powerful muscles in the right shoulder area, and for most beginners, at the top of the swing, this area feels most able to deliver a solid blow to the ball. But the shoulder and back muscles are big and slow and cannot produce enough club head speed to hit the ball a long way. The looping action again sets the swing across the ball from out-to-in and with good hand action missing, once again you have the blueprint for a slice.

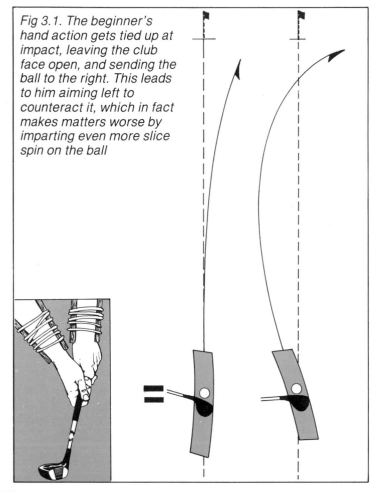

Fig 3.1. The beginner's hand action gets tied up at impact, leaving the club face open, and sending the ball to the right. This leads to him aiming left to counteract it, which in fact makes matters worse by imparting even more slice spin on the ball

CHAPTER FOUR

The correct grip

The purpose of the grip is to return the club face squarely to the ball without any undue or independent manipulation of the hands. The technique of the game of golf has evolved over many years, matching the evolution of the equipment used, and whereas fifty years ago players may have had to employ a hand action that facilitated the hickory shafts of their era, today's

equipment allows a simpler method of playing golf and one that advocates quite simple hand action. However, without first gripping the club correctly, the hands are unable to work either in the right direction or in harmony and this is how problems may begin.

Each of us may have hands that work at different speeds; certainly those people who use their hands quite actively at work will have developed strong muscles and consequently will be able to derive a great deal of power from them. But the power will lie dormant or be destructive if the grip is technically suspect and does not naturally return the club face square at impact.

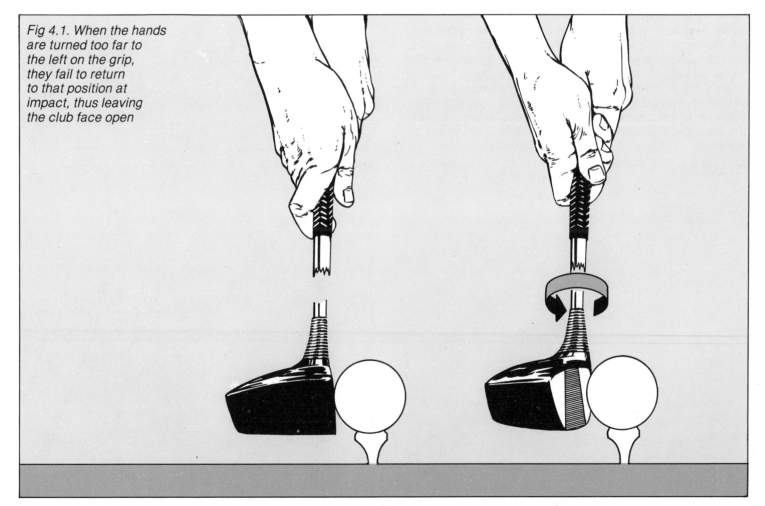

Fig 4.1. When the hands are turned too far to the left on the grip, they fail to return to that position at impact, thus leaving the club face open

Constructing the grip

The slicer is usually born as a result of poor hand action, which usually results from placing the hands on the grip incorrectly, with either one or both hands turned too much to the left so that the 'V's formed by the thumb and forefinger point too much towards the chin or left ear. At impact, the hands fail to return to their address position and instead are facing more to the right. Of course, the club face matches this change and it too faces right of the target (Fig 4.1).

To correct this, place the left hand on the grip with the shaft across the palm of the hand and the end of the grip under the fleshy pad at the heel of the hand and cradled in the forefinger (Fig 4.2). Close the last three fingers round the grip, and make certain that when you look down you can see at least two to two-and-a-half knuckles (Fig 4.3). The thumb should sit just to the right of centre of the front of the grip, and there should not be a large gap between the base of the thumb and the forefinger, since this part of the hand must provide much of the support at the top of the swing. You may find it easier to check if the grip

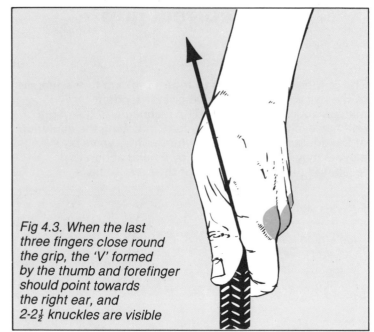

Fig 4.3. When the last three fingers close round the grip, the 'V' formed by the thumb and forefinger should point towards the right ear, and 2-2½ knuckles are visible

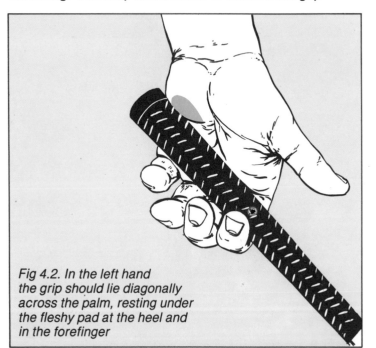

Fig 4.2. In the left hand the grip should lie diagonally across the palm, resting under the fleshy pad at the heel and in the forefinger

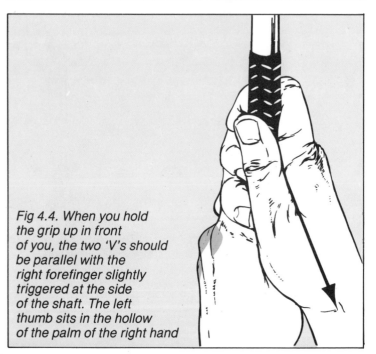

Fig 4.4. When you hold the grip up in front of you, the two 'V's should be parallel with the right forefinger slightly triggered at the side of the shaft. The left thumb sits in the hollow of the palm of the right hand

conforms to these standards by holding the club up in front of you. The 'V' between the thumb and forefinger should point in the region of your right ear, and when you place the right hand on the grip make sure that the 'V' is parallel to the left hand 'V' (Fig 4.4). The right hand grips the club more in the fingers than the palm and fingers, so that it can provide maximum power. Again, do not allow a gap to develop between the thumb and forefinger, and rest the thumb just to the left of the centre of the grip. The forefinger should feel slightly triggered on the grip and you will find that the left thumb will rest in the hollow of the right hand. Whether you overlap, or interlock the right little finger, or even grip with ten fingers on the club, is a matter of personal preference. Personally, I would recommend the overlapping grip but if either of the other two feel more comfortable, then so be it.

Placed on the club in this fashion, you will find that if you uncurl your fingers, then the hands are practically parallel, with the back of the left and palm of the right facing the target.

The very strong grip

It is also possible to slice with a very strong grip, i.e. both hands are turned well to the right so that you can see three or four knuckles on your left hand (Fig 4.5). What happens with this type of grip is that the hands are blocked through impact with the heel of the left hand going towards the target. If the hands were to release you would hook the ball quite viciously since they are in such a strong position. You need to adjust the grip to suit the recommendations above by moving both hands round to the left.

Grip pressure

Grip pressure is applied by the last three fingers of the left hand and the middle two of the right, and should be light rather than tight. It is difficult to be exact about grip pressure but you are gripping too tightly if the muscles in your forearms feel hard and taut. For muscles to work most efficiently, they must be relaxed and soft. Grip the club in your left hand only and place your right hand on your left forearm. By increasing the left-hand grip pressure

you will feel the muscles tighten and harden. Now slacken the pressure until they feel relaxed and you will be nearer the correct grip pressure.

At this stage, the new grip will feel far from comfortable since any change of grip feels extremely awkward initially but the sooner you decide to commit yourself to this change, then the sooner and quicker you will progress. Try to practise the grip for at least 5 to 10 minutes a day so that you quickly get used to the unaccustomed position.

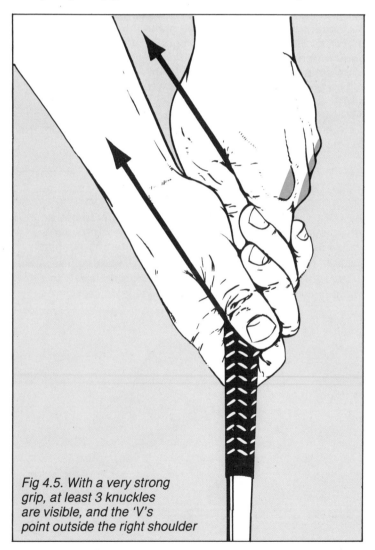

Fig 4.5. With a very strong grip, at least 3 knuckles are visible, and the 'V's point outside the right shoulder

CHAPTER FIVE

Correcting the set up

As a natural reaction to the ball curving to the right, many players who slice start to aim left. When you address the ball, ideally you should try to set yourself parallel to an imaginary line between the ball and target. This will then enable you to swing the club head on the correct in-to-in path. In clock face terms, the ball to target line is from 3 o'clock to 9 o'clock, and you stand parallel to that (Fig 2.1). However, the slicing golfer who aligns his or her body much more along the 2 o'clock to 8 o'clock line, consequently swings from out-to-in.

The golfer who aims a long way to the right sets the body more along a line in the 4 o'clock to 10 o'clock direction, but then inserts a looping action into the swing so that the club head inevitably approaches more from the 2 o'clock direction (Fig 5.1).

Intermediate target

One of the easiest ways to set up correctly is to use an intermediate target, which is approximately three feet ahead of the ball on the target line. So standing behind

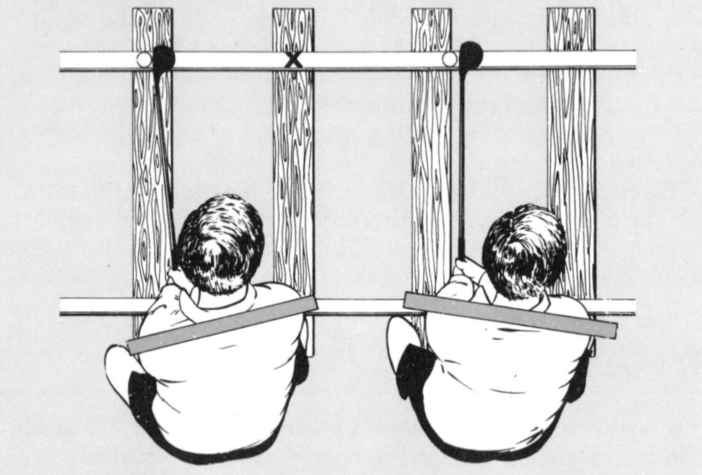

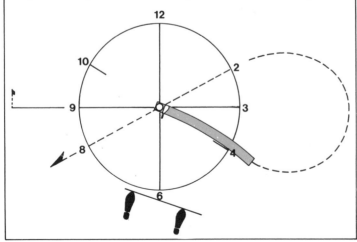

Fig 5.1. The golfer who aims a long way right, tends to loop his swing onto an outside path in the downswing

Fig 5.2. The golfer on the left shows the ideal set up to slice, with the shoulders open. To counteract this use an intermediate target to aim over, and a slightly closed shoulder and eye line to encourage an inside takeway

In order to have a good mental image of the set up, liken it to a railway track where the ball and clubhead are on the far rail, and you stand on the near one

the ball and looking towards the target, pick out a divot or leaf just ahead of the ball. Then standing opposite the ball, place the club head behind the ball square to this imaginary line and the target. At this stage of your progress, it would be useful either to place two clubs down, one just outside the ball and the other about 18 inches nearer to you and parallel to the target, or to work on your set up standing on square patio slabs or kitchen floor tiles where the straight lines will help considerably. The new address position will feel strange initially, and any endorsement you can get to assure you that you are now square to the target and not aiming miles to the right or left will enhance your progress and belief in what you are doing.

It is important for you to check first that the club face is square. It is often difficult for the player to appreciate that the blade may be misaligned, but with the help of clubs on the ground, or the square tiles, this should become obvious.

Next position your feet, knees and hips parallel to the ball to target line. The most important parts of the body in determining the swing path are the shoulders, and ideally these too should be parallel, but since you are trying to cure an out-to-in swing path, it would be beneficial at this stage to align your shoulders a little closed, so that a club placed across them would point more towards the target than parallel to it. This over-correction will help you to keep the club on an inside path, and when that becomes more automatic you can consider re-aligning the shoulders back to the parallel position. However, I must stress that the shoulders should be only slightly closed and not aimed a long way right (Fig 5.2).

As a similar aid to encouraging the correct inside

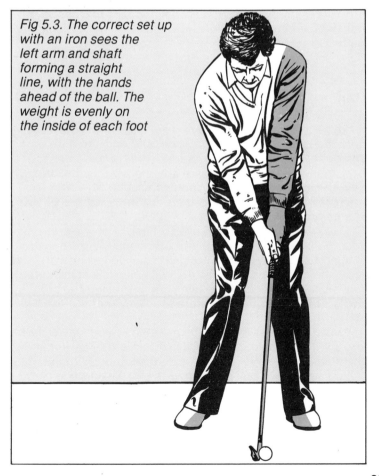

Fig 5.3. The correct set up with an iron sees the left arm and shaft forming a straight line, with the hands ahead of the ball. The weight is evenly on the inside of each foot

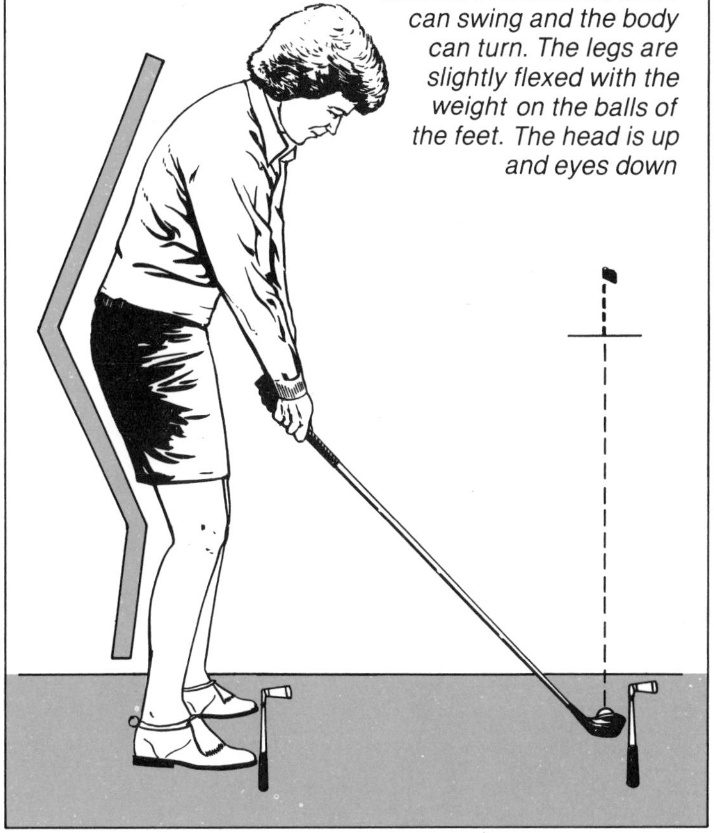

Fig 5.4. By bending forward from the hips with the seat pushed back as counterbalance, a space is created in which the arms can swing and the body can turn. The legs are slightly flexed with the weight on the balls of the feet. The head is up and eyes down

backswing path, and also to visualizing it, set your eye-line so that a club held across your eyes and under the bridge of your nose would aim just right of the parallel.

Most golfers who slice have trouble making a good turn in the backswing, and so to make this easier, angle your right foot out about 15 to 20° at address, but make sure that the left foot is fairly square to the line of flight, or only just turned out.

Whereas the left arm is straight at address, the right arm should feel soft to enable it to fold easily on the backswing, so allow it to bend very slightly, with the elbow pointing towards the right hip bone. Check your set up in a mirror, and when viewed face on your left arm and the shaft should form a straight line. The shaft must slope towards the target so that your hands are ahead of the ball (Fig 5.3). Many golfers who slice, start with their hands behind the ball with the left wrist kinked inwards, which leads to a hands and arms only backswing with no shoulder turn. By setting up correctly, you have a much better chance of a good shoulder turn.

If you stand with the mirror to your right, you should just be able to see your left shoulder in it, which will indicate that the shoulders are slightly closed.

In order to have a good mental image of the set up, liken it to railway lines, where the ball and club head are on the far rail and you stand on the near one (Fig 5.2).

Fig 5.5. The player who slices often has bad posture and stands too close to the ball, which leads to an out-to-in swing path

Good posture

In order that your body and arms can work correctly throughout the swing, good posture is essential. Therefore you must bend forward from the hips to create a space in front of you in which your arms can swing. At the same time your seat must push back as a counter-balance, the weight must be towards the balls of your feet, and your knees will be slightly flexed and knocked towards each other. Keeping your chin up off your chest and eyes down will complete good posture, thereby ensuring that your body turns out of the way to allow a free arm swing (Fig 5.4). If you set up in this manner you will be more likely to get your distance from the ball correct. Many players who slice stand far too close to the ball, which almost certainly guarantees an out-to-in swing path (Fig 5.5).

Ball position

It is highly likely that you have been playing the ball too near the left foot. This is a chicken and egg situation, but any golfer who has open shoulders will have the ball too near the left foot, and likewise anyone with the ball too near the left foot will have open shoulders. So you must now play the ball from a position nearer the centre of your stance (Fig 5.6).

This will have a two-fold effect. First, it will help to square up the shoulder line and consequently the swing line; and secondly, when the ball is played too near the left foot, the club head reaches the ball when it is starting to move back inside the target line and is moving towards the left of the target. Therefore it is likely that the ball will start left of target.

I would suggest that for the meantime, you play all iron shots with the back of the ball just forward of centre and the driver about two inches inside the left heel.

You can check ball position either by placing one club down across your toes and another behind the ball, or by doing that and placing some tee pegs to mark your feet position and then moving away and looking from the other side. It is always easier to see the ball position from an onlooker's viewpoint rather than from standing at the ball, although personally I prefer to check my set up by looking in a mirror. By playing the ball more centrally, you will find that the right shoulder does not want to stretch forward and out of line but will feel much lower than the left and further back than usual.

Weight distribution

The distribution of your weight at address can affect the swing significantly, and, in fact, weight distribution should change to match the shot you are playing.

With short irons, there is slightly more weight on the left side than the right.

With the rest of the irons and fairway woods, it is about even. When driving, there is slightly more weight on the right side than the left.

The slicer tends to keep too much weight on the left foot at address for all shots, which restricts the shoulder turn and encourages a steep out-to-in swing. I would like you to set up with a 6 iron, and try to feel that your weight is even and towards the inside of each foot (Fig 5.3). Probably you have not been conscious of this before, and you can check it more easily by looking in the mirror.

Summary

The shape of the swing and the resultant shot are largely pre-determined at address. With a poor set up even the best golfers in the world will not hit the ball straight, so do not think that improving your set up is purely cosmetic — it is essential if you wish to improve.

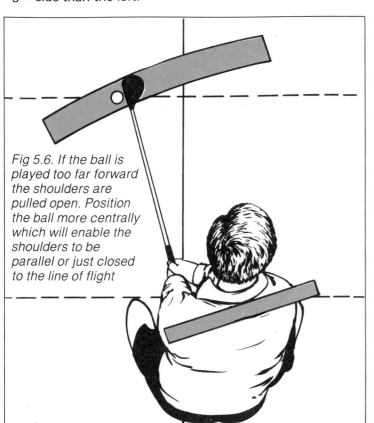

Fig 5.6. If the ball is played too far forward the shoulders are pulled open. Position the ball more centrally which will enable the shoulders to be parallel or just closed to the line of flight

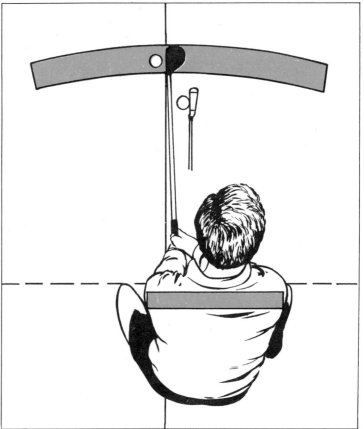

CHAPTER SIX

Correct hand action

Before you tackle the full swing, it is important that you have a clear understanding of the correct hand action. By now you should have a good grip, showing about two to two-and-a-half knuckles of the left hand and not gripping too tightly, and an improved set up. Therefore, you can now concentrate on just how the hands and arms should work in the impact area.

Swing the club back and stop when your hands reach hip height. At this point the back of your left hand should face forward and the toe of the club should be in the air, with the leading edge at right angles to the horizon (Fig 6.1). Due to the swinging weight of the club head, your wrists will be starting to cock upwards so that your left thumb is hinging towards the inside of your left forearm and the shaft is beyond the horizontal position. Provided that everything is correct here, then it should also be correct at the top. If the club face points towards the sky, then you have rolled your wrists and the club face open and you can regard this as being one of the major contributory factors to your slice (Fig 6.2).

Now swing the club head into the ball, allowing your forearms and hands to rotate slightly to the left and your wrists to uncock. This action will square the club face at impact, and you should find that by hip height on the through swing, the back of the right hand faces forward, and the toe of the club will again be in the air. As the right hand and arm rotate over the left after impact, the wrists will start to cock upwards and the left elbow will bend inwards and downwards, much as the right elbow does on the backswing. This will be an unfamiliar position to many of you since it is quite possible that your right hand has been working under rather than over your left through impact.

To emphasize the hand and arm action, put your feet together, which will help to keep out unwanted upper body action, and make this half-swing, quite gently at first, checking that everything is correct at hip height. Depending on how bad your hand action has been, you will feel that your hands, wrists and arms are much more active and freer, creating a slinging action of the club head into the ball. Club head speed will increase and, although at this stage the quality of strike may vary, the ball should

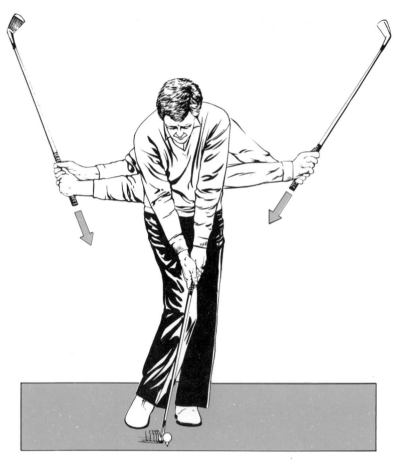

Fig 6.1. To develop good hand action, using a 6 iron with the ball teed low, swing back to hip height, where the back of the left hand should face forwards, toe of the club is in the air with the leading edge at right angles to the horizon. At hip height on the through swing the club should be in a similar position with the back of the right hand facing forwards. At the end of each half of the swing, the end of the grip should virtually point to the ball

start to fly with less curve on it. If this exercise is done correctly, you will find that the end of the grip points virtually at the ball at the completion of each half of the swing. Do not worry if at the end of the through swing the club face points slightly towards the ground — that is acceptable. What is unacceptable is a club face that points even slightly towards the sky (Fig 6.3). Once you have hit a few shots that fly straight, or with a slight right to left draw, you will have experienced correct hand and arm action through the impact zone, and the shot will feel sweeter off the clubface and will also fly further and lower than those that curve to the right.

This drill is best performed with the ball on a low tee, gripping down slightly on a 6 iron, which has just about

Fig 6.3. This is an incorrect position where the club face points towards the sky. Check this against Fig 6.1

Fig 6.2. This shows a correct, square blade and an incorrect open blade position. In the correct position the back of the hand faces forward, not skyward

NO
YES

the right amount of loft to allow sidespin to be more effective than backspin, and enabling you to get a true idea of how square the club head is at impact. The exercise serves to highlight hand action and hopefully starts to make your hands and arms less tense. It will also help you to swing the club on the correct plane and path. However, once your arms, body and legs start to play their part in the full swing, this hand action becomes somewhat diluted and less obvious as the swing gathers width. But without first being able to rid yourself of tension and the incorrect action, you would find it difficult to appreciate or incorporate the correct movements.

CHAPTER SEVEN

Starting correctly

By adopting the grip and set up described, you have every chance to start the backswing correctly, but I think it is important that you have a good picture in your mind's eye of what you are trying to do.

To correct any error in golf, it is usually necessary to feel that you are overdoing the correction, initially at least, and generally the change is not as big as it feels. As a slicer, your swing path has been very much from out-to-in, and in order to correct it you must try to swing from in-to-out. In clock face terms, you must convert from a 2 o'clock to 8 o'clock direction more towards the 4 o'clock to 10 o'clock line (Fig 2.1). As you address the ball it is essential that you can visualize where the club head should swing. When practising you can lightly score a mark in the grass in the 4 o'clock to 10 o'clock direction and try to swing along that line, or place some tee pegs in the ground just outside the correct line and try to swing just inside them.

Thus your pre-shot thoughts are important: if you can imagine where the club head should swing you have a better chance of making it happen.

The initial move

Most slicers do not turn the body sufficiently but make the backswing simply by swinging their arms and hands, so now you must feel that the left shoulder, left arm and shaft move away from the ball together (Fig 7.1). For most golfers, it is not natural to use the left arm, but by doing so you will engage the left shoulder muscles and start the turn correctly so that the triangle formed by the shoulders and arms at address moves away as one unit. The hands at this stage should feel passive and you must concentrate on turning your shoulders as the arms swing backwards and then up. You will notice that the club head will start back in a straight line and then turn inside much more than usual, and I would suggest that you lay another club down just outside the ball so that you can check this easily. The club head should move straight back without touching the club on the ground and then start to move inside. The slightly closed eye line will also help you to envisage the correct path. Try to keep the club head lower

Fig 7.1. Feel that you start the backswing with the left arm and shoulder so that the triangle of the arms and shoulders remains intact. Starting in this manner will help keep the club head low to the ground

to the ground than usual as this encourages the backswing to become a combined action between the shoulders and arms. Avoid any conscious hand or wrist action, especially excessive rotation to the right which will roll the clubface open. Since the shoulder and back muscles are large, they move slower than those in the hands and arms, so do not rush the backswing or you will not give the shoulders time to turn.

At the top

As the backswing continues, your body will be turning out of the way as your arms swing up, so that at the top of the swing your back will be turned 90 degrees and your hips about 45 degrees (Fig 7.2). I have no doubt that you

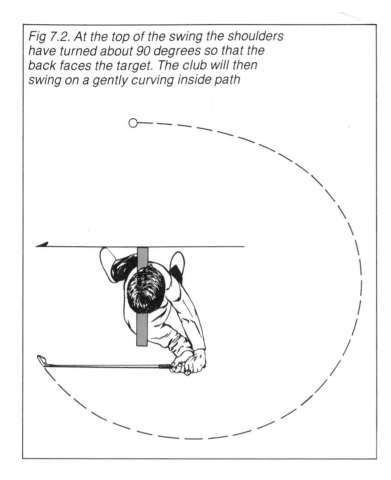

Fig 7.2. At the top of the swing the shoulders have turned about 90 degrees so that the back faces the target. The club will then swing on a gently curving inside path

perfectly straight or bent at the elbow, and the right arm should be folded with the elbow pointing to the ground. Main pressure will be felt in the last three fingers of the left hand which must not loosen on the grip. The left hand should have cocked so that the angle between the shaft and left arm is approximately 90 degrees. Provided that it has cocked correctly, i.e. flexed sideways rather than back on itself, the back of the left hand, arm and club face should be more or less in line. If your wrists have collapsed and there is excessive cupping at the back of the left wrist, you will probably find that the club face has turned open, i.e. the leading edge will be almost at right angles to the horizon (Fig 7.3 inset). This needs correcting. You may find that you have loosened the last three fingers of your left hand so keep them firm. If this is not the answer, then you may have turned your wrists open too much, possibly just as the club moved away from the ball. If this applies to you, then you must make certain that you initiate the backswing with the left shoulder, left arm and shaft moving away together, keeping your hands passive. Check the club position halfway back, making sure that the blade is at right angles to the horizon. Alternatively, you may just need to control the clubhead better at the top of the swing. When the shoulders fail to turn, there is a great deal of pressure on the wrists at the top of the swing, and inevitably they tend to collapse under this pressure. Now by turning your shoulders more fully, you are spreading the load of the swing and should control the club head better at the top.

As a reasonable guide, the arms should swing into the gap between your right shoulder and head, and for those of you who have been lacking a decent shoulder turn, your hands will feel lower and further behind you than usual. This is because the shoulders have provided an unaccustomed turning element to the swing, consequently altering its entire feel. The plane, i.e. the angle of incline of the swing, is flattened, making your attack on the ball shallower and providing more forward and less downward force to result in more powerful shots.

However, the 'wrist rollers' among you may feel that your arms have swung higher than usual, and this is correct. Excessive clockwise hand and arm rotation in the backswing flattens the swing and thus when you eliminate the roll, the plane becomes slightly more upright which is correct. Your action now should feel that you swing your arms much more up and down in the swing, thus preventing you from casting the club to the outside. You

will feel a stretching sensation in your back muscles never before experienced. However, by closing the eye line it means that your head has rotated slightly to the right, which will make it easier to achieve a full turn. Check your swing in the mirror and you should find that the club shaft is virtually parallel to the line of flight (Fig 7.3) whereas many slicers have the shaft aimed left of target at this stage. This parallel position is vital if you are to be able to return to the ball from an inside path. Your weight should be mainly on the inside of your right leg, which should retain the flex it had at address and, depending on your flexibility, you may need to lift the left heel just off the ground. As the hips have turned, the left knee should now point just behind the ball.

The left arm should be slightly bowed, rather than

should check this new position in a mirror so that you can see how good it looks — just like a professional!

There are two good exercises that will help you to improve your backswing. Place a club behind your back and under your arms and then, bending slightly forward as in the good address position, turn to your right and left. This will help to stretch your back muscles and put you into the correct position at the top of the backswing.

Find a sidehill slope, where the ball would be positioned above your feet and practise swinging there. This will make your shoulders turn more readily and flatten your arm swing, causing you then to swing from in-to-in. Or alternatively, imagine that the ball is teed at shoulder height so that you hold the club horizontally in front of you. From this position, swing the club making sure that your shoulders turn to the right and then to the left as your arms swing. By gradually lowering the height of the imaginary tee and repeating the swing, you will start to appreciate and experience how the shoulders must turn in the swing.

Although golf is not a series of positions, but a continuous swing, it is necessary when altering your game to be able to isolate and feel new positions. You will be able to groove your backswing by being aware of the correct new position at the top. By checking it in a mirror you will also get a visual input which will serve as an additional reminder as well as helping you to see that everything looks as it should.

Fig 7.3. Ideally the shaft at the top of the swing is parallel to the target, the club face is still square and in line with the back of the forearm with the right elbow pointing to the ground. In the inset drawing, due to the wrists collapsing the club face has been turned open so that the leading edge is almost at right angles to the horizon

CHAPTER EIGHT

The change of direction

The change of direction from backswing to downswing is perhaps the most crucial part in the swing as even with a perfect backswing, things can still go wrong at this point. For most beginners, it is hard to appreciate that the hands and arms are going to provide most of the power when in fact they feel so weak. What you must realise is that it is club head speed that is of the essence, and hands and arms can move much quicker than the body. However, clubhead speed is only of consequence if the face is square and travelling from the correct angle and in the direction of the target at impact — all factors that you are working towards.

Remember, however, that you are trying to *swing* the club head back to the ball and *not* heave your body towards the target. Unfortunately for the beginner and higher handicap player, it is the right shoulder area at the top of the swing that feels most powerful, and so often the downswing is initiated by throwing the right shoulder forwards towards the ball (Fig 8.1). This only serves to set the swing onto a steep out-to-in path, and the hand and arm action gets blocked.

The correct way down

On the backswing, the right side of your body should be turned out of the way to create a space in which your arms should swing backwards and upwards, and it is into this same space that they must swing on the way down. You must feel that instead of moving the right shoulder first, your arms should swing *down* into this gap and your back should stay turned to the target (Fig 8.2). To you it will feel as though you are liable to hit the ball a long way to the right, which indeed might well happen initially, but do not worry about that for the moment. Instead, concentrate on pulling down with your *left* arm, without your shoulders turning back. This, of course, will not be what is happening, but remember that until now your shoulders have been far too active at this point, and so you must feel that the start of the downswing has no shoulder motion at all. In clock face terms, you will now be able to swing the club down more from the 4 o'clock, rather than 2 o'clock, direction.

Fig 8.1. *At the top of the swing it is the right shoulder area that feels most powerful and is usually thrown forward casting the club onto an outside path*

Downswing faults

Many problems with the change of direction come about because the player is so keen to hit the ball *forward,* and this translates into a forward movement with the right side creating an outside approach to the ball. If instead you can think of the downswing as being a *downward*

103

movement of your arms, then you are more likely to keep the club head on an inside path. The right shoulder will then turn much more under the left, rather than forward and across it. The forward element of the swing will come about naturally as your body eventually turns through the shot.

Another cause of throwing the club head onto an outside path is rushing from the top, which tends to allow the right side to overpower the left. Instead, the change of direction should be smooth and unhurried so that the left arm can keep control. As your arms swing down you must feel that your left knee moves towards the target, which will start to transfer your weight onto the left side. However, this must not be a jerky or violent action but should be a smooth movement, complementing the arm swing. It is easy to overdo leg action, which can spin the left side out of the way too much, and pull the right side forward creating the out-to-in swing that you are trying to cure. So feel that the left knee moves laterally towards the target at the same time as the left arm pulls down. You can practise the correct change of direction movements without the ball, perhaps with the mirror to your right, so that you can check that the club stays on that inside path.

The head position can also help or hinder at this stage. Prior to the backswing, you set the eye line closed by rotating the head slightly to the right; at the start of the downswing, try to maintain that same position, so that you are looking at the ball mainly with your left eye and your head does not move towards the target either laterally or in a rotary motion. This will help to keep you on that inside track, but once you approach the impact zone it is quite in order for it to be rotating fractionally to the left.

Fig 8.2. At the start of the downswing the arms should swing down into the space created by the right side moving out of the way on the backswing. It may help you to keep the club on the inside by feeling that your back stays turned to the target as your arms swing down. The left knee should move laterally towards your target which will encourage an inside attack

CHAPTER NINE

Impact and beyond

Having started the downswing on the correct track, i.e. from the inside, you must now allow your hands and arms to work through the impact zone much as described earlier in Chapter 6. So as the club head approaches impact, both hands and arms will be rotating to the left and your wrists will be straightening, squaring the club face. To the better golfer, who has trained his or her hands to work correctly in the swing, this becomes very much a matter of free-wheeling through impact to the finish, allowing the centrifugal force of the swing to assist in the squaring of the club face. But to the golfer who has been gripping the club too tightly and has not experienced a decent club head release too often, it will mean consciously having to work on squaring the club face. At this stage it is important also to remember the swing path

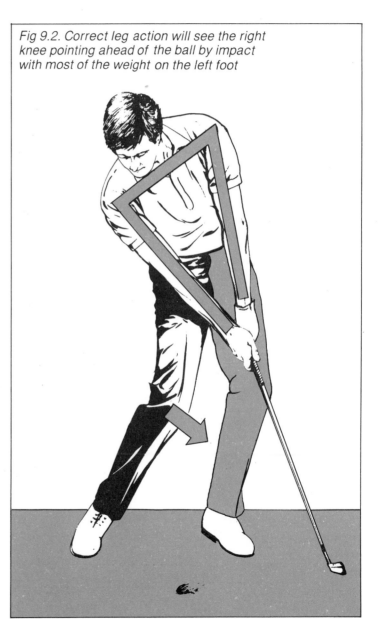

Fig 9.2. Correct leg action will see the right knee pointing ahead of the ball by impact with most of the weight on the left foot

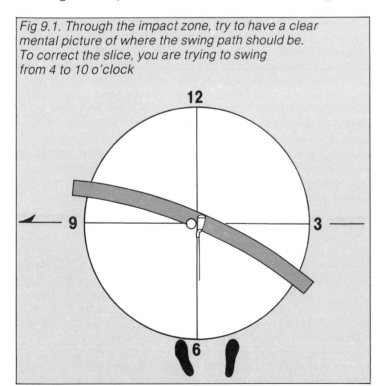

Fig 9.1. Through the impact zone, try to have a clear mental picture of where the swing path should be. To correct the slice, you are trying to swing from 4 to 10 o'clock

Fig 9.3. The golfer who does not use his legs correctly leaves too much weight on the right leg on the downswing and through impact

direction, i.e. 4 o'clock to 10 o'clock (Fig 9.1) and feel that as your arms are swung down towards the ball, they are not only rotating to the left but also swinging away from your body towards the right of the target. This is the way that someone who draws the ball plays, and it is a good antidote to the slice. As the arms swing past the ball the body must continue turning so that both at impact, and just beyond, the triangular relationship between the arms and shoulders is intact.

Leg action

I wrote that at the start of the downswing you should move your left knee towards the target, and as the swing progresses you must allow the right knee also to move in this direction so that by impact it is pointing ahead of the ball (Fig 9.2). Many golfers who slice lack any leg action, and if you are someone who has most of their weight on the right foot at impact (Fig 9.3) then you must emphasize the leg action somewhat so that you finish with most of your weight on the outside left foot with the right heel off the ground and the right toes providing the balance. It is helpful to move your right knee towards your left at impact in order to get to this position. You must also allow your head to rotate towards the target once you have hit the ball so that you finish looking forward with your body in the same direction. Most of my pupils create good leg action by trying to swing to this balanced finish position, because if you can get to that position, then your legs must have worked well (Fig 9.4). Timing them to move at exactly the right moment comes with practice, but once you realise what the legs should be doing, at least you have a sporting chance of attaining the correct action.

Left side strengthening

Most people who play golf right-handed are right-handed, which usually means that their left side is quite weak. It is therefore beneficial to strengthen the left side, as it plays an important guiding role in the swing. Grip a 6 iron with the left hand only and place the right hand over the left instead of on the grip. Without a ball, make your backswing and you will naturally be using your left side, just as you should in the two-handed swing. As you swing down you will feel your left arm pulling, rather than the

Fig 9.4. By trying to swing to a balanced finish, where most of your weight is on the outside of your left foot and the right heel is off the ground, you should develop better leg action

right side throwing the club. Complete the swing, but at impact take your right hand off the club. You will automatically swing through the ball, rather than stop at it, and finish facing your target with your weight on your left side and the right heel off the ground. This exercise not only promotes left side control but also encourages the body and legs to work correctly beyond impact. If at the beginning, the club feels too heavy, grip down it slightly. Gradually build up the number of swings, but take care not to over-exercise at first — perhaps 10 to 15 swings twice a day would be sufficient, depending on your strength.

Action and reaction

At first it will be hard for you to accept that in order to stop the ball going to the right, you need to have the feeling of hitting in that direction. Earlier in this book, I explained in some detail how the slicer is born, i.e. lack of correct hand action leaves the club face open — spinning the ball to the right so that the golfer starts to hit across to the left. But if you work on developing your hand and arm action to square the blade at impact, the ball will no longer curve to the right and this will encourage you to start to attack the ball from the correct inside path. I have suggested that you envisage this as being in the 4 o'clock to 10 o'clock direction, but some people may even have to exaggerate that example so that at first you *feel* as though you are swinging from 5 o'clock in order to correct your extreme out-to-in swing. Eventually, as your hand and arm action improves, you will have more confidence to commit yourself to that feeling of swinging to the right of the target and will ultimately be able to start the ball just right of the target and draw it back.

If you find that it starts consistently too much to the right, you will know then that a lot of your hard work is over and that you can now swing the club head back to the ball from the inside. You may need to move the ball a little nearer the left foot and square up your shoulders at address so that your swing path will be more in the 3.30 to 9 o'clock direction.

As your hand action improves you may have to weaken the grip if you find that the ball is now curving too much to the left. This is fine tuning and very much a personal thing.

CHAPTER TEN

The pull

The pull is the shot that starts left and continues in that direction with no curve to the flight (Fig 2.4a on page 87). I am dealing with this now as it belongs to the same family as the slice, i.e. the out-to-in swing path, and, generally speaking, someone who slices will also pull some shots. Remember that the straighter faced clubs will impart more sidespin than the lofted clubs, and so if you slice with your 4 iron you may well pull your 9 iron, since the strong backspin from the shot over-rides the sidespin and the ball flies straight left (Fig 10.1). If your shots fall into this category, then really you should consider yourself

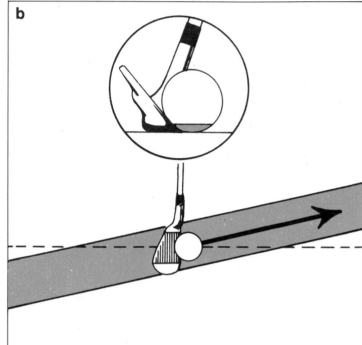

Fig 10.1b. The same swing with a more lofted club will pull the ball straight left of the target because the more lofted club strikes the ball low down, imparting strong backspin which over-rides the sidespin

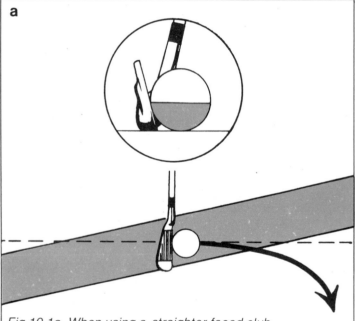

Fig 10.1a. When using a straighter faced club, swinging on an out-to-in swing path with an open club face, the ball will start left then fade to the right. Because the ball is hit nearer its equator, more sidespin is imparted which eventually curves the ball to the right

a slicer rather than someone who pulls shots.

However, if you tend to pull all of your shots, then it would seem that your hand action, and consequently club face alignment, is fine but the direction of the swing path is incorrect. First you muct check your set up, using the methods in pages 94–97. You may discover that you have been aiming straight left instead of at the target. Therefore you should practise with the two clubs on the ground until the new line up becomes familiar. In this new set up you will be more aware of seeing your left shoulder in your vision when you look towards the target.

You might have been aiming left because the ball was

too far forward in your stance, which has the effect of pulling the shoulders open at address and thereby setting the swing path out-to-in in relation to the target (Fig 10.2a). Place the ball more centrally in your stance and check that your shoulder line is parallel to the target.

If your shoulders are square but the ball is still too far forward, you will hit it when the club head starts to move back to the inside rather than when it is travelling directly towards the target (Fig 10.2b). Adjust the ball position until your shots start on target.

Alternatively, you could be aiming too far right, and then coming over the top of the ball (Fig 10.2c). Just like the golfer who slices, you can either be aiming too far left or right and create a pulled shot.

Whichever set up error you make, it will be helpful if you have clubs on the ground in order to convince you that the adjustments are correct. If your set up and ball position seem satisfactory but your shots still go left, it must be because you are swinging from out-to-in. If this is the case, you should re-read pages 100-107 and work to improve both the takeaway and downswing, making sure that you have a strong mental picture of where the club head must swing on that corrective 4 to 10 o'clock path. Do not make the backswing just by lifting your arms up; be certain that you also have a good shoulder turn which will help to keep the club on an inside path. Do not rush

the change of direction for the downswing, but concentrate on swinging your arms *down*, feeling that the club is swung to the right of the target. Hitting shots that *feel* half- to three-quarters power will help to keep the club on that correct inside track.

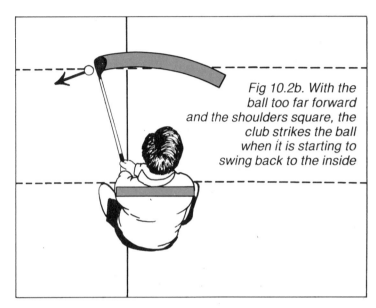

Fig 10.2b. With the ball too far forward and the shoulders square, the club strikes the ball when it is starting to swing back to the inside

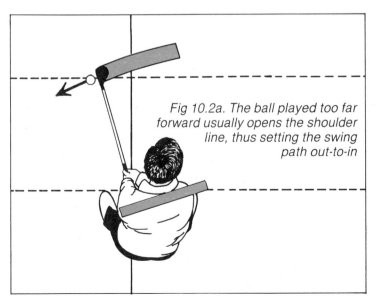

Fig 10.2a. The ball played too far forward usually opens the shoulder line, thus setting the swing path out-to-in

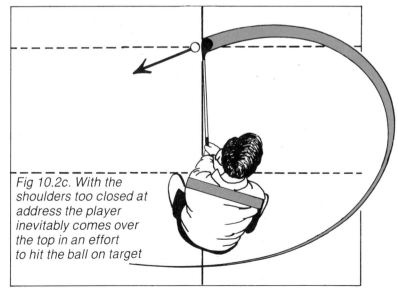

Fig 10.2c. With the shoulders too closed at address the player inevitably comes over the top in an effort to hit the ball on target

CHAPTER ELEVEN

The pull hook

Fig 11.1. If the body stops turning and arms stop swinging through the shot, the hands will quickly turn the club face closed resulting in a shot that curves from right to left

It is important to differentiate between the beginner who hits the occasional pull hook and the golfer who hits it more regularly. As a beginner, if you swing from out-to-in and are inconsistent with club face alignment at impact, you will inevitably hit a few shots that start left and then curve left (Fig 2.4c on page 87). The club face was closed, i.e. facing left of the swing path at impact. For the beginner the shot will usually go quite low and not very far, and is a symptom of the fact that until you have played and practised a little longer you will continue to hit a variety of shots. The main cures have already been detailed and you must go back to checking the basics, such as grip, set up and ball position. You must try to

swing along the 4 to 10 o'clock swing path line and make certain that you keep your hands and arms swinging through the ball — not just at it. If the body stops turning or the arms slow down, the hands carry on and close the club face too quickly (Fig 11.1). So instead of thinking about hitting at the ball, look upon the swing as making a big circle with the club head, and striking the ball within that circle.

The consistent pull hook

However, if you consistently hit shots that go quite a long way but always start left and turn left at the end of their flight, apply the same corrections as for the pull (see pages 108–109) to correct your swing path. You should also check that your grip is not too strong, i.e. hands turned too far to the right, and experiment with a weaker grip. It is quite acceptable to draw the ball under control, i.e. where the ball curves only a few yards in flight, as this is, in fact, a powerful shot, but if the club face becomes too closed at impact a hooking flight is the result, which is usually very destructive. You may also need to smarten up your foot and leg action, ensuring that as you swing your arms down, your weight is transferred from your right foot back to the left (Fig 9.2) and that your hips continue turning towards the target so that your hands and arms have room to square the club face gradually (Fig 17.1). You should also practise the following half swing drill, which will emphasize quieter hands in balance with the correct body turn and arm swing.

beginner should practise this exercise as well as the one outlined on pages 98–99 in order to ingrain the right balance of hand, arm and body action.

However, one word of warning about this exercise: whereas the wider stance encourages firmer wrists, it tends also to restrict leg action, so make sure that you do not swing flat-footed! To further promote awareness of swinging *through* the ball, practise the left side strengthening drill (see page 106).

Fig 11.2. To correct an over-active hand action make a half swing ensuring that the triangle relationship of the arms and shoulders remains intact throughout. The hands should work within this swinging action, not independently. The swing will feel wooden but will highlight how the arms and body work

Half swing exercise

Using a 6 iron, grip down the handle and take a wider stance than normal for the club. Practise a half swing in which the triangle of the shoulders and arms at address turns to the right, then swings through impact and remains intact until hip height on the follow through (Fig 11.2). Feel that you are trying to swing the club more by the effort of your body turn and arm swing (which the set up should encourage) than by active hand action. You are trying to educate your hands and arms rather than just swish them about aimlessly in the swing. The swing should feel wider than your normal action both on the backswing and through swing. Hit about 20 shots like this and then make your usual swing. You should feel that your hands are working more within the body turn and arm swing rather than independently. The more erratic

The straight slice

We have now covered all shots possible from an out-to-in swing path, and before tackling the in-to-out family of shots, I want to deal with those players whose swing path is correct, i.e. in-to-in, but whose shots start towards the target and then veer to the right. This is because the clubface is open at impact.

If your shots are in this category you should check first that your grip is not too weak, i.e. your hands are not turned too much to the left on the grip (Fig 12.1). If this is the case, you should move them until you can see two to

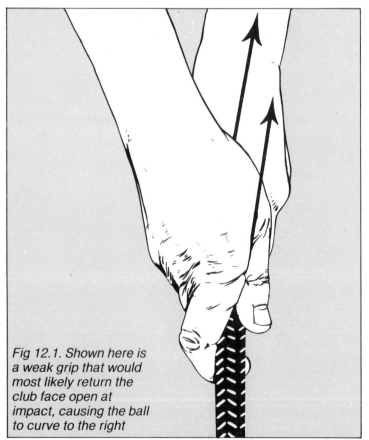

Fig 12.1. Shown here is a weak grip that would most likely return the club face open at impact, causing the ball to curve to the right

two-and-a-half knuckles of the left hand, which should then square the club face (see pages 91–92).

Also check that you are addressing the ball with the club face square to the target; it is easy to fall into bad habits in this respect and not to realise that the face is out of line.

If your grip and club face alignment seem okay, make certain that your hand action is correct and lively enough, since you may be opening the clubface on the backswing with excessive hand and arm rotation and/or blocking the action through impact. Practice as in pages 98–99 until the shots go straight, allowing the right hand and arm to rotate over the left just after impact. If your grip is good and you feel that you are rotating your hands and arms correctly, you could be doing one of two things: either not transferring your weight sufficiently on the backswing (Fig 12.2) and/or moving too much towards the target on the downswing. On the backswing, the weight must transfer to the right side so that about 80 per cent rests on the right leg at the top of the swing. As the downswing starts, the weight moves back to the left so that all momentum is in the direction of the target. The left hip and the body continue turning out of the way, giving your arms a clear passage to swing through and square the club face. If you fail to transfer your weight to the right on the backswing — often brought about by trying to keep the head still — it will move onto the left leg and will then transfer back to the right during the downswing. Consequently the left side does not clear out of the way and the hands and arms cannot fully release to square the club face. If you are in this category, the correction will make you *feel* that you are swaying to the right in the backswing as you turn the right side out of the way. Do not worry about keeping your head absolutely still but keep it steady with your eyes on the ball, and make certain that you feel the weight going onto the right leg, which must retain its original flex. Having turned on the backswing you will now be able to transfer your weight back to the left side and then continue turning the left side out of the way as the arms swing through. Feel that the

your leg action. There are plenty of photographs of top professionals who use a strong leg action at the start of the downswing. They match this with a very strong hand and arm action that few club golfers possess. Do not be lulled into copying this strong leg action when all it will do is prevent your hands and arms delivering the club head squarely into the back of the ball at impact. Practising hitting balls with your feet together will make you appreciate the role of your hands and arms.

Fig 12.2. If the correct weight transference is not made in the backswing, too much weight remains on the left foot, often brought about by trying to keep the head absolutely still

Fig 12.3. If you move too much ahead of the ball, you will not be able to release the club head at impact and it will remain open

right knee moves towards the left at impact, which helps to turn the left side smoothly out of the way.

If you feel that you make a good weight transference but still slice the ball, it might be that you are getting ahead of the ball at impact (Fig 12.3) and in that position the hands are unable to release. You will have to feel that from the top of the swing, you look at the back of the ball very carefully and try to stay behind the shot. You may need to put more emphasis on an arm swing and less on

CHAPTER THIRTEEN

The in-to-out swing

If you consistently manage to swing the club head along an in-to-out path then you should not be too far away from becoming a reasonably good golfer. You may find it hard to believe if you fall into this category since you may also be capable of hitting the most horrendously destructive shots as well, and so may quite possibly possess a high handicap. As you will realise by now, the ideal swing path is from in-to-in, and for the beginner, the hardest part in golf is to bring the club head back to the ball from an inside path. You can already do this but cannot yet hit the ball while the club head is travelling towards the target since your club is still travelling towards the outside, i.e. right of the target, at impact. Having conquered the hardest part, you will be pleased to learn that your corrections are far easier to master than for the inveterate slicer. It will be helpful to review the sort of shots that are likely from an in-to-out swing path:

▶ When the clubface is square at impact, the ball will go straight right (Fig 2.5a on page 88).
▶ When the clubface is open the ball will start right and then turn to the right (Fig 2.5b on page 88).
▶ When the clubface is closed, the ball will start right and then turn to the left (Fig 2.5c on page 88).

The player who has a well developed hand action has no problem in squaring the clubface at impact, and indeed very often closes it. He/she is therefore more than likely to start to swing from the inside, knowing that the ball will turn to the left in flight. Under control, this type of shot, the draw, is one of the most powerful, and indeed most satisfying, of golf shots, which I am sure would satisfy all golfers. However, when the draw becomes too strong, it turns into a hook with which no golfer would be happy.

Players who swing from in-to-out are often those who underwent a course of golf lessons and consequently understand the need for an inside attack and good hand action. Therefore, rather than suggest they have bad habits they have simply exaggerated the good ones. They generally hit the ball a fair distance but might experience trouble with shots from bare lies. They may also be better hitting a 3 wood than a driver, since closing the clubface on a driver can produce an unpleasant duck (quick) hook

quite easily. If the club face becomes excessively shut at impact, the ball will hook low and left very quickly, despite the player swinging to the right of the target. In this instance, the very shut club face has over-ridden the swing path and sent the ball immediately left.

The in-to-out swing tends to be on the flat side often causing the club head to swing through the impact zone on a sharply curving path. As the club head curves sharply, it is not travelling directly towards the target for very long before it swings back to the inside (Fig 13.1). It is therefore quite common for someone with a flat swing to be able to hit shots a long way right or a long way left, depending on the part of the arc in which contact is made with the ball.

We will analyse the factors that can cause a hook in the same way in which we dealt with the slice, i.e. getting the basics right first.

Fig 13.1. The player who hooks tends to swing the club head on a flat, sharply curving arc so that it does not travel directly toward the target for very long. It is therefore easy to hit shots that go right and left of target

CHAPTER FOURTEEN

The strong grip

The purpose of the grip is to return the club face to the ball in a square position without any undue or independent manipulation. The player who flights the ball from right to left has his/her hands on the grip in such a way that the club face is closed at impact (Fig 14.1), and the more closed it is, the stronger the curve in flight.

I would recommend you re-read pages 91–93 in which I described the most important aspects of the grip. However, in your case, you should grip with only two knuckles of the left hand showing and the 'V's pointing more towards the chin and right ear (Fig 14.2). The right hand, especially the triggered forefinger, must sit much more to the side of the grip than underneath it, with the club resting more at the base of the fingers than in the palm of the hand. Make certain that the left thumb sits snugly into the hollow of the right hand as this will help to

make the two hands work as a unit. With your hands in this position, the palm of the right and back of the left will be facing towards the target. If by any chance you grip with two hands completely on the club, I would suggest that you try the overlapping grip, where the little finger of the right hand sit on top of the left forefinger. This change will again make your hands act as more of a unit and put a little more authority in the left hand. You may also find that a *slightly* firmer grip will help to stabilize your hand action, which previously may have been working too independently of the rest of your swing.

The player with a very strong grip who has virtually four knuckles on the left hand showing might read the above explanation of the grip and wonder how it is that he/she still hits the ball with left to right curve on it. This player has turned the hands so far to the right that at impact the heel, instead of the back, of the left hand is facing the target. By rotating the forearms and hands correctly, he/she would be lucky to get the ball off the ground, as the club face would be so closed. His/her grip allows and indeed encourages swinging the club to the inside on the backswing, but then blocks his/her action through impact. It may sound strange but to square the club face this player must weaken his/her grip. I will outline the swing corrections in Chapter 18.

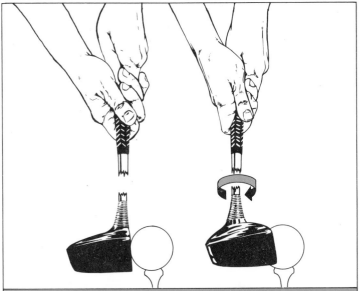

Fig 14.1. When the hands are turned too much to the right on the grip, they return to a more neutral position at impact thus closing the club face

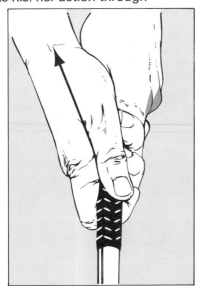

Fig 14.2. The player whose shots curve too much from right to left should grip the club so that he can see about 2 knuckles of his left hand. The 'V's point between the chin and right ear and the right forefinger sits at the side of the shaft, not underneath it

CHAPTER FIFTEEN

The closed set up

The golfer who closes the club face at impact, curving the ball to the left, will soon start to aim to the right to allow for the curve (Fig 15.1). But much like the slicer who believes that aiming left is the cure when in fact it compounds the error, so the golfer who hooks, makes matters worse by aiming to the right. Not only will the club face be shut at impact but the club head will approach so much from inside the target line that additional hook spin will be imparted on the ball. It becomes a vicious circle (and a vicious hook for that matter) and one that is first broken by checking the grip and then the set up.

Since you tend to swing along the line of your body, ideally you should try to stand parallel to the intended line of flight so that you may swing correctly from in-to-in, i.e. the club head approaches the ball from between 3 and 4 o'clock and strikes the ball whilst swinging towards 9 o'clock. In the closed stance, a line across the shoulders would point considerably right of the target, more in the direction of 4 to 10 o'clock, which will then tend to set the swing from in-to-out.

Checking the address position

With a target to aim at, address the ball and then place a club down across the line of your toes. You will be able to see if your stance is closed. But also check your shoulder line, either by holding a club across the shoulders yourself or by getting a friend to do this and telling you exactly where the shaft points. Remember that it should be parallel to the target. You can also check this in a mirror, standing with the mirror to your right, and if they are closed, you will be able to see quite a lot of your left shoulder and a club across the shoulders will point to the right.

To help correct your set up, place two clubs on the ground, one just outside the ball and the other about 18 inches nearer to you, both parallel to the ball to target line. Now address the ball, trying to get your feet, knees, hips and most importantly your shoulders parallel to the clubs. Look towards the target several times, so that you become familiar with how it should appear, no longer are

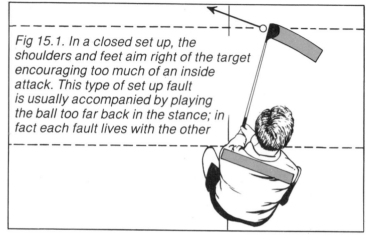

Fig 15.1. In a closed set up, the shoulders and feet aim right of the target encouraging too much of an inside attack. This type of set up fault is usually accompanied by playing the ball too far back in the stance; in fact each fault lives with the other

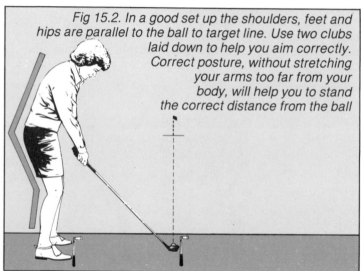

Fig 15.2. In a good set up the shoulders, feet and hips are parallel to the ball to target line. Use two clubs laid down to help you aim correctly. Correct posture, without stretching your arms too far from your body, will help you to stand the correct distance from the ball

you looking over your left shoulder at it (Fig 15.2). You will also find it helpful to use an intermediate target, about 2 to 3 feet ahead of the ball over which to aim.

An adjustment of the angle of your feet may also be worthwhile. Most golfers who swing from in-to-out, make a good backswing turn, but often fail to clear their body, i.e. turn sufficiently through the shot. You might benefit from placing your right foot at right angles to the line of flight but angling your left foot towards the target at about 15-20°. It may also help to have your feet just a touch open as this will restrict any excessive backswing turn and make it easier to clear your hips on the through swing.

A strong grip with the hands turned well under the club tends to make the right shoulder drop much lower than the left and also closes the shoulders. Hopefully your correct grip will now make shoulder alignment easier.

It is also worthwhile for you to check that your eye line is not aimed too far to the right, giving you a distorted view of the correct target line.

In correcting the set up for the slice, I recommend that it would be helpful for the player to practise the address position standing either on square patio slabs or kitchen floor tiles, or by using two clubs laid down parallel to the target. The same holds true for the player who sets up closed, as these guide lines will help to convince you that you are now lined up correctly. They will also prove useful in checking that the club face is square at address.

Ball position

A closed set up is often accompanied by playing the ball too far back in the stance, which in itself will encourage the shoulders to close (Fig 15.1). Check that the ball for your iron shots is played forward of centre in your stance, which will help to square the shoulders (Fig 15.3). Play the ball for the driver only just inside the left heel. It is difficult to be exact about ball position because so much depends on the width of stance, but experiment with playing it in a more forward position for all shots. With the ball back you may have found that your hands were a long way ahead of the ball at address so that there was a forward angle

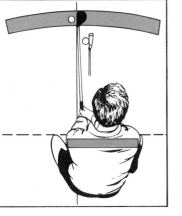

Fig 15.3. With the ball positioned correctly, i.e. forward of centre for iron shots and just inside the left heel for the driver, it will be easier to get the shoulders parallel to the target and the swing on line

Fig 15.4. By standing too far away from the ball and streching your arms away from your body, you will encourage a flat in-to-out swing

between your left arm and the shaft. This situation tends to make the club head swing too much to the inside at the start of the backswing. Therefore when you re-position the ball, check that your hands for the irons are only just ahead of the ball with the left arm and shaft forming a straighter line than before. With the driver, I would recommend that the straight line still exists with the back of the left hand approximately level with the front of the ball. Apart from the ball being too far back in the stance causing a closed shoulder line, you are also more likely to strike the ball whilst the club head is still swinging from the inside and so the ball starts out to the right. By moving it forwards, you have a better chance of making contact while the club is swinging directly towards the target.

Distance from the ball

The golfer who hooks will often be standing too far away from the ball at address (Fig 15.4) which will encourage a flat, in-to-out swing. To correct this, stand erect with the club held out horizontally in front of you with your hands at waist height. Now lower it to the ground by bending from the hip bones. Do not stretch your arms too far away from your body — the upper part of the arms should be quite close to your body. If you bend sufficiently from the hips, the arms will just hang more or less in the space created. Now flex your knees slightly and you should be in a good address position, having the correct posture and distance from the ball (Fig 15.2).

CHAPTER SIXTEEN

The swing

In your corrected address position, it is important for you to be aware of the new direction of the target. Until now you have looked at it over your left shoulder, which is no longer the case. Take two or three glances towards the target and then try to see the direction in which the club head must approach the ball. This will help to give you a better picture of the overall swing, and consequently you will be better equipped to start the backswing on the right track.

Swing path

In clock face terms, you need to see that the swing path is more in the direction of 3.30 to 9 o'clock rather than 4 to 10 o'clock (Fig 16.1). To this end, it will probably help if you can start the club head back towards 3 o'clock for a

Fig 16.1. From the improved set up you need to visualize the correct backswing path. Ideally for the golfer who has swung too much on the inside, he should imagine it as 3.30 to 9 o'clock

Fig 16.2. At the top you will find your hands and arms are higher than before, more above your head than behind it, with the club face square to the plane

longer period of time than before, and feel that your arms swing more up and down rather than behind you. Most golfers who swing too much from the inside have a good enough shoulder turn, so concentrate a little more on what your arms are doing.

The top of the swing

At the top of the swing, your back should be turned to the target and your arms should be positioned in the gap between your right shoulder and your head. If you have had a flat arm swing, your hands will now feel more above your head than your right shoulder (Fig 16.2). Again, this is only a relative feeling and ideally they will be in the correct slot. If you can practise on a sidehill lie with the ball below your feet, this will make you swing your arms more upright in the backswing and put less emphasis on

your body turning too much. The club should also be about parallel to the target line, but golfers who hook often find that it points to the right at the top of the swing. Hopefully the improved set up and backswing path will have gone a long way to curing this problem, but if the shaft still points excessively to the right, check that for the first twelve inches of the takeaway the club swings away on a *gently* curving inside path. If that seems satisfactory but the shaft is still well across the line, you might be collapsing your wrists at the top so make certain that there is not excessive cupping at the back of your left wrist (Fig 16.3). It should be almost in line with the left forearm. If you are very supple, you may just be swinging rather a long way which inevitably means that the shaft must cross the line. This is acceptable provided that you can turn back in a co-ordinated fashion. However, you would probably benefit by putting more emphasis on your arms swinging rather than the body turning, and by

Fig 16.3. Excessive cupping of the left wrist will raise the right elbow and cause the shaft to aim well right of the target with the club face open

making what feels to you to be a three-quarter length backswing from which you will find it easier to swing the club more towards the target through impact. This will emphasize your through swing rather than your backswing and make the swing feel more controlled.

Club face alignment

You should also ensure that the club face is square, i.e. positioned between facing the sky and facing forwards, and approximately in line with the back of the left hand and forearm. If it points to the sky, i.e. closed, check that your grip is still not too strong. If you have arched the back of your left wrist, then this will close the club face and you should adjust this position until the left thumb is under the shaft at this stage. Check that at hip height the club face is at right angles to the horizon and not pointing towards the ground.

However, it is also possible to hook the ball from an open club face position at the top of the swing. The hands, having turned the club face open by working too independently on the backswing, respond in a similar manner on the downswing and turn the club face closed prior to impact. You must try to make the initial part of the backswing more co-ordinated with the triangle of the arms and shoulders moving away together, and allow the wrists to cock purely in response to the swinging weight of the club head. Do not roll the hands but ensure that the left thumb moves sideways towards the inside of the left forearm.

The downswing

With your hands hopefully now in a higher position at the top of the backswing, you will inevitably be able to swing back to the ball on a better path, not so much from the inside but more straight on towards the target. Therefore, at the start of the downswing, you should feel that the left arm is in command and pulls down at the same time as the left knee moves laterally towards the target (page 104). You may be someone who flattens the plane of their swing too much on the downswing, by dropping the right elbow in towards the right hip. This action, if not overdone, is commendable but since you swing too much from in-to-out, guard against jamming the right elbow into

your side at this stage. Instead you should feel that you are pulling the end of the grip directly towards the ball so that the club will approach from a steeper but more correct plane than before and not so much from the inside.

Since you hook, or over-draw the ball, it is possible that your leg action has not been sufficiently lively, which has allowed your hands and arms to become too active through impact, thus closing the club face. In the downswing you should feel your weight move onto your left side as your arms swing down, but do make sure that your head remains steady throughout.

Impact and beyond

In the impact area you must feel that as your *arms* are swinging *through* the ball, you allow your body to turn through as well, preserving the triangular relationship (Fig 9.2 on page 105). Often a player who hooks, stops his/her arms swinging and the body from turning. Consequently the right hand closes quickly over the left, shutting the club face (page 110). Players who swing too much from in-to-out usually have well developed hand action, but in order to be effective this action must work on swinging arms, so always be sure to keep the left arm moving through the swing.

The right side of the body turns out of the way in the backswing and the left side must react similarly in the downswing (page 121), thus creating a space in which the arms can swing and enabling the club face to remain square to the target for just a split second longer rather than becoming closed too quickly. Provided that you have a neutral grip, as already described, at impact you should feel that the back of the left hand is facing the target for a longer period of time. You should also sense that the club head is swinging down the target line, i.e. towards 9 o'clock, rather than to the right of it. The ball will go higher than before because a square club face has more loft than a closed one.

Ideally what you are trying to achieve is a shot that starts just a little right of target and then draws back, since not only is this one of the most powerful shots in golf but if you can be reasonably certain that you can reproduce this shape, then the whole game becomes simpler as you can then disregard, to a great extent anyway, any hazards on the right-hand side of the course.

CHAPTER SEVENTEEN

The push

The push shot starts right of target and continues in that direction with no curve in the flight (Fig 2.5a on page 88). This is so close to being a good shot that you should not make too much adjustment for it to become so. To produce a push shot, the club head is swinging from in-to-out, i.e. from 4 to 10 o'clock, with the club face square to that direction.

First, check your aim; it could be that you are simply aiming further right than you thought. Also check that the ball position is not too far back in your stance as this will tend to send it to the right (see page 116).

Once you have confirmed that your set up is satisfactory, if the ball still flies to the right then you have a swing fault. You could still be swinging your arms too much to the inside on the backswing, so re-read the previous chapter which dealt with this at some length.

If you feel that your backswing is satisfactory, you could be blocking your left side on the through swing, which will prevent the club head from moving towards the target through impact. At the start of the downswing the left knee moves laterally towards the target and then, as the downswing progresses, the left side has to turn to the left to clear a passage for the arms (Fig 17.1). You may be exaggerating the lateral element and therefore be deficient on the turn. It is not correct to turn the left hip out of the way as the initial action of the downswing — this is inclined to spin the whole body, resulting in an out-to-in swing path, so do not convert from a 'blocker' to a 'spinner'. You should feel that, as your arms reach impact, your left hip is now turning out of the way. You may be able to achieve this best by swinging to the finish position where most of your weight is towards the left heel, as this will encourage you to turn through (Fig 9.4). Alternatively, feel that the right knee moves towards the left at impact, which pushes the left hip out of the way.

Often by moving too laterally towards the target you will get ahead of the ball, which can restrict hand action and may convert what would have been a gently drawing shot into a straight push. This sometimes happens if you try to hit the ball too hard. Try hitting some smooth three-quarter shots, keeping your head more behind the ball at

Fig 17.1. As the club head approaches impact the left side is clearing so that the hand and arms have a clear passage and can gradually square the club face

impact. This will allow your left side to clear better and thereby enable your hands and forearms to correctly rotate slightly to the left through the impact zone in a powerful free-wheeling action.

The push slice

This shot is a result of an in-to-out swing path, with the club face open (Fig 2.5b on page 88). The line of the swing is more in the 4 to 10 o'clock direction, but the player has not managed to square the club face to that line at impact. This shot can be caused by having a very strong grip, i.e. both hands turned well to the right with four knuckles of the left hand showing when you hold the grip up in front of you. Whereas you might imagine that this type of grip would close the club face at impact, what it actually tends to do is to block the hand action completely so that at impact the heel of the left hand is moving towards the target (Fig 18.1). Because the hands are turned so far to the right in the first place, the club head goes back naturally on an inside path and the outcome is a shot that starts right and then turns right.

To correct this action, the grip must be adjusted since it is the root cause of the problem. Unfortunately, this process will feel neither comfortable nor natural, and initially the shots may not be very encouraging either, but stick with it if you want to improve. Move your hands to the left on the grip until you can see only two to two-and-a-half knuckles of the left hand, with the right hand more at the side of the shaft (Fig 14.2 on page 115). Become aware of how your hands should be working through impact so, using a 6 iron, carry out the hand action exercise in pages 98-99. It may be difficult for you at first to grow accustomed to rotating you hands so much to the left through impact since you have always led with the heel of the left hand. Indeed it may take considerable hard work before you can repeat the action consistently. To give you another swing thought while you practise this exercise, try to feel that the toe of the club is going to beat the heel of the club back to the ball — for that to happen, the hands and arms must rotate to the left.

Once you can hit the ball off a tee so that it does not curve excessively in either direction, you can concentrate on the swing path. Despite the grip change, it is more than likely that you will still swing the club head to the inside on the backswing but, hopefully now, not quite as inside as with the strong grip. Imagine the backswing path initially to be towards 3 o'clock before it turns inside

Fig 18.1. With a very strong grip the heel of the left hand pulls towards the target at impact, leaving the club face open and the left side of the body fails to turn out of the way

towards 4 o'clock.

You will then be able to swing the club back to the ball from a better line and feel that you are clearing the left hip to the left at the same time as your arms are swung towards the target. If you are someone who hits the right going right shot you may move laterally towards the target, so you should re-read page 121 on the push shot, paying particular attention to the advice on the hip action from the start of the downswing. Once you start to square the club face, you will also find your shots going a little lower and further.

The straight hook

Having now covered all the shots possible from an in-to-out swing path, the last curving shot is the one that starts towards the target and then curves to the left. In this instance the ball is struck from an in-to-in swing at the moment the club head is moving towards the target, but the face is closed at impact (Fig 2.2c on page 86).

It is possible that you are addressing the ball with the club face closed, so check whether this is the case before making any other adjustments. If all seems well with the club face alignment, then check your grip. It may reveal that the hands are turned a little too far to the right. Move them to the left so that the back of the left hand and palm of the right face more towards the target (Fig 14.2 on page 115). This enables you to use the good hand action you have developed but without closing the club face.

You will need to experiment to find exactly the right grip, but do so allowing yourself to swing aggressively through the ball. Do not stifle your hand and arm rotation to correct the hook — instead, see if a grip change will do the trick.

If your grip seems satisfactory, then you must have a swing fault. Your hand and arm action is too strong, which suggests that the left side might not be controlling things as it should. Make sure that as you start the downswing, you lead with the left arm, keeping the back of the hand facing in the same direction as it was at the top of the swing (Fig 19.1). If the right side becomes too dominant too early, the arms will begin rotating to the left which will cause the back of the left hand to face the target too soon, thus squaring the blade too early. Change direction in an unhurried manner and keep pulling with the left arm right through impact so that the right hand will square the club face at, rather than before, impact.

I have already detailed leg action and how the body should turn out of the way through the impact zone, so re-read page 110–111, which contain a half-swing exercise to help control hand and arm action, which you should practise.

Once you have turned your shot from an uncontrollable straight hook into a gently drawing shot, you may like to experiment a little more by putting the ball back in your

Fig 19.1. As the downswing starts feel that the back of the left hand remains looking more skywards to prevent your arms rotating to the left too early

stance, say a ball's width to begin with, and see if you can make the ball start just right of target and draw back. I stress that you need to rid yourself of the hook first, but you can benefit from your over-active hands when they have become more educated.

CHAPTER ONE

Downhill lies
from the fairway

The most important point to consider when playing a shot from anything other than a flat lie is how to adjust your set up and how you can expect the ball to react. I firmly believe that a correct address position for whichever shot is to hand is essential if you are to play the shot well. However, the beginner may experience some problems remembering how to adjust the set up. Naturally, the longer you play, the easier it is to remember what to do, but it does surprise me how often even established club golfers seem to have little knowledge of how to cope with sloping lies.

Club selection

The first thing to consider is the severity of the slope and how that will affect your choice of club. Any downhill lie will de-loft the club, so that a 7 iron could be more like a 5 or 6 iron, depending on just how steep the slope is (Fig 1.1). If you have a very long shot, be careful about

Fig 1.2. For the downhill shot, the body is set at right angles to the slope with more weight on the left foot and the ball back in the stance. The club head is swung back more steeply than usual to avoid hitting the ground behind the ball

Fig 1.1. On a downhill lie, the loft of the club is reduced so a 7 iron can become more like a 5 iron, depending on the severity of the slope

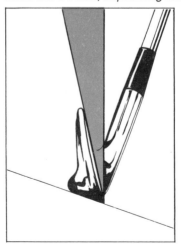
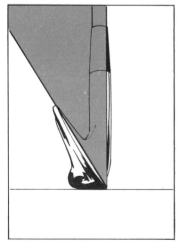

selecting a 2 or 3 iron, since their reduced effective loft would make them extremely difficult to use. You would be better playing a 4 or 5 iron, which will effectively become more like a 3, or to consider using a lofted wood such as a 5 or 7 wood.

The set up

For the downhill shot, you are trying to set your body in the same relationship to the ground as for the level lie. Normally on a shot from a level lie, your spine is at right angles to the ground, so to retain that relationship for a downhill lie, you must allow your weight to be more on your left than right foot, with the right knee more flexed than normal to accommodate the change. Your shoulders will then be more parallel to the slope and the left will feel considerably lower than normal, which will help you to swing the club in the correct manner for the shot. You should position the ball back in the stance, which will help you to make good contact. Again, how far back depends on the severity of the slope, and a little experimentation on your part will help you to discover the necessary degree of adjustment.

The swing

The set up adjustments will help you to make the correct swing, but you must also understand what you are trying to achieve. If you were to take the club away from the ball in the normal manner, i.e. initially fairly low to the ground, because the ground behind the ball is higher than usual, it would obstruct the club's progress. Therefore, it is essential that you swing the club more upright in the backswing, following the line of the slope (Fig 1.2). Your set up will help to a great extent but you should always

Fig 1.3. After impact you should try to swing the club head down along the contour of the ground, allowing the right knee to be more active than usual

have a couple of practice swings so that you know just how upright the backswing needs to *feel* in order to avoid hitting the ground behind the ball. Having swung up the slope on the backswing, you must have the feeling of swinging down the contour of the slope through the impact zone, and for this to happen your right knee may need to be more active than normal (Fig 1.3). It is possible that you will finish off balance — in extreme circumstances even taking a step after having hit the shot. This it why it is essential to have a couple of practice swings so you know what to expect and can therefore balance your body accordingly.

The ball's flight

Since the backswing will be more upright than normal, you will not turn your body as much which, together with the fact that you start with more weight on the left leg, means that you will not transfer as much weight to the right side as usual.

Consequently it is very easy for the left side to be a little ahead of its usual position at impact, and indeed the slope makes it easy for the left side to move out of the way. This action tends to leave the hands and arms behind, which can cause the club face to be open at impact, resulting in a shot that curves to the right. The situation is made worse by the fact that the ball is positioned back in the stance, which tends to send it to the right. So in extreme circumstances, you can get a shot that starts right of target and then curves even further to the right. You must allow for this by aiming to the left and trying not to let yourself move ahead of the shot. Feel that the swing is made primarily with your arms, allowing your legs to work at the moment of impact so that you can swing the club head down the slope. The ball will also fly lower than normal for the club you are using.

Summary

Be conservative with your choice of club; do not make the shot more difficult by taking a 3 wood or a 3 iron. Remember also that the ball will fly lower and will be inclined to go right of the target. Put more weight on the lower foot and the ball nearer to the high. Swing within yourself and try to remain balanced.

CHAPTER TWO

Downhill shots
around the green

These are the shots when the ball is on a mound surrounding the green, quite often sitting down in the grass, which has prevented it from rolling back onto the green. At the best of times, shots from around the green require a delicate touch, but when your balance is affected by the slope and the ball's lie is less than perfect, then producing an action that makes ideal contact with the ball is relatively difficult. Perhaps the secret, if there is one, is to know how to allow and adjust for the slope's effect on the outcome of the shot and, of course, to practise.

Which club

Your choice of club will be affected by the severity of the slope and how much green lies between you and the hole.

Fig 2.1. Set up with your spine at right angles to the slope, weight mainly on the left leg and the right more flexed than usual. With the ball back in the stance, the swing follows the contours of the ground

More often than not you will be near the edge of the green, but judging just how far the ball will run is marginally more difficult than normal. As with the downhill lie on the fairway, whichever club you choose will have a less effective loft so a 9 iron could be more like a 7 iron. Therefore, since you need to be able to control the shot, and unless you have perhaps 30 to 40 yards to the pin, I would suggest that you use either a wedge or a sand wedge for this shot. If you are, say, 30 yards away, then perhaps a 9 iron may be better so that the ball will roll most of the way to the hole. Whereas the downhill lie will send the ball lower, whenever you chip to a green below you the ball will not run as much as usual, which will help you to control the shot better. Take this into account before selecting your club and deciding how hard to hit the shot. Practice will help to cultivate your visualization of just what will happen to the ball.

The set up and swing

As with the shot from the fairway, you must try to set your spine at right angles to the slope by putting more weight on your left side, flexing your right knee more and playing the ball nearer to the right foot than normal. You will find that a wider stance than you usually employ will give you a more secure and balanced set up (Fig 2.1).

Aim yourself left of target, grip down the club, even to the extent of placing the right hand on the shaft if necessary, and open the face of the club a little so that you have more effective loft to play with. Make the swing, mainly using just your hands, picking the club head up abruptly in the backswing to avoid the ground behind the ball. Keep the blade open through impact and do not let the grass twist it shut. This is a delicate shot so do not rush it — stay down after impact and try to swing the club head down the slope. Avoid all temptations to see the results of your efforts too soon as this will make you come up off the ball, most likely thinning it or leaving it on the bank.

Shots from severe slopes

You may have to play shots from such severe slopes that it is not possible to lean away from the slope without falling over. In these situations, try to adopt an address

Fig 2.2. On severe slopes the spine remains at right angles to the horizon and weight mainly on the right leg. With the ball positioned even outside the right foot, and the blade slightly open, the shot is played mainly with the hands and wrists

position that is as balanced as possible, which enables you to make the best contact under the circumstances. You will have to set your spine more at right angles to the horizon and may well find that your right leg is extremely bent. Aim left of target and play the ball well back in the stance, even outside the right foot so that you are able to hit the ball first instead of the ground (Fig 2.2). You will have to grip down on the club, perhaps even onto the shaft itself, and because of the ball's position, the club will have reduced effective loft causing the ball to fly much lower than normal. You can, of course, open the blade a little to gain extra height on the shot but on the severest of slopes, you will still have less loft on the club than from a flat lie.

For this shot, the swing is made just with the wrists and hands chopping down on the ball, so an accurate shot, especially from a bad lie, can be difficult to judge.

127

Downhill bunker shots

This is one of the most difficult and therefore most feared shots in golf. When the ball is on a downhill lie, it is usually near the back of the bunker, possibly with the lip of the bunker impeding the backswing, and thus you are confronted by two problems:

1 The downhill lie makes it more difficult to get sufficient height on the ball that it at least gets onto the green, even though it may be some distance from the pin.
2 Because the ball is often near the back of the bunker, the over-hanging lip can make it difficult to make an unimpeded backswing.

Consequently, there may be circumstances when it would be more prudent to settle for the green than to play towards the pin. Alternatively, if the shot is really fearsome, your best route may even be sideways or backwards — better to be out of the bunker with the first shot than to attempt the impossible and take several shots.

Fig 3.1a. When the blade of the sand iron is opened, the flange comes into play, preventing the club from digging too deeply into the sand b. When the blade stays square, the club digs deeper into the sand

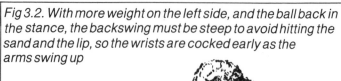

Fig 3.2. With more weight on the left side, and the ball back in the stance, the backswing must be steep to avoid hitting the sand and the lip, so the wrists are cocked early as the arms swing up

The set up

As with the other downhill shots you are trying to set your spine at right angles to the slope so that you avoid hitting the ground, or in this case the sand, behind the ball. So set up slightly open with more weight on the left leg than normal, the right knee well flexed and your shoulders virtually parallel to the sand (Fig 3.2). Position the ball more centrally than for a flat lie and grip down on the club, but do not open the blade too wide. The sand iron has a flange which is designed to stop the club digging too far into the sand. Instead it produces more of a skimming action (Fig 3.1). The wider the blade is opened, the more the flange comes into play. However, when the ball sits on a downhill lie, there is more sand to penetrate behind it. Therefore, if you open the blade wide and bring the flange into play, you will make it more difficult to hit down through the sand. But because the downhill lie reduces the effective loft of a club, you may be tempted to open the blade to offset this. Weigh up the situation carefully, trying to balance the height needed on the shot by how much sand lies behind the ball. Again by experience and practice you will get to know just how much you can afford to open the face and still hit down through the sand without thinning the ball. If the bunker face is not too steep and the pin is set 25 yards away, you have no real problems. If the bunker face is steep and the pin is just 10 yards away, then you do have problems and will just have to accept that the ball may not finish near the hole. Getting the ball out with the first shot is your main objective.

The swing

You must swing your hands and arms up steeply away from the ball so that you do not hit the sand (Fig 3.2). Although you cannot take a proper practice swing in a bunker, I would suggest that you have a couple of practice backswings, just so that you can judge and feel how steep it needs to be. On very steep slopes, you may well have to break your wrists and even bend the left elbow as the first movement to avoid hitting the sand. Try to hit the sand about 2 inches behind the ball, and be absolutely certain to hit down and through, trying to follow the contour of the sand. Do not allow the right hand and arm to overpower the left which will close the club face. Instead, keep the left hand and arm accelerating, following the contour of the sand so that at the finish, the back of the left hand faces more towards the sky than the ground. Allow your knees to move towards the target as you strike the ball, which will help you to stay down through the shot (Fig 3.3). Whatever happens, do not be tempted into trying to scoop the ball out of the bunker; keep your hands leading the club head and trust the loft of the club. You will not finish with as full a follow through as on a normal shot — instead, your hands will probably finish about hip height and you might well be a bit off balance, but this does not matter if the

Fig 3.3. After impact the club must swing down the slope, so make sure the right knee moves towards the target

ball is out of the bunker. The ball will come out lower than usual and consequently run more on landing.

Summary

The most important point about this shot is to be realistic in what you can hope to achieve. Do not regard it as an admission of defeat to play out sideways or even backwards, I have seen top professionals do that, simply because they knew that to go for the pin or the green would be foolhardy. Spend some time practising the shot so that you can get used to the unaccustomed set up and the sort of action that is necessary for success.

CHAPTER FOUR

The uphill lie
on the fairway

To most golfers this is an inviting lie and one that in certain circumstances can allow you to hit the ball a long way. If the ball settles on a slight uphill lie along a reasonably flat fairway, this is the time to hit a 3 wood or, in some cases, even a driver for the better golfer if maximum distance is needed. However, as with any shot from a lie other than level, adjustments need to be made and a good sense of balance maintained in order not to waste the inviting lie.

Club selection

An uphill lie will increase the effective loft on a club, thus turning a 5 iron into a 6 or even a 7, depending on the severity of the slope (Fig 4.1). Consequently the shot will tend to go higher and not as far as normal, so select a club

with less loft. As already stated, if you have a long shot, provided that the slope is not severe and the ball is sitting up on a tuft of grass (what luck!), you can even hit a driver.

The set up and swing

Following the same principle as for the downhill lie, you need to set your spine at right angles to the slope, so put more weight on your right leg and flex your left leg more than usual (Fig 4.2). This will bring your shoulders more parallel to the slope and thus enable you to swing along the contour of the ground. If you do not make this adjustment, you will just dig the club head into the ground at impact and not strike the ball very well. To ensure that you sweep the ball from the turf, position it a little nearer

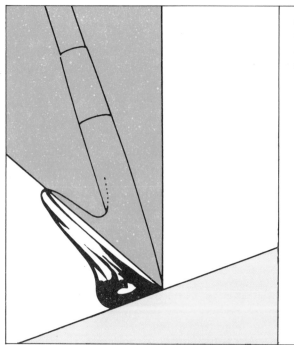

Fig 4.1. On an uphill lie the club becomes more lofted so that a 5 iron can become more like a 7 iron, depending on the severity of the slope

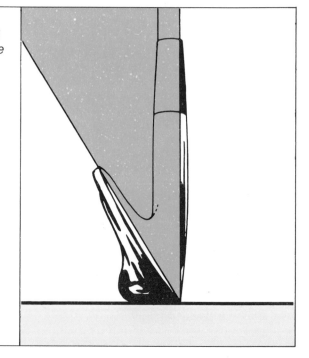

Fig 4.2. The spine is set at right angles to the slope, with more weight on the right leg and the left more flexed than normal. With the ball played more forward in the stance, the club head is swung along the contour of the slope as much as possible

NO

YES

Alternatively, where accuracy rather than length is important, play the ball more centrally in the stance and restrict the backswing somewhat by making it mainly with the arms. Through the impact zone, concentrate on moving your legs and holding your hands squarer, preventing the right hand and arm from rotating over the left.

To help you remember how to adjust for uphill and downhill lies from the fairway, this short rhyme might help you.

'From an uphill or a downhill lie,
Weight to the low foot, ball to the high'

If you have trouble thinking of that, remember that 'weight' and 'low' both contain a 'W'.

Fig 4.3. Through impact it is difficult to transfer your weight back to the left side, and so the hands and arms tend to close the club face, creating a shot that goes left of target

the left foot than for a flat lie.

As you swing the club head away, do not swing it up too steeply but try to swing down the slope. You will find it easy to make a good turn in the backswing and will have a lot of weight on the right leg at the top of the backswing. The main problem arises in trying to move your legs and hips through the shot sufficiently. Consequently, the arms and shoulders can tend to overtake them (Fig 4.3), creating a pull, draw or hook shot, so allow for this by aiming to the right at address. The practice swing will help you to gauge just how aggressive you can be with the shot and still remain balanced.

CHAPTER FIVE

Uphill lies around the green

Just how accurate you can be with these shots will depend usually on how good a lie you have. Because the ball has remained on the slope, inevitably the grass may not be very short and so the ball may be lying badly, which makes the shot more difficult to judge. You may either hit a shot that flies out of the grass, or one that is rather dampened by the grass and falls short of the target. You have to decide, depending on how much grass will be between the blade and the ball at impact, which is more likely to happen. Having said that, from this lie you should be able to hit a reasonably good shot onto the green since it will not be difficult to get height on the ball, which means it will land fairly softly. However, you may have to deal with this shot in two different ways, depending on the severity of the slope.

Club selection for gentle slopes

On the uphill lie, where the degree of slope still permits you to set your spine at right angles to the slope, effective loft is added to the club so that the ball will go higher. A 9 iron might be more like a wedge so you can use either a less lofted club for the shot, or just make sure that you hit the ball sufficiently hard. Usually from an uphill lie, you are playing to a green above you, and whenever this happens the ball will run more. Luckily the additional loft that you can expect from the shot will help to control the ball, which, if the hole is cut close to you, will be most welcome. Club selection will depend on how much green you have to play with, and how you *feel* and *see* the shot.

The set up and swing for gentle slopes

Again, set yourself as much at right angles to the slope as possible, with more weight on the right foot, the left knee well flexed and the ball just forward of centre in your stance (Fig 5.1). Grip down on the club for extra feel and control, and make the swing with the hands and arms. There is no need to break the wrists too much on the

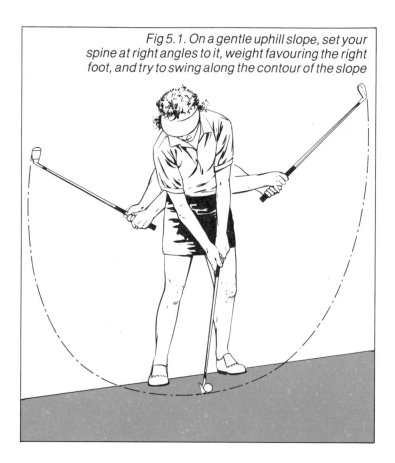

Fig 5.1. On a gentle uphill slope, set your spine at right angles to it, weight favouring the right foot, and try to swing along the contour of the slope

backswing. Make sure that you swing through the ball, allowing the club head to swing along the contour of the slope. However, take care that you do not swing *up* too much on the shot and thin the ball. Try to stay balanced and keep the eyes focused on the spot where the ball was a little longer than usual to prevent coming up too soon.

If you are faced with this shot and the ball is sitting on a tight lie, I would suggest that unless you are a very low handicap player, you should play the shot as described for the steep uphill shot which follows — otherwise, you could easily thin the shot.

Club selection for steep uphill slopes

On steep slopes you will not be able to add effective loft to the club face by your set up, since you will have to lean into the slope rather than away from it. But you can add loft by opening the club face at address, thus increasing the height of the shot. Most of the time you will need to use a wedge or sand wedge for this shot. Since you need height to clear the slope in front of you, if length is also needed you must consider the angle of the slope before deciding to hit a less lofted club.

The set up and swing for a steep slope

The severity of the slope will prevent you from setting yourself at right angles to it without falling over! Instead you must lean into the hill with your spine virtually perpendicular to the horizon, setting more weight on the left leg and also flexing it more than usual (Fig 5.2). You will have to grip down the club considerably, even onto the shaft in some cases, which may also prevent you hitting this shot very far. The ball is played just forward of centre. Do not attempt to swing down the slope in the backswing — just swing your hands and arms back quite naturally. Through the impact zone, feel that you are dragging the club head into the ball, keeping your hands ahead of the club head throughout the shot. The club head will tend to dig straight into the bank so be sure to keep a firm grip. The ball will still go high, but if it has been in a grassy lie it will lack backspin and will run on landing.

Tips for the higher handicaps

Newcomers to golf and higher handicap players usually attempt to hit a ball into the air by trying to scoop or lift it. First you must dismiss any thoughts of scooping or lifting from your entire approach to the game. The ball flies into the air by applying backspin, which is attained by striking *down* on the ball. Any time you try to hit up on the ball with an iron, you will impart topspin, which is what makes the ball nosedive along the ground. When faced with any shot from an uphill lie, because of the particular set up where the spine is virtually at right angles to the slope,

there is a sense of hitting up on the ball. If you are someone who tends to thin shots in these instances, I would suggest that for all the shots around the green from uphill lies, you set your spine at right angles to the horizon with more weight on your left leg. This set up will help to guarantee a downward strike, and although the ball will not go as high as it would when set up at right angles to the slope, it will help you to strike correctly and produce a very satisfactory shot. By opening the club face a fraction before gripping the club, you will get extra height on the shot. Once you can master the shot from this set up, then, where the slope and lie permit, you can progress to tilting your spine at right angles to it and you will find that the ball will go higher and land softer.

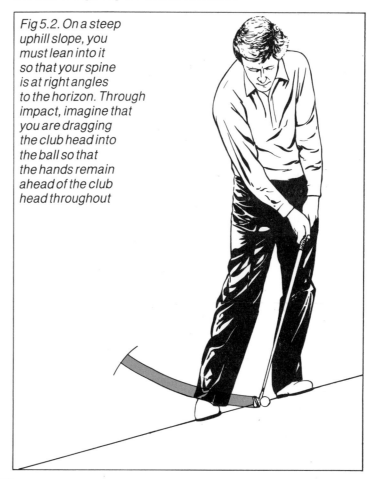

Fig 5.2. On a steep uphill slope, you must lean into it so that your spine is at right angles to the horizon. Through impact, imagine that you are dragging the club head into the ball so that the hands remain ahead of the club head throughout

CHAPTER SIX

Uphill bunker shots

Having now read five chapters on downhill and uphill lies, I hope that you will have a clear idea of how to hit this shot. You should by now have a much better picture of how the set up and the resultant swing should look. However, I have no intention of denying you a description of how the uphill bunker shot should be tackled, so read on!

The set up

Once more you must set your spine at right angles to the slope so that there will be more weight on the right foot than usual, the left leg will flex more, and the right shoulder will feel considerably lower than the left (Fig 6.1). On short shots, set up slightly open to the target but stand squarer for the long shots. You will naturally have more effective loft on the sand iron, so depending on the steepness of the bunker face, you may not have to open the club face as much as you think. Position the ball just inside the left heel.

The swing

Your set up will now allow you to swing along the contour of the sand with your normal bunker shot swing. Let the club head enter the sand about 2 inches behind the ball, and have the feeling of swinging up the slope (Fig 6.2a). The ball will come out higher and land more softly than usual so you will have to hit it harder, and also take less sand for longer shots. On severe slopes you may fall backwards after the shot so be sure to maintain your balance long enough to hit the shot well.

One of the most common mistakes is to bury the club head too deeply into the sand, which usually results in leaving the ball in the sand (Fig 6.2b). This occurs because the player fails to set up correctly — instead of leaning away from the slope, he/she leans into it. The correct set up dictates that you swing along the line of the slope, i.e. down in the backswing and up on the through swing,

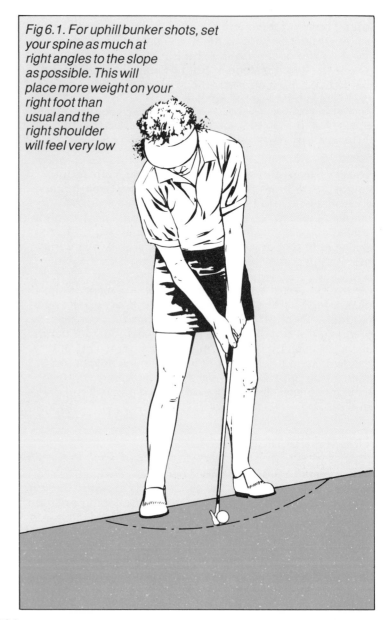

Fig 6.1. For uphill bunker shots, set your spine as much at right angles to the slope as possible. This will place more weight on your right foot than usual and the right shoulder will feel very low

taking a shallow divot of sand from around the ball. So do not argue with the slope; swing along it!

Playing from severe uphill lies

If the ball is on a severe slope, and this often occurs when the ball is near the top of the bunker face, then you may not be able to adopt the above set up and remain balanced. In this case you must lean into the slope so that most of your weight is on your left foot and the ball is fractionally more central in your stance. Open the club face a little to ensure that you have sufficient loft for the ball to clear the lip of the bunker and then swing the club quite aggressively into the sand behind the ball, trying to

swing through as much as possible. As already explained, the extra amount of sand beyond the ball will make it difficult for you to swing through very far and the whole action will feel like a stabbing motion.

Summary

However many words are written on the subject, you will only learn exactly how to tackle less straightforward shots by playing them, so spend some time hitting shots from a variety of lies. Armed with the knowledge of how to play them, once you have successfully done so in practice, you will be more confident when faced with the shot on the course.

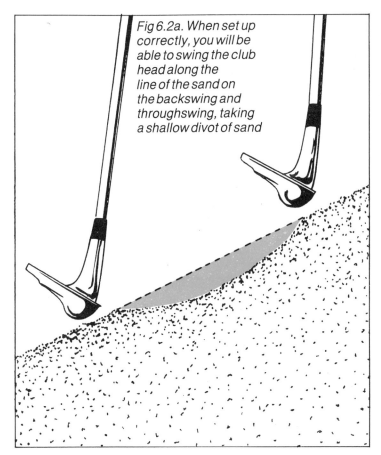

Fig 6.2a. When set up correctly, you will be able to swing the club head along the line of the sand on the backswing and throughswing, taking a shallow divot of sand

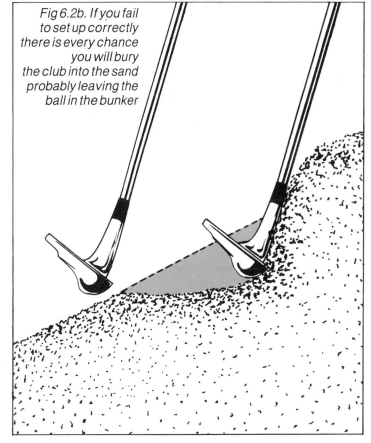

Fig 6.2b. If you fail to set up correctly there is every chance you will bury the club into the sand probably leaving the ball in the bunker

CHAPTER SEVEN

Fairway shots with ball below feet

This shot has to fall into the category of one of the least liked shots in golf. It is definitely not one to 'have a go' at. Indeed, caution must be the watchword or disastrous results may ensue. Whereas the uphill and downhill shots require a change in weight distribution at address in order to play them successfully, it is your posture that must be adjusted when the ball is above or below your feet. Since so many golfers fail to achieve good posture even for a shot from a level lie, it is no wonder that the sidehill shots, particularly when the ball is below the feet, cause so many problems.

Set up

When the ball is below your feet, it is further away from you than on a flat lie, so to compensate you stand closer to it and lower the club head down to it by bending forward more from the hips, making sure that you grip at the end of the club and flexing your knees a little more (Fig 7.1). You need an upright swing for this shot and thus it is essential that you increase the angle of tilt from your hips — just bending your knees will not provide the correct plane to the swing. You must be well balanced to prevent any possibility of falling forward when playing the shot, which could result in a shank. The severity of the slope will dictate weight distribution, and although you will feel more weight towards your toes than for a shot from a level lie, you must have sufficient weight towards your heels to prevent over-balancing. However, do avoid sitting back too much on your heels as this has a tendency to ruin the correct spinal angle necessary for the shot. It is best to establish that you have a secure stance by having a couple of practice swings, which will also enable you to find out how hard you can safely hit the shot and remain balanced. You can improve the strike also by playing the ball nearer the centre of your stance. Be conservative on club selection — now is not the time to pull out a 3 iron — and be content with using mainly the middle irons, unless the slope is not too severe and the ball is sitting extremely well. If you need distance, use a 5 or a 7 wood.

Fig 7.1. When the ball is below the feet, you must angle your spine forward by bending more at the hips and then flex your knees. You must have sufficient weight on your heels so that you remain balanced when you swing

The swing

You make the swing mainly with your hands and arms and there is little body turn (Fig 7.2). This, combined with the fact that the set up demands that the swing is upright, will inevitably lead to an out-to-in swing path causing the ball to fade, so aim left to allow for this (Fig 7.3). Swing at no more than three-quarter pace or length, and try to stay down through the shot for as long as possible. On steep slopes you may even fall right off balance after the strike, so do not swing too aggressively. The fading flight of the ball, plus the three-quarter length swing, will naturally restrict the distance the ball goes, so always balance your choice of club between what you can safely expect to hit from the lie and the distance to the hole.

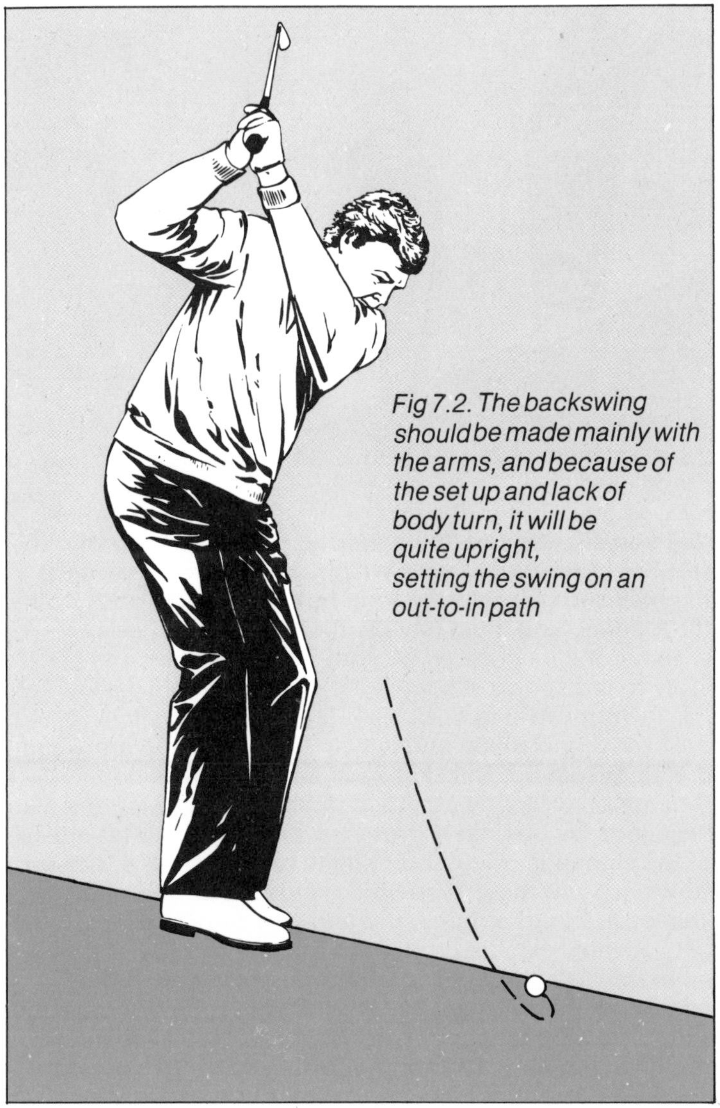

Fig 7.2. The backswing should be made mainly with the arms, and because of the set up and lack of body turn, it will be quite upright, setting the swing on an out-to-in path

Fig 7.3. Like the backswing, the follow through will also be upright and three-quarter length. The out-to-in swing path will cause the ball to fade

Ball below feet around the green

As with the shot from the fairway, maintaining your balance will help you to hit this shot well. Perhaps it is because it is one of the least common shots that you may be called upon to play that makes this shot even more difficult. Setting up in a balanced position so that you can swing the club back without hitting your right knee with the shaft is often the main problem.

Set up and swing

Because you are near the green, you are more likely to be using a short iron for this shot. So set up in a similar manner as for the shot from the fairway, standing closer to the ball and bending forward more from the hips with your knees sufficiently flexed (Fig 8.1) You should not

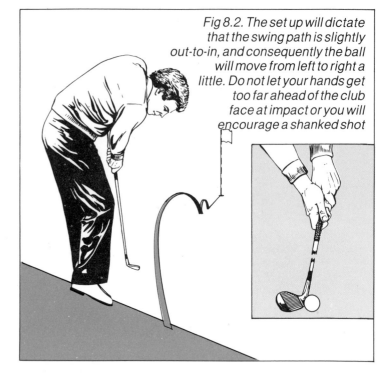

Fig 8.2. The set up will dictate that the swing path is slightly out-to-in, and consequently the ball will move from left to right a little. Do not let your hands get too far ahead of the club face at impact or you will encourage a shanked shot

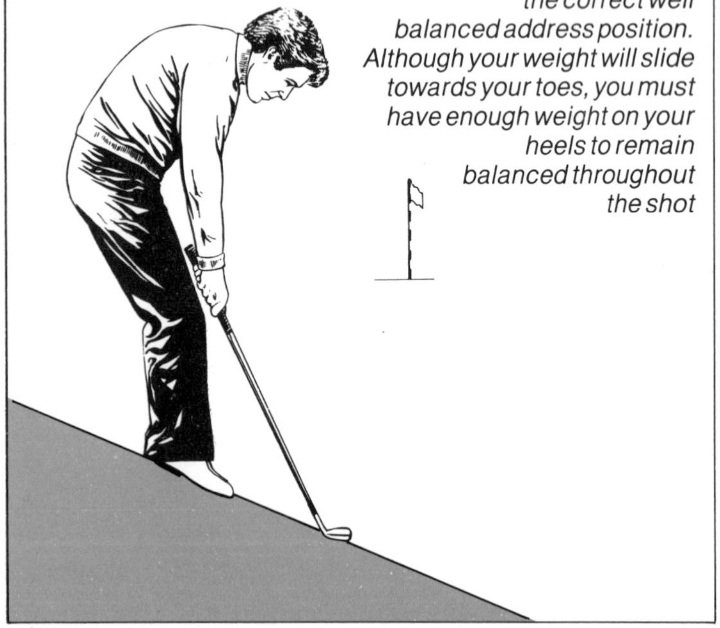

Fig 8.1. Grip down the shaft a little, bend forward from the hips and flex the knees more than usual to get the correct well balanced address position. Although your weight will slide towards your toes, you must have enough weight on your heels to remain balanced throughout the shot

have to grip right at the end of the club, but make sure that you are comfortably balanced. Depending on the severity of the slope, your weight will be forced towards the toes and balls of your feet, but, as with the shot from the fairway, you must have sufficient on your heels to ensure good balance. Even with this short shot, the ball is likely to fade or go slightly right of your target so allow for this in your aim (Fig 8.2).

The swing is made purely with the hands and arms and, due to the set up, the club head is swung back and through on a slightly out-to-in path. As you swing the club head into the ball, do not let your hands get too far ahead of the club face or you may shank the shot (Fig 8.2 inset). However, you must keep both hands moving through impact so that the right hand and arm do not fold over the left. It would also be prudent to address the ball slightly more towards the toe end of the club rather than the middle, as this will give you a little more room for error should you fall forward at all. The most crucial point about the shot is to stay down throughout and try to listen for the ball landing before you raise your head or your spine.

CHAPTER NINE

Ball below feet
in a bunker

This can be one of the most awkward shots to play since very often the ball will have come to rest at the edge of the bunker, thus preventing you from standing in the bunker to play the shot. However, you have to accept such difficulties as part of the challenge of the game, and instead of bemoaning your luck, you should concentrate and decide on the best way to tackle the shot.

The set up

One way that you can help to off-set the ball being below your feet is by working your feet into the sand more than usual. This will naturally lower you towards the ball even though you might get sand in your shoes! Having done

Fig 9.1. When the ball is close to the edge of the bunker, you may have to stand outside it. You will then need to take a very wide stance and bend forward a long way in order to stand any chance of getting the ball out

that, you must make the same adjustments for this shot as for the others with this stance, i.e. stand closer to the ball, bend sufficiently from the waist, grip a little nearer the end of the club than usual and get yourself well balanced. With most bunker shots you aim left of target so that you can swing from out-to-in, but since this particular stance encourages an out-to-in swing anyway, do not aim yourself too far left. Instead, have the club face just open and position the ball nearer the centre of your stance than for a bunker shot from a flat lie. If the ball is so close to the left edge of the bunker that you have to stand outside to play it, you just have to take your stance as best you can. It may mean that you have to spread your feet very wide apart, and bend forward more (Fig 9.1) or, if you can somehow get one foot in the bunker, kneel with the other leg. Take your time over this, and have a few practice swings *without touching the sand,* until you feel that you are in the best possible position. Should you decide that to try to play the ball towards the pin is beyond your capabilities, then play sideways or backwards — *this is not accepting defeat,* but using your head wisely. All that anyone is really interested in is the final score, so better to get out in one shot than try to accomplish the shot of the century and need several attempts.

The swing

If the ball is not too far below your feet, then you can expect the shot to be as good as one from a flat lie. But realising your limitations in golf is sometimes one of the harder lessons to learn, and if the ball is considerably below your feet or you are having to stand outside the bunker, then do not expect miracles. Be satisfied with getting the ball out with the first shot (hopefully in the direction of the hole) but if the pin is quite a distance away, you may be wiser to concentrate on just getting out rather than going for distance. On severe slopes, the more effort you put into this sort of shot, the more likely you are to mishit it. The swing is made with the hands and arms, with the wrists breaking immediately the backswing starts. This usually happens because the sand behind the ball is quite steep and you must avoid hitting it. Thus the backswing is very upright. The club head should enter the sand about 2 inches behind the ball, and through impact you *must* keep down through the shot. Try to imagine

that the club head is going underneath the ball and coming out of the sand about 4 or 5 inches ahead of where the ball was. Concentrate on this rather than being too keen to see the results of your efforts (Fig 9.2). You must retain the same angles of your knees and back that you set at address; if you rise up at all you will most likely play the next shot from the same bunker. Do not allow the right hand to cross over the left, which would close the club face. Concentrate instead on accelerating both hands through the shot. You may fall off balance once you have hit the ball but this is of no consequence — just make sure that you keep your balance long enough to hit the ball. Try to make the swing as smooth and unhurried as possible.

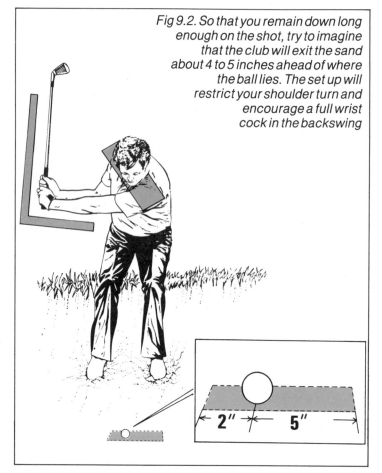

Fig 9.2. So that you remain down long enough on the shot, try to imagine that the club will exit the sand about 4 to 5 inches ahead of where the ball lies. The set up will restrict your shoulder turn and encourage a full wrist cock in the backswing

CHAPTER TEN

Ball above feet
on the fairway

As long as the slope is not too steep, this can be one of the more inviting shots in golf and tends to encourage a good attacking swing. So often the beginner fails to make a good shoulder turn in the swing, producing instead a rather weak 'arms only' type of action. When the ball is above your feet, it encourages a good shoulder turn and consequently a more powerful shot is the result. So if the lie is not too extreme, you can look for a good shot. If you are unlucky enough to find the ball considerably above your feet, then you may have to sacrifice power for accuracy, depending on what lies ahead.

Now that you understand how to compensate for the ball being below your feet, you can understand also how best to play those shots from above your feet. In fact, we tend to make almost exactly opposite compensations, so if you can remember how to play the shots below your feet, then you need only try to make the reverse alterations.

Fig 10.1. When the ball is above your feet, keep your spine more erect, grip down a little on the club and make sure you are well balanced with a little more weight on the balls of the feet.

The set up

When the ball is above your feet, it is closer to you than on a flat lie. Therefore, you will not need to bend from the hips as much as usual in order to ground the club. Consequently your spine will be more erect, with more weight on your heels than on a level lie (Fig 10.1). However, do not lean away from the hill but feel that your spine is more at right angles to the horizon than normal. Depending on the severity of the slope, you may like to grip down on the club a little, so that the swing does not become too flat. If the ball is only slightly above your feet you can probably play it in its usual position, but where the slope is steep, play it nearer the centre of your stance. You can be quite attacking with this shot, and very often a wooden shot is most successful since its rounded sole will adapt better to the lie.

The swing

Because of your erect spine and the fact that the ball is above your feet, the plane of the swing will be flatter than normal. You will be more aware of the rotary movement of the body and, indeed, the hands and arms will swing on a flatter plane as well (Fig 10.2). These changes should occur naturally and you would be wrong to try to prevent them. Take a couple of practice swings so that you know how the swing will feel. It is almost as though the ball was teed on a very high tee-peg, where you would have to swing more horizontally in order to strike it correctly. At the top of your backswing, you will feel that your arms are more behind your head than normal, and likewise on the throughswing, they will finish more around your body than above your head (Fig 10.3). The outcome is a swing path that is more in-to-in than normal, resulting in a shot that is liable to draw or even hook, so aim right to allow for this. If you want to hit the ball hard but need a fairly straight shot, you could either open the club face a little at address or hold your hands squarer through the shot, preventing the right hand and arm rotating over the left. If you allow the ball to draw, it will fly lower than normal and run on landing so you can probably play one less club than usual.

If the lie is rather severe, you will have to make a more controlled three-quarter length swing. Always take a couple of practice swings, which will help to tell you how aggressive you can be and still maintain your balance.

Fig 10.2. The set up will mean that the backswing is flatter than usual, with the hands and arms more behind than above your head. This creates an exaggerated in-to-in attack on the ball

Fig 10.3. The through swing must also be flatter with the hands and arms finishing lower than usual. The ball is liable to draw or hook, so allow for this by aiming to the right

CHAPTER ELEVEN

Ball above feet around the green

This shot is usually played from a mound around the green, invariably onto a green below the ball. Unfortunately, it is not always easy to be accurate with this shot, especially if the ball is lying badly. The very set up encourages a shot that is hard to control, and the prospect of the ball lying poorly adds another difficult factor to the shot. Whilst you should always be able to get the ball onto the green, the degree of difficulty of stance and lie may mean that getting the ball close to the hole can be something of a lottery. Furthermore, many golfers will not necessarily experience playing this sort of shot very often, especially if you play most of your golf on a well manicured parkland course. Those golfers who play links-type coastal courses will undoubtedly be faced with this type of shot quite regularly and will therefore know more about its problems.

The set up and swing

As with the shot from the fairway, your spine is more erect than normal, so much so that for extreme examples of this shot where the ball might be about waist high, you are standing almost totally upright. You will always have to grip down the club, sometimes with both hands on the shaft rather than the grip. Your weight will be more towards your heels but you will feel quite a strain at the front of your shins since your feet are likely to be angled upwards. You will feel as though you are leaning more towards the slope than away from it, and be certain that you have a secure footing for although the shot may not require much force, your body and stance need to remain as steady as possible. Position the ball near the centre of your stance.

The shot is played with the hands and arms, with the club being swung fairly horizontally depending on the degree of slope (Fig 11.1). If the grass is cut short the shot is not too difficult, but if you are in short rough you may need to pick the club up with your hands in the backswing to avoid catching the club in the grass. You must feel as though you are dragging or pulling the club head back into

the ball so that you attain the same impact position as you had at address, with the hands ahead of the club face. The wrists need to stay firm through the impact zone so that you feel the forearms rather than the hands swinging the club, and you keep the blade in a square or open position, never letting it close. In a very bad lie, the grass can easily twist the club face closed which will cause an inaccurate shot, so be very firm with the left hand and do not let the right roll over the left. In most instances, the ball is likely to be pulled, so aim slightly right of target.

Fig 11.1. When the ball is very much above your feet, your spine is virtually straight. To help control the shot, grip well down on the club. The flat swing will make you pull or hook the ball left, so aim right to allow for this

CHAPTER TWELVE

Ball above feet in a bunker

Although this shot is not so formidable as the ball below the feet shot, nevertheless it is not always as easy as it seems. Greenside bunker shots are best played using a rather steep out-to-in swing, which produces a shot that flies high without too much run on landing. However, as explained in the previous two chapters, when the ball is above the feet it produces a flatter in-to-in shaped swing. For bunker shots this can make it rather difficult to contact the sand at the predetermined spot, resulting in a shot that is not as good as might have been expected.

The set up and swing

If the slope is gentle and the ball is not too much above your feet, I would suggest that you stand a little further away from the ball and set up with your body aimed left of the target as for a normal bunker shot and the blade just open. Do not wriggle your feet too deeply into the sand but grip a little further down on the club to prevent it digging too deeply into the sand. The gentle slope will not prevent you swinging your arms up in the backswing, which means you will make an adequately steep swing and provided that you do not allow the right hand to roll over the left through impact you should be able to hit a shot that does not roll too much on landing. As the club is shorter than normal, you may have to hit the shot slightly harder than from a flat lie.

Where the ball is considerably above your feet, you make the same adjustments as for the fairway shot, i.e. stand more upright and further from the ball so that your arms are slightly extended, grip down on the club and play the ball nearer the centre of your stance. Since the lie will encourage a shot that hooks or pulls, you should aim right of target and maintain a fairly square set up with your feet and shoulders. Do not dig your feet into the sand too much as this will make you even lower than the ball, but do make certain that your stance is secure. Open the blade as appropriate for the shot so that you get enough height on the ball. As I have already explained, the swing for this shot will be flatter than usual, and you should allow for this action rather than fighting it. While your arms and body turn more horizontally in the backswing, allow your wrists to break. On the downswing feel as though your arms are pulling or dragging the club head back into the sand — do not throw the club head at the sand with your hands as you will only strike the sand too far behind the ball. You will feel that your body is turning through the shot more than usual, and due to the flatter plane, you may find that your hands and arms want to rotate to the left through impact. This will tend to shut the club face causing the ball to come out lower than usual with right to left spin on it so that it will run on landing.

You must concentrate on the spot where you wish the club head to enter the sand and be certain to swing right through the shot. If you find that you are taking too much sand before the ball, adjust your intended entry point closer to the back of the ball. The fact that you have gripped down on the club may mean that you need to hit the ball harder, but this factor can be offset if the ball has a little draw flight on it and thereby runs more on landing.

Bunker shots from flat and perfect lies need to be practised in order for the ball to land near the pin each time, so do not expect these more difficult bunker shots to land where you want them without practising regularly.

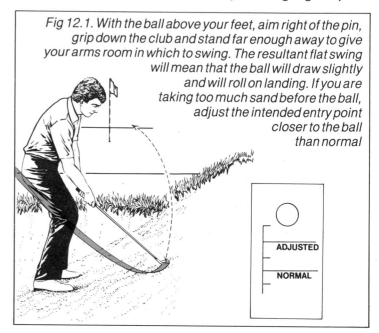

Fig 12.1. With the ball above your feet, aim right of the pin, grip down the club and stand far enough away to give your arms room in which to swing. The resultant flat swing will mean that the ball will draw slightly and will roll on landing. If you are taking too much sand before the ball, adjust the intended entry point closer to the ball than normal

CHAPTER THIRTEEN

Making full use of fairway woods

Certainly for the beginner and probably for the majority of club golfers, the long irons are the hardest clubs to hit. The small bladed heads of the 1, 2, 3 and 4 irons do not immediately inspire confidence. Added to this, the longer shafts in these clubs can tend to make them more unwieldly, and their lack of loft only exaggerates unwanted sidespin. So often the shots with these clubs are poor which leads to lack of confidence, resulting in the golfer thrashing at the ball in a most unco-ordinated fashion. Something of a stigma was once attached to the player who *resorted* to using a 5 wood instead of a long iron, but in recent years this trend and thinking has been reversed, helped considerably by players like Lee Trevino extolling the value of the 5 and 7 woods. Fairway woods are versatile and their extra loft, compared to that of a long iron, will not create as much unwanted sidespin. With a good understanding of how they should be hit in specific circumstances, you also will be singing their praises.

Fairway woods from a good lie

When faced with a long shot from the fairway with the ball sitting up on a cushion of grass, you should be aiming to sweep the ball from the top of the grass, just taking a few blades of grass after the strike rather than a large divot. In order to sweep the ball away rather than hit down on it, you should position it opposite your stance at the point where the club reaches the bottom of its arc. Thus it will be slightly nearer the left foot than for iron shots and just back from where you would play your driver.

It is impossible to be definite about the exact point and you will need to experiment a little yourself, but with the ball somewhere just inside your left heel you should not be too far out (Fig 13.1a). Your weight should be about 50:50 on each foot, although if you are lucky enough to find an exceptionally good lie — sometimes this happens in light rough where the ball is really sitting up — you could put a *little* more weight on the right foot.

Fig 13.1a. Position the ball at the lowest point in the arc so that the ball is swept away from the turf. The arms and body move away together so that the clubhead is kept low to the ground at the start of the backswing

When viewed face on, your left arm and the shaft should form a relatively straight line, and the sole of the club should sit flat on the ground (Fig 13.1a). Many players make the mistake of raising the back edge of the club and hooding the face by getting their hands too far ahead at address. Although there are times when you may need an address position similar to this (which I will cover later), it does in fact encourage a steeper attack on the ball, which is not ideal for a good lie.

The wood should be swung on a fairly shallow, wide arc so that in the initial stages of the backswing you should feel your arms and shoulders swinging away *together*. Do not just swing the club head up in the air with your arms;

try to keep it low to the ground at least until it has passed your right foot so that at the top of the swing you have made a full turn with your shoulders and your weight is predominantly on your right leg. As your arms swing down, you must sense that you are going to sweep the club head into the back of the ball and continue into a full, well balanced finish.

Due to a certain lack of strength, and often poor technique, many lady golfers fail to strike iron shots crisply enough, failing to take a divot after the ball. Therefore, the gently sweeping action of their swings lends itself most appropriately to fairway wood shots, and they should maximize their use of these clubs.

Which club you use will depend naturally on the distance to be covered and the lie of the ball. Most sets these days include a 3 and 5 wood, but you will also find that more manufacturers are making 7 woods, which

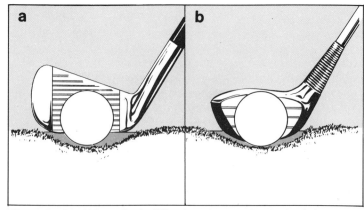

Fig 13.2a & b. When the ball lies in a depression in the fairway, the rounded soled fairway wood is better suited to the shot than the long bladed iron

would be the equivalent of a 3 or 4 iron. To vary the distance you hit the woods, naturally you can change the amount of force in the swing, but also by gripping down the shaft you will find that you can play shots of a great variety of lengths. It would be a good exercise to hit some 4 irons on the practice ground and then use your 5 and 7 woods to try to cover the same distance. This will teach you how to conjure up shots by a combination of different grip positions, swing paces and lengths.

Fairway woods from the rough or a bad lie

If the ball is sitting in a slight depression on the fairway or sitting down a little in the rough, a fairway wood will almost always be the best club to use if you have a long distance to cover. On the fairway, the shape of the fairway wood is more suitable than the long blade of an iron (Fig 13.2), whilst in the rough the broad sole tends to flatten the grass out of its way, and the grass will not tangle around the wood like it does with an iron. Because the ball is sitting down, you will need a steeper angle of attack than for a good lie, so position the ball nearer the centre of your stance. This will allow your hands to be more ahead of the club head and the ball and encourage the steep attack. In this instance the club face might become slightly hooded with the back edge off the ground (Fig 13.1b). You may also need your weight to favour the

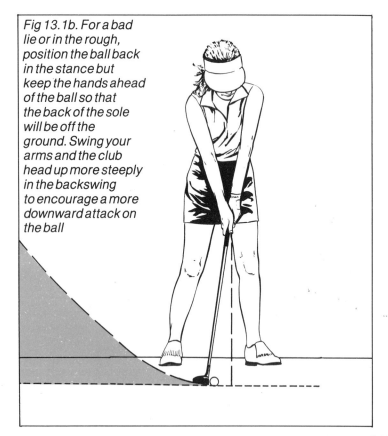

Fig 13.1b. For a bad lie or in the rough, position the ball back in the stance but keep the hands ahead of the ball so that the back of the sole will be off the ground. Swing your arms and the club head up more steeply in the backswing to encourage a more downward attack on the ball

left foot *slightly*, depending on just how bad the lie might be. As you swing the club head away, try to swing your arms a little more upright than usual, or if you are in the rough you may need to pick up the club head quite quickly with an early wrist break. Your downswing force will be directed downwards rather than forwards so that it feels more like a chopping than a sweeping action. I would not suggest that you use a 3 wood in such situations but depending on the lie and distance required, a 4, 5 or 7 wood should be ideal.

Woods from a bunker

If the ball is sitting well towards the back of a bunker that does not have a steep face, you can use a 5 or 7 wood to good effect. Take a firm stance but do not bury your feet too much in the sand, and grip down the club a little to compensate for the stance. Play the ball just forward of

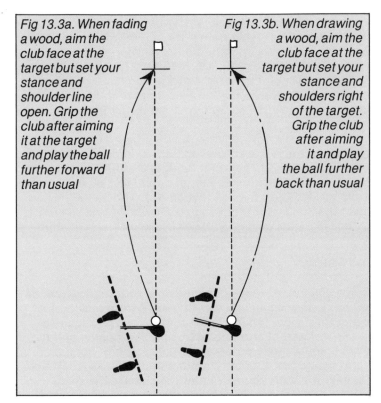

Fig 13.3a. When fading a wood, aim the club face at the target but set your stance and shoulder line open. Grip the club after aiming it at the target and play the ball further forward than usual

Fig 13.3b. When drawing a wood, aim the club face at the target but set your stance and shoulders right of the target. Grip the club after aiming it and play the ball further back than usual

centre and, with a firm wristed swing, smoothly clip the ball from the top of the sand. Keep your arms swinging throughout the shot rather than trying to flick at the ball with your wrists, as you will more than likely hit the sand before the ball. Looking at the top of the ball rather than at the back, may help you to hit it cleanly. If you catch the sand before the ball the shot is dampened and you might just as well have played more conservatively. This is not a shot for the beginner, and no matter what standard of golfer you may be, a little practice will tell you when to gamble and when to be less attacking. You will also find it an easier shot to hit from firm rather than soft sand.

Woods in the wind

If you are playing downwind, the woods will send the ball higher than their equivalent irons. For example, a 5 wood will hit the ball higher than a 2 iron so you will be able to take more advantage of the wind. Of course, the reverse might be true when playing into the wind, but provided that the lie is reasonable, a 3 or 4 wood will not hit the ball too high. If you grip down on the club with a firmer grip than usual, you will produce a firmer wristed swing that will hit the ball lower. Do not be tempted to hit the ball very hard as this usually results in more backspin and sends the ball higher. Whilst your companions may be happy hitting a 2 iron into the wind, in these circumstances any unwanted sidespin is accentuated and the ball needs to be struck quite purely. You would undoubtedly be better off playing a fairway wood in which you have confidence and which will tolerate a certain degree of mis-hit more readily than the long iron.

In cross winds it is better to aim off to allow for the wind rather than shaping the ball against the wind. But sometimes you may feel that in order to control the ball better, a certain amount of intended fade or draw would be an advantage. This really only applies to the better player — the higher handicap golfer should just allow for any crosswind in his/her aim.

Shaping the shots

If you need to fade a long shot with a wood, you will get better results from a 3 or 4 wood than the 5 or 7. When fading a shot the club face is open to the line of the swing, adding loft to the club face. The higher numbered woods already have more loft than the 3 or 4, and the additional loft added will make them more liable to add backspin and not sidespin to the shot. That is not to say that you cannot fade the 5 or 7, just that it is easier with a 3 or 4.

To fade or slice the ball you must align yourself and consequently the swing path left, i.e. out-to-in, in relation to the intended target, with the ball further forward in your stance than usual (Fig 13.3a). Thus a club placed across your shoulders should point left of the target and not parallel to it. Having set up in this position, just open the club face so that it points more towards the intended target, and then re-grip it so that your hands are in their

normal position but the club face is open. The amount of curve will depend on how far left you aim, and how far right the club face is positioned at impact. Do not allow the right hand and arm to cross over the left through the impact zone but keep the left in command throughout, allied to slightly more emphasis on your leg action (Fig 13.4a). The shot will go higher than normal and will not run much on landing. Thus you will lose some distance on the shot.

When you need to hook or draw the ball, you will find that you have more control with the more lofted woods. Trying to hook the 3 wood may result in a shot that barely gets off the ground or runs into trouble. When drawing or hooking a ball, the club face needs to be closed to the swing path, and consequently effective loft is deducted from the club face. Since the 4, 5 and 7 woods have a reasonable amount of loft already, they will be better suited to curving the ball from right to left in a controlled manner with the ball flying through the air and not along the ground.

To draw or hook the ball, aim yourself, and consequently the swing path right, i.e. in-to-out in relation to the intended target, with the ball further back in your stance than usual (Fig 13.3b). A club placed across your shoulders will point at or right of the target. Once set up, close the club face so that it faces more towards the target, then re-grip it so that your hands are in their normal position but the club face is closed. Again the amount of curve will depend on how much the club face is pointing to the left of the swing path at impact. You may need to encourage your right hand and arm to rotate over the left through the impact zone, depending on how much curve you need on the ball (Fig 13.4b). The ball will fly lower than usual for the club you are hitting and will roll on landing, thus gaining you some distance on the shot.

Fig 13.4a. When fading the ball, make certain that the left hand leads through impact and just beyond. You may need more leg action than usual to help keep the blade open

Fig 13.4b. When playing a draw, depending on how much the ball needs to curve, you may have to encourage the right hand and arm to rotate over the left through the impact zone

Summary

I hope you can now see how versatile your fairway woods can be. Ladies especially would benefit from making full use of their more lofted woods. Long irons do require a certain amount of strength to be struck properly, and the lady beginner rarely possesses the strength of hand or technique to feel totally at home with them. Be smart and get to know both your own and the clubs' capabilities, and the fairway woods will become your secret weapon.

CHAPTER FOURTEEN

Trees: over, under, round, through

Someone has created a rumour that trees are 75 per cent air. Ask any golfer if he/she agrees with that statement, and I am sure that the answer would be 'no'. Whilst not all courses have trees that come into play, it is inevitable that sooner or later you will play a course where trees are a considerable hazard. Having played a shot that puts a tree between you and the target, you must first decide which is the most sensible route either to the hole or back onto the fairway. I know that I may have written this already, but the wise golfer is one who knows his/her limitations. Luckily many professional tournaments are televized these days and we see international stars playing incredible shots from deep in the woods or around trees. Unfortunately, many golfers seek to emulate their heroes and, armed with the same intent but not the same ability, they too try to perform miraculous shots. If you do not escape from the trees at the first attempt, invariably the ball will hit a branch and can land up anywhere. Sadly 'anywhere' is often an unplayable lie from where you have little chance of even swinging the club. I would not like you to think that I believe in playing sideways or backwards onto the fairway whenever you find yourself in the trees. This would be far too defensive and would also deny you the thrill of planning and executing the best shot possible. So this chapter aims to help you decide which shot to choose and how best to play it.

How to assess the shot

The first point to check is the lie of the ball, which will have an important influence on which types of shots are possible.

1 If the ball is lying well in light rough or on the fairway, your choice is not really restricted with the only danger being that you may try to be over-ambitious. If you can strike the ball without too much grass getting between the blade and the ball, you should be able to shape the shot left or right. Hitting the ball high or low should pose no problems (Fig 14.1a).

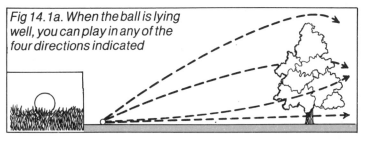
Fig 14.1a. When the ball is lying well, you can play in any of the four directions indicated

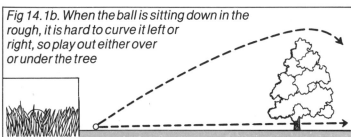
Fig 14.1b. When the ball is sitting down in the rough, it is hard to curve it left or right, so play out either over or under the tree

Fig 14.1c. When the ball is in the trees, lying on grass, you will easily be able to hit it out low, but should only hit it out up through the trees if the lie is good and the route not too obstructed

Fig 14.1d. When the ball is on a bare lie, choose the low route

2 If the ball is sitting down in the rough, you will have difficulties in curving it right or left, since too much grass will intervene between it and the blade. You may still be able to hit the ball high enough to get over the tree, provided that it is not sitting down too deeply, whilst hitting low will present no problems (Fig 14.1b).

3 If the ball is in the trees and lying in grass, for the reasons given above you will not be able to curve it but will be able to hit it high if the lie is not too bad and there are no intervening branches. You will also be able to hit it low (Fig 14.1c).

4 If you are in the trees and the ball is lying on bare earth, you would be best advised to hit it out low. Only attempt a lofted shot if there are no intervening branches and to hit it low is impossible (Fig 14.1d).

The human factor

The options suggested above have not taken into account your particular ability to hit each of the recommended shots, and this is where you must be honest with yourself. If you are an inveterate slicer, no matter how many words I may write here on how to hook the ball around the trees, you would be well advised not to attempt the shot without first being able to produce it on the practice ground. If you habitually move the ball from left to right, or vice versa, always try to do what comes naturally, especially under pressure. Accept that if you have never drawn or hooked a ball in your life, wherever possible you should choose an alternative shot to get yourself out of trouble until you have had a chance to experiment on the practice ground.

The best tactical shot

Having outlined which shots are possible from different lies, you must then consider which will be most advantageous. If you choose to hit over the trees, you may have no trouble hitting the ball high enough but can you hit it far enough to clear the trees? It is always best to have a look at the shot from the side so that you can see just how far the ball must fly.

When playing a low shot from the trees, the main danger can be hitting the ball too far so that it runs into

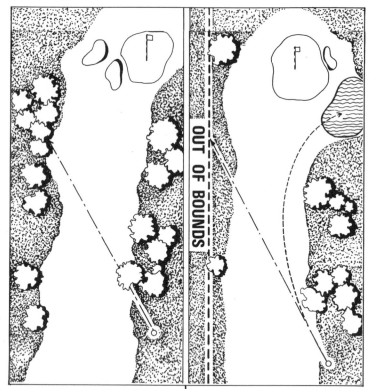

Fig 14.2. Do not be tempted to make up for a bad shot by being greedy for distance, since you might just hit the ball back into trouble

Fig 14.3. If you decide to curve the ball and do not hit it correctly, are you going to be in more trouble? In this example, if the ball does not fade enough, it could go out of bounds, whereas if it fades too much, it could land in the water

trees on the other side of the fairway (Fig 14.2). One can easily be tempted into trying to 'make up' for the errant shot and opt for as long a shot as possible. If you cannot get the ball onto the green, you must look for the spot from which you would ideally like to play the next shot.

If you elect to fade the ball around the tree and do not manage to get the right amount of turn on it, are you likely to hit the ball out of bounds or into a lake or bunker (Fig 14.3)? Whilst you might have envisaged and have the opportunity to play this shot, the fact that if you over- or under-cut the ball will be disastrous may in itself prevent you from playing the shot to the best of your ability. You would be putting yourself under pressure, and only you know how well you can withstand pressure. A matchplay situation may demand different tactics from those employed in stroke play. This, together with your own particular form on the day, should help to determine how you tackle the shot.

Trying to play up through the trees perhaps presents the biggest chance of failure. It is easy to recall Severiano Ballesteros playing many superb shots from such

positions, but remember that he is a genius and has the ability to match his attacking spirit for the game. He can execute such shots in the almost certain knowledge that he can play them successfully. If you are playing through the trees, you really must consider what might happen if you do not make good contact. Will the outcome be very costly or is it worth the gamble? If you have no alternative shot, okay, but consider this shot as a last option unless you are a very low handicap golfer with a good lie!

The 'over' shot

This presupposes that the ball is sitting on a cushion of grass rather than bare ground. In this example, I will take it that the target, whether it is the green or a certain part of the fairway, is about 140 yards away and that you are at least 15 to 20 yards back from the tree. You must decide with which club you can best gain the required height and distance, remembering that the shot will not carry as far as usual as you will be hitting it higher.

Position the ball forward of centre, open the club face a little, aim slightly left of target and feel that your right shoulder is lower than usual. With a fairly narrow stance, keep your weight a little more on your right foot (Fig 14.4). These adjustments will help you to get height on the shot. At address keep your hands fairly level with the ball so that you can initiate the backswing with an early wrist break, which, together with the open stance, will help to create an upright swing and a steep attack on the ball. The shot will feel more 'handsy' than normal, but through impact you must not allow the right hand to cross over the left as this would de-loft the club face. Your arms should finish high. The length of shot, lie, height of the tree and your skill must together determine how long a club you can risk playing. You should practise with each club down to about your 5 iron to see how high and how far you can hit the ball. Only then will you really know whether you are taking a risk or are being sensible with your club and shot selection.

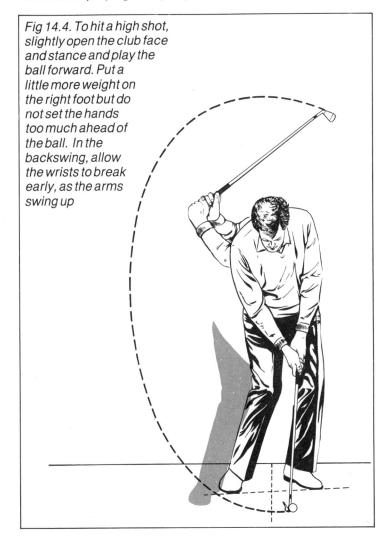

Fig 14.4. To hit a high shot, slightly open the club face and stance and play the ball forward. Put a little more weight on the right foot but do not set the hands too much ahead of the ball. In the backswing, allow the wrists to break early, as the arms swing up

The 'under' shot

Since you want to play the ball out low, you should choose a club with little loft, perhaps anything between a

3 and a 7 iron. The problem you may face when playing a ball out low is that although you wish to avoid hitting overhead branches, you also want to clear any long grass or other obstructions lower down. A shot that travels almost completely along the ground may therefore not be the best choice. You may want one that flies about two feet off the ground, which may mean using a 6 or 7 iron depending on the lie and where you play the ball in your stance. Having selected the correct club, position it well back in your stance nearer your right foot to ensure keeping the ball low. This will reduce the effective loft of the club making a 7 iron react more like a 5 or 6 iron. Keep your hands well ahead of the ball so that the shaft slopes considerably towards the target, with your hands opposite your left thigh (Fig 14.5). Make sure that you keep the blade square, since with your hands so far forward it is easy to turn the blade open. With a wider stance than normal, place more weight on the left foot and make the swing in a firm wristed manner, feeling that you punch the ball out. Keep your hands ahead of the club at impact and beyond, finishing with the club head quite low to the ground. The ball will naturally run considerably so always have a couple of practice swings in order to judge the shot better.

The 'round' shots

In the last chapter I outlined how to shape shots with your fairway woods, and you would find it helpful to re-read that section of the book. However, if you have a shot of, say, 130 to 140 yards, you will not want a wood.

A shot of 130 yards that needs to curve from left to right, i.e. fade or slice, is best played with an iron that does not have too much loft. The fading family of shots requires a club face that is open to the swing path at impact, which consequently becomes more lofted and less likely to impart sidespin. To ensure that you get sidespin and not just additional backspin, select a straighter faced club, perhaps a 5 iron, and if necessary grip down on it and alter the length, pace and power of the swing to adjust the distance. Do not forget that a fading shot does not travel as far as a straight one. One of the pitfalls of this shot is not aiming sufficiently to the left at address. The path of the swing usually determines the initial direction of the ball, but when a club face is opened a lot, the ball will

tend to start out between the line of the swing and where the club face is pointing. The set up is the same as for the fairway wood shot, but in the swing try to exaggerate the up-and-down movement of your arms. This action, together with keeping the body turn to a minimum in the backswing, will produce a more upright swing, which will encourage a fading flight on the ball (Fig 14.6). A firmer grip than usual will help to prevent unwanted hand action so that through impact you feel as though you are dragging the club head across the ball mainly with your arms, preventing the forearms from rotating anti-clockwise. The golfer who naturally slices all shots will probably not have to think too much about this shot but

Fig 14.5. For a low shot, play the ball back in the stance, keeping the weight more on the left side, hands well ahead of the ball and the club face hooded. Make the swing very firm wristed, punching the ball out keeping the club head low to the ground after impact

should just take care with aiming the shot. The golfer who naturally hooks or draws the ball will definitely need to observe the above points and make full use of a couple of practice swings to experience how the action should feel.

A shot of 130 yards that needs to curve from right to left may be played with a more lofted club than you would normally use from that distance, when the ball is required to hook or draw, the club face will have less loft on it than normal, so an 8 iron could be more like a 7 or 6 iron. Your

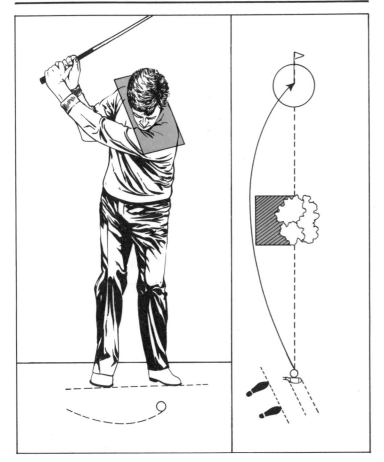

Fig 14.6. When fading the ball with an iron, slightly restrict the shoulder turn and make a more upright arm swing. Make certain that you aim enough to the left as the open club face means the ball starts out just right of the swing path

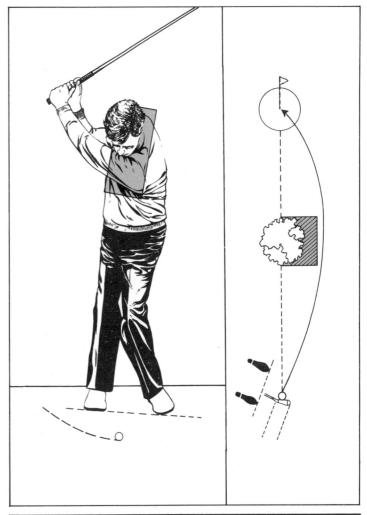

Fig 14.7. When drawing the ball, make a good shoulder turn and a flatter arm swing. Be sure to aim far enough to the right as the closed club face will make the ball start left of the swing path

set up will be similar to that described for shaping the fairway woods but do make certain that you aim enough to the right of the obstacle to avoid hitting it. Do not grip the club too tightly, and make a good shoulder turn in the backswing (Fig 14.7). Through impact feel that your hands and arms are rotating to the left. Your arms will finish more round your body than normal, and the ball will go further and lower than usual and run on landing, The golfer who naturally imparts draw or hook spin on the ball will not need to over-emphasise these points, but the slicer should take a couple of practice swings concentrating on allowing the hands and arms to be more active through the impact zone.

With each of these 'round' the tree shots, you should always assess whether you would be better off over-curving or under-curving the ball and let that dictate the degree to which you try to bend the shot.

The 'through' shot

For the high shot that emerges from a gap in the trees, you are more likely to use one of the short irons, and what you have to match is the angle at which the ball leaves the club with the gap through which you are planning to hit (Fig 14.8). If the lie is bare, the ball will fly lower, whereas a good lie will encourage height. Try to make the swing as smooth as possible and resist the temptation to look up or come up on the shot too early. Lining up the shot is crucial so do take time on this and use an intermediate target about a yard ahead of the ball to assist you.

If you are in the middle of the trees and decide to play out low, you may have to thread the ball between several trees to get back to the fairway. In this instance lining up is crucial since you may have only a few inches through which to squeeze the ball. As you will be playing the ball back in your stance, there is a chance that you could hit it slightly right of where you are aiming. You should either close the blade a little or aim a bit further left to compensate (Fig 14.9).

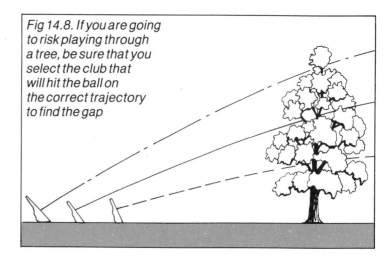

Fig 14.8. If you are going to risk playing through a tree, be sure that you select the club that will hit the ball on the correct trajectory to find the gap

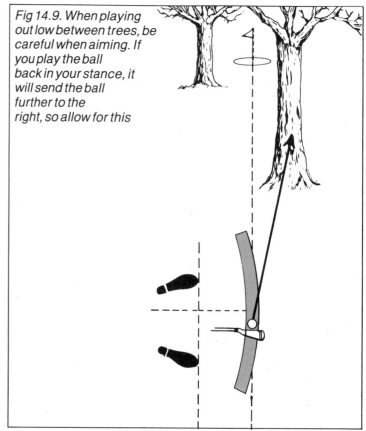

Fig 14.9. When playing out low between trees, be careful when aiming. If you play the ball back in your stance, it will send the ball further to the right, so allow for this

CHAPTER FIFTEEN

Playing from the rough

It never ceases to surprise me how poorly many club golfers play shots from the rough. Possibly having hit what could at best be described as a 'weak' shot into the rough, they try to make up for the bad shot and proceed to take out their 3 wood and hit a ball that is barely visible. Then sadly, and inevitably, they take at least two or three more shots to move the ball anywhere near the fairway and thus pay the penalty for playing the wrong shot at the wrong time. There is no one club that is the correct one to use from rough — it will always depend on your lie, how far you have to go, how strong you are and what will happen if your chosen shot fails. In the chapter on trees, I highlighted how you must think about the shot and weigh up all the possibilities before you choose your club and exit route, and much the same advice applies to playing out of the rough. However, here are some points that are worth remembering next time you stray from the fairway.

Long shots from rough — club selection

The ideal club to gain maximum distance from the rough is a lofted wood. The loft on the same numbered woods does vary, and thus a 3 wood in one set may not have exactly the same loft as a 3 wood in another set but, generally speaking, unless the ball is sitting up in the rough, leave the 3 wood in the bag. You would do better using a 4, 5 or 7 wood, and the worse the lie the more lofted the wood you should use. Strong men players do have an advantage over ladies when it comes to shots from the rough because regardless of how good your technique may be, the success rate from really bad lies will, to a large extent, depend on brute strength, so it is especially important for the ladies not to attempt shots beyond their physical capabilities. However, fairway

Fig 15.1. For long shots from rough, a fairway wood is usually the better club to use, since it glides through the rough, whilst the long grass wraps itself around the hosel of an iron

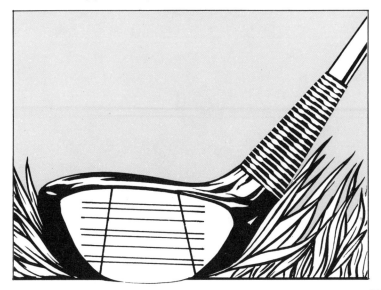

woods come to the rescue as they glide through the rough rather than getting tangled in it(Fig 15.1).

The exit route

So having decided which club is the best to use, select the best line on which to play, which in many cases will not be directly towards the hole. You would be wise to avoid having to carry a bunker if the lie suggests that the ball might come out rather low (Fig 15.2). Likewise, if the lie is reasonably good, you must aim down rather than across the fairway so as not to land up in the rough on the other side.

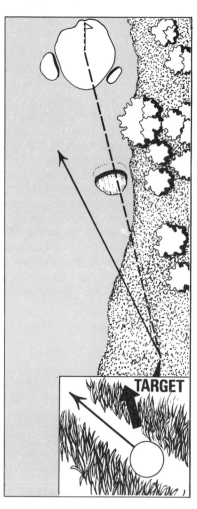

Fig 15.2. The ball will often come out low from rough, so avoid having to carry bunkers. You may also benefit from adjusting your aim if it allows you to swing the clubhead along a channel of shorter grass

Grass in the rough does not lie uniformly and very often you will see that the grass directly behind the ball is long and thick, whereas if you were to hit the ball in a slightly different direction, perhaps swinging along a line on which someone else had hit, you would stand a better chance of making good contact and good distance (Fig 15.2).

Remember that if it is not possible to reach the green, you want to play your next shot from the optimum position, which may mean hitting an easy 5 or 7 wood to

lay up short of a bunker rather than trying to thrash your 4 wood and finishing in the bunker.

The set up and swing

Play the ball nearer the centre of your stance than usual, grip down the shaft a little and also grip more firmly. Keep your hands well ahead of the ball and put more weight on your left leg. Make the swing more upright so that the club does not catch the grass at the start of the backswing. Concentrate on swinging your *arms* up and down rather than making a good turn, and swing through the shot as much as possible, keeping your left hand leading for as long as possible.

Another way to play these shots when the lie is not very good is to open the club face and aim yourself slightly left of your target, with the ball fairly central in your stance (Fig 15.3). This set up will enable you to make a steep backswing and cut across the ball. There will not be much left to right spin imparted because there will be too much

Fig 15.3. To cut the ball out of the rough, slightly open the club face and stance, and swing along your body line, i.e. out-to-in to the target

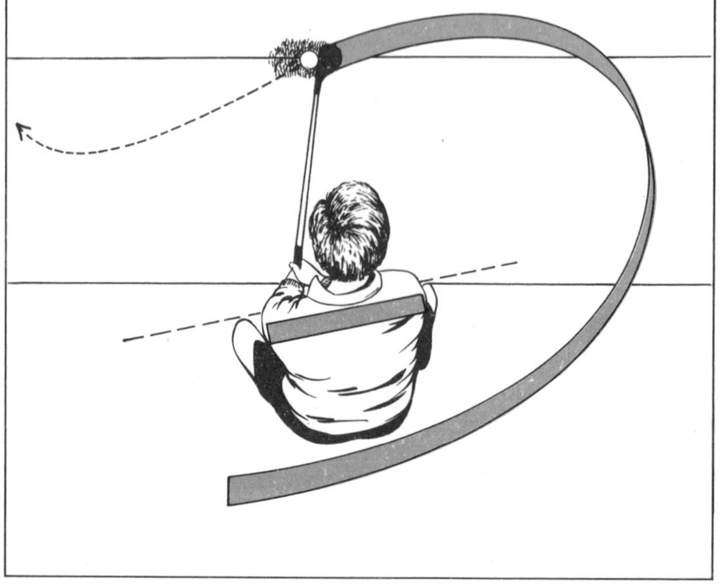

Fig 15.4. For a short low running pitch from the rough, set up with your shoulders square, stance just open and the ball central. The hands are ahead of the ball at address and impact. The ball is punched out, with the back of the left wrist remaining firm

grass between the club face and ball for clean contact. But the ball will come out on a line between the path of the swing and the direction of the club face. This resembles the fade shot with a wood described in pages 147–148.

If the lie is too bad for a wooden shot, you must accept this and take an iron. The only exception to the rule might be if you were only a yard or so into the rough and the fairway ahead had no hazards to concern you. The worst shot that you might hit with a wood would be a semi-topped shot, which would come out low and run. This shot is quite acceptable at the right time, expecially if the fairway ahead is downhill.

If you play an iron, you have decided to sacrifice distance for strategy, so do not ruin your wise decision by taking a long iron. Select a middle or short iron that you know you can definitely hit well. Play it in either manner described for the wood, but since the grass is likely to catch around the hosel, do have a firmer grip than normal.

For any shot in the rough you should have a practice swing in order to feel how the grass will affect the club. If the grass is lying towards you, the resistance is quite severe and you must be prepared for it — otherwise the club head will twist excessively. When the grass lies with the shot, the resistance is not so severe and the club head, especially with woods, will tend to glide through quite easily.

Any ball played from the rough will run more than a shot from the fairway, and this, at least, will help to make up for lost distance.

Short shots from the rough

Here I refer to shots of 100 yards and under where control and not distance is of greater importance. The type of lie will determine how accurate you can expect to be, since from a really bad lie even the best golfer in the world cannot be certain of what will happen.

The running pitch from short rough

A pitch shot from 70 to 80 yards where the ball is not lying too badly can be tackled in two ways, depending on whether or not height is essential. If there are no bunkers to carry then set up with your shoulders and hips parallel to the target, feet slightly open with your weight favouring the left foot. Keep the blade square with your hands well ahead of the ball, which should be central in your stance. Break your wrists early in the backswing and swing your arms up steeply. As you swing down keep your hands ahead of the club head and feel that you 'stab' the club head into the back of the ball (Fig 15.4). There is not much to follow through the shot but the ball will come out quite readily, lower than a normal pitch, and run on landing. There is very much a 'hit and stop' feeling about this shot, with the hands taking most of the strain.

The high pitch from short rough

The difficulty of a pitch shot from 70 to 80 yards that has to carry a bunker depends on the lie of the ball. When it is sitting quite well with a nice cushion of grass beneath it, the shot presents no real problems. However, from a bad lie, the outcome is less certain and perhaps only the stronger and lower handicap player ought to attempt the shot.

To guarantee height, open the face of the appropriate club, then take your grip, keeping the left hand firmer than usual. Set up aiming slightly left, with the ball forward of centre in your stance but your weight evenly distributed. Keep your hands fairly level with, rather than too far ahead of, the ball so that you make full use of the club's loft. This type of address position creates an out-to-in swing, which helps to hit the ball on a higher trajectory (see Fig 14.4). The arms swing up steeply and the wrists break early in the backswing causing an upright action. As you swing back to the ball, feel that the right hand works *under* the left so that the blade remains open (Fig 15.5). Try to swing to a full finish with your hands high. Due to the fact that most of the force of the shot was designed to send the ball upwards, it will land softly and should not run too much. You must not be afraid to hit the ball quite hard, since the open stance and club face, hand action and thick grass will all reduce the distance of the shot. If you hit the ball too softly it will either remain in the rough or land in the bunker so do not try to be too clever — make certain that you get on the green. This shot requires rather more skill than the average higher handicap player might possess, and players in this category would be better advised to play a firmer wristed shot, starting with the hands ahead of the ball and the weight more on the left side. A slightly open stance and club face should provide adequate loft for the shot.

Thick rough

If the ball is lying in thick rough, the strength factor becomes more important, and so you must assess whether to carry a bunker will present too much of a problem. For men with a decent technique, the rough will not be as limiting as it is for women players, and particularly for the beginner. If reaching the green is out of the question, just play the ball back onto the fairway. The sand iron, with its heavy flange, is ideal for getting out of thick rough so do not be afraid to use it. Keep your weight and hands ahead of the ball, which is placed well back in an open stance opposite the right foot. Always have a practice swing as thick rough will want to severely twist

the club head through the impact zone, and you must be prepared for this by gripping firmly. The upright arm swing, accompanied by an early wrist cock, will enable you to hit down on the ball. You will probably be unable to hit the ball but will strike the grass behind it, which will slow up the club head, reducing the power of the shot, so do not expect miracles from very bad lies.

Shots from around the green

Shots from the rough about 5 to 10 yards off the fringe, especially when the pin is not very far onto the green, can be difficult to judge. Unfortunately, sometimes the ball comes out 'hot', i.e. it flies off the club face and runs a lot on landing; at other times the grass behind the ball 'kills' the shot and the ball barely lands on the fringe. Consequently, you may be torn between being too firm

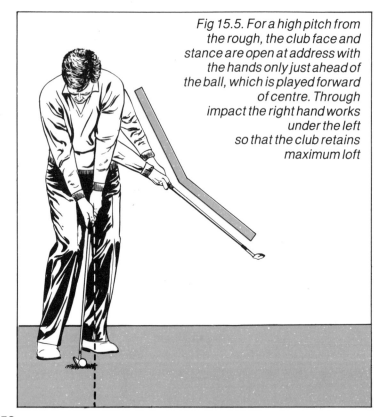

Fig 15.5. For a high pitch from the rough, the club face and stance are open at address with the hands only just ahead of the ball, which is played forward of centre. Through impact the right hand works under the left so that the club retains maximum loft

Fig 15.6. For a soft shot around the green from a reasonable lie in the rough, use an open set up and a passive handed action. Too much wrist cock in the backswing will give too much club head speed

I hope that by now you can imagine the set up needed — an open stance and club face with the body aimed just left of target, so that by swinging along the line of your body you will cut across the ball from out-to-in. Let your weight just favour the left foot, or keep it even on both feet if the lie is good. Position the ball centrally for reasonable lies, and slightly more forward for good lies. Although the club head needs to swing upwards away from the ball, swing your forearms up, keeping your wrists quiet (Fig 15.6). They will in fact break a little, but this should happen naturally rather than consciously. The whole swing should be very smooth, so take the club back far enough to keep the backswing and downswing almost at one pace. Do not be tempted to hit *at* the ball with your hands at the last minute, fearing that you do not have enough power for the shot. The back of the left hand should lead throughout so that both it and the club face finish facing more towards the sky than the ground. To maintain good rhythm, be sure to ease your knees towards the target at impact.

Having a mental image of playing the shot in slow motion helps create the correct feel for the shot. At first you will be tempted to hit the ball with your hands, but the feeling is very much one of dragging the club head *through* the ball with the forearms. By gripping a little firmer with both hands you will be able to keep your hands more passive. The more you play this shot, the more you will appreciate just how delicate you can afford to be with it. The main problem can be not having sufficient momentum in the swing, so that the club does not accelerate through the ball enough, and gets stuck in the grass. Good lies do not usually present this problem, but if the ball is sitting down slightly, make sure that you have enough force in the swing to keep swinging through the grass. By trying to make the length of the backswing and throughswing the same, you should then accelerate enough through the shot. The ball comes out quite softly and should not run too much on landing.

with the shot or swinging too easy. The best club to use for the majority of these shots is the sand wedge, since its maximum loft and heavy flange will readily add height to the shot. Always grip down on the club, which allows you to be more positive without hitting the ball too far.

The passive handed shot

If the lie is not too bad, play the shot with passive hands. By this I mean that you must concentrate on swinging the club mainly with your arms, with no conscious strike with your hands. You thereby limit club head speed and can control the shot better. Having read this far in the chapter.

The very short chip

For very short shots, from, say, 2 or 3 yards off the green, use a sand wedge and set up as for the short pitch above, but grip well down on the club, even to the extent of having one or both hands on the shaft. For this delicate shot you just need to break the right wrist a little to make the backswing, and then be sure to hit through the ball, working the right hand *under* the left. Do not stab *at* the ball but keep the club head swinging through the grass, even with such a short swing, or you may leave the ball in the grass.

The grass 'bunker' shot

If the ball is lying badly around the green, you should consider playing the shot as though it were a bunker shot, i.e. aim to hit the grass perhaps an inch or two behind the ball rather than the ball itself. The shot is played using the same set up as for the passive handed pitch, with the ball positioned a little nearer the front foot. As you swing your arms up steeply, allow your wrists to break a little, and aim, and therefore look, at a spot in the grass behind the ball, concentrating on hitting it (Fig 15.7). You must hit right through the shot, keeping the back of the left hand looking towards the sky and swinging a little harder than you would do if you were hitting the ball itself. There is a little weight transference in the backswing but make sure that your legs move through the shot so that you finish

with most of your weight on the left leg. At first you will find it hard to accept that you can hit the ball quite hard, even though you are so near to the hole. The grass that intervenes between the club head and ball cushions the force considerably, but you need to practise so that you can be confident that the extra power in the shot will land the ball on, and not over, the green.

Summary

I have tried to cover several options for escaping from the rough, but obviously you must decide for yourself which shot is not only the right one but the one that you feel happiest playing. I know many club golfers will play better long shots from the rough just by adopting my recommendations. Not too much practice is needed for these shots to improve — you just need to adapt to the situation. Do not try to be too clever around the green; remember that you are always better off *somewhere* on the green rather than off it. So let that always be the standard you bear in mind before deciding which shot to play.

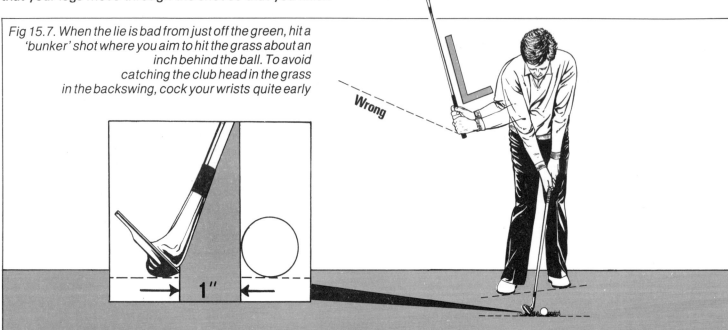

Fig 15.7. When the lie is bad from just off the green, hit a 'bunker' shot where you aim to hit the grass about an inch behind the ball. To avoid catching the club head in the grass in the backswing, cock your wrists quite early

Wrong

1"

CHAPTER SIXTEEN

Two-tier greens

Choosing the right shot at the right time in golf is half the battle of low scoring. All of us develop shots that we feel we can play without too much fear or the need for excessive concentration, and more often than not you are better off playing the shot you find easiest. However, on occasions you may have to opt for your least favourite shot to have any chance of getting the ball near the hole. In learning the correct aspects of the short game, the best maxim to adopt is to putt the ball if possible. However, if it is not possible, then chip it and leave the pitch shot as the last option. This advice is based on the fact that usually a bad putt will give a better result than a bad chip, and a bad chip will give a better result than a bad pitch. Always consider both the lie of the ball, the intervening ground and the pin position before making a decision how to play the shot. This, of course, holds true for the short game department but in this chapter I want to cover in some detail how best to play shots that involve two-tier greens.

Putting to a two-tier green

For the first example, let us assume that you are just off the green on the closely mown fringe, which is fairly smooth and even with the hole cut in the middle of the top tier. In this situation you would be best advised to putt the ball since it is the easiest shot to play (Fig 16.1).

Most two-tier greens are fairly deep and it is more than likely that you will have a very long putt, which needs striking quite firmly. To assist in this, stand a little taller and grip nearer the end of your putter than usual. You may need to add a little extra wrist break to your putting action in order to get enough speed into the shot. So in the backswing allow your right wrist to hinge a little, but be sure to keep the back of the left wrist firm at impact and beyond. With more action from the right hand it is easy to drag or pull the putt left, so try to keep the putter head moving towards the target at least 18 inches after impact. Pace will be difficult to judge and obviously will depend on the total length of the putt as well as the severity of the slope between you and the hole. Naturally

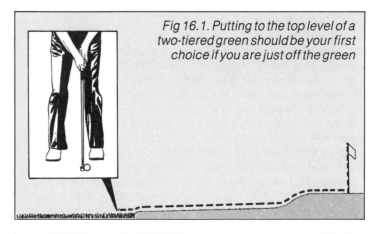

Fig 16.1. Putting to the top level of a two-tiered green should be your first choice if you are just off the green

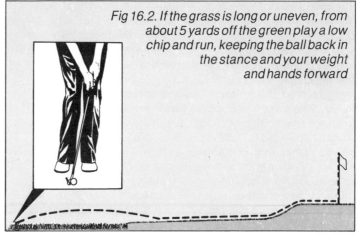

Fig 16.2. If the grass is long or uneven, from about 5 yards off the green play a low chip and run, keeping the ball back in the stance and your weight and hands forward

the slope will slow the ball so do not be afraid to strike the putt firmly. I am sure that you would be better off 5 feet past the hole rather than 'babying' the shot only to see the ball roll back down the slope and be faced with the same shot again. So strike the ball crisply, trying to keep the putter head accelerating towards the hole. If you are not putting straight up the slope but across it, remember that the ball will break in the direction of the lower level of the green. One tip to help you judge the pace of the putt is to imagine that the slope does not exist and that the putt is on a flat green with the hole further away. So, for instance, you could imagine that a 16 yard putt up the slope is perhaps an 18 yard putt on a flat surface.

Chipping to a two-tiered green

When the ball is further off the green, perhaps 3 or 4 yards, and the grass is not smooth enough to allow you to putt, and the hole is on the top tier, then you should chip and run the ball. Using a less lofted club, perhaps a 5, 6 or 7 iron, depending on your preference, set more weight on your left leg and play the ball back of centre of a narrow, open stance (Fig 16.2). Keep your hands ahead of the ball opposite your left thigh, which means that the 7 iron will become hooded, making it more like a 6 iron. This set up makes it easy for you to hit the ball on a slight descending arc. Of course it is impossible for me to tell you how hard you should hit the ball as this will depend not only on the depth and speed of the green but also on the steepness of the slope. These are factors that you must consider while assessing the shot and taking a couple of practice swings. However, the same principle applies as with the putt — that you are better off on the top level but past the hole rather than on the lower level of the green. As with putting, you may find it helpful to imagine that the green is flat but that the pin is further away. The stroke should be firm-wristed and smooth. Try to make the backswing and throughswing the same length, and you will then produce a more rhythmical stroke rather than a stabbing action. On the throughswing allow the right knee to ease towards the target, which will enable you to keep the back of the left wrist firm and moving towards the target. The ball will land on the lower level, then run up the slope to the top tier. These shots need practice for although the technique is simple, judging the distance accurately is essential for success.

To pitch or chip and run?

Imagine that the ball is 70 yards from the hole, which is cut on the top tier. How you choose to play this shot will depend greatly on how good a player you are. Certainly the higher handicap player would be better off trying to land the ball on the lower tier and letting it run up the

slope (Fig 16.3) whereas the better player might well be able to judge pitching it onto the top tier provided that the circumstances are right (Fig 16.4).

To play the lower running shot, you should select perhaps anything from a 9 to a 7 iron depending on how you see the shot and how fast the ground is running. Ideally you still want to land the ball on the front on the green since you are less likely to get an awkward bounce. If the fairway is close cut and flat, then you could safely land the ball there and your choice of club will be influenced by this factor. Set up with a fairly narrow open stance, but with your shoulders parallel to the ball to target line. With your weight favouring your left side, perhaps 60:40, play the ball in the centre, or just back of centre, in your stance and position your hands ahead of the ball. The swing should be made mainly with your arms, keeping your hands fairly passive and firm and ahead of the ball at impact. There is no need to swing your arms up steeply in the backswing; instead, just swing them back quite naturally so that the clubhead makes more of a 'U' than a 'V' shaped arc. The throughswing will

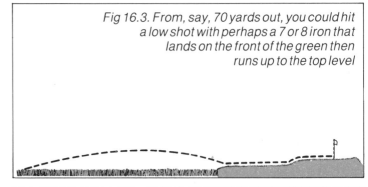

Fig 16.3. From, say, 70 yards out, you could hit a low shot with perhaps a 7 or 8 iron that lands on the front of the green then runs up to the top level

Fig 16.4. The more advanced player could hit a high pitch shot onto the top tier, where the ball lands softly without much roll

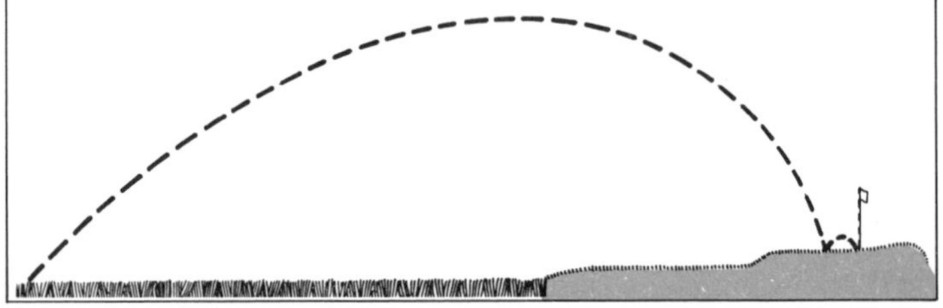

be abbreviated somewhat so that the whole action feels more like a punch shot. The length and power of your swing will be governed by the length of the shot and choice of club. It would therefore be a very valuable exercise to hit balls varying distances of, say, between 50 and 100 yards with different clubs. Naturally it would be best if you could carry out this practice onto a two-tiered green as you would then be able to see how the ball reacts on landing. However, if this is not possible, simply practise hitting to a target, e.g. an umbrella, and you will learn to judge how hard to hit a 9 iron 50 yards, or a 7 iron 80 yards. How far the ball runs on landing will come with experience, and also will vary according to the conditions.

Remember that a less lofted club, such as a 6 or 7 iron, will fly lower and run more on landing than a more lofted club such as a 9 iron. Once you can judge how hard to hit the ball so that it lands on or near the front of the green even if the strength of the shot is slightly misjudged, you will be able to build on your experience. If there are no serious hazards over the back of the green such as out of bounds, a deep bunker or very thick rough, you may be better erring on the side of hitting the ball too hard rather than too soft. Often a two-tier green is banked at the back so that any shot hit too hard will be prevented from going too far, or may even roll back down off the bank onto the green. Take all these points into consideration before playing the shot and you may find that being slightly more attacking will result in a much improved shot.

If you are a lower handicap player, then you may prefer to pitch the ball onto the top tier. This shot requires more precise judgement of distance than the lower running shot, but if you know how far you hit your sand iron, wedge or 9 iron, and are good at judging the depth of a shot, then you might well get better results from pitching the ball all the way. However, before deciding to play this shot, I would recommend that you consider the following points carefully:

1 The ball needs to be lying well — if it is in the rough, it will run on landing and you may not be able to stop it on the green.
2 If it is on a bare lie, you will probably not be able to use your sand iron as the flange will tend to bounce off the ground and you risk thinning the shot.
3 If the green is very hard, and especially if the top tier is quite shallow, you will find it difficult to stop the ball on the green.

4 If you misjudge the shot and hit the ball beyond the green, you may be in a worse position than being on the lower tier.

So ideally to pitch to the top tier, you need it to be sufficiently deep, the green to be yielding, and to have a decent lie. Whilst backspin will help to stop the ball, if the shot is not very long, say, less than a full sand iron, you will not be able to hit the ball hard enough to get maximum backspin and must therefore use elevation as well to stop the ball. To ensure this, address the ball with your weight 60:40 in favour of your left side, a slightly open stance and shoulder line, and the club face open a little. This set up will create an out-to-in swing path which adds height to the shot. Swing your arms up in the backswing allowing your wrists to break naturally. As you swing down make certain that your knees ease towards the target as you strike the ball. Keep the left arm and hand in charge, but do not become too wristy on the shot — your set up should guarantee enough height.

However, if you are lucky enough to find a very good lie where the ball is sitting on a cushion of grass, set your weight more evenly or slightly in favour of the right leg at address, and this will increase the height of the shot.

It is absolutely essential that you hit the ball far enough; the height of the shot means that it is most unlikely to roll up the slope. You should practise using the short irons until you become adept not only at hitting the ball the required distance but also at judging the distance on the course. The fact that all pins are not the same height can lead you to misjudge the depth. It is often helpful to walk half-way to the hole, then pace back to your ball. By doubling the number of paces you will have a good idea of the length of the shot. Of course, this presupposes that you already know how far you hit each club, and also that you do not hold up play.

Whichever shot you choose to play to a two-tiered green, you must be 100 per cent certain and confident when you stand over the ball that you are playing the right shot. Indecision will undoubtedly lead to a poor result.

CHAPTER SEVENTEEN

Banked and elevated greens

If you just miss a banked or elevated green, you will be faced with a shot that can be played in several ways. Which shot you choose must be decided not only by your standard of play and which shots you are most capable of executing well, but also by how the ball lies and how much green you have to work with.

Let us assume that you have hit the ball 5 to 10 yards wide of the green and that the hole is in the middle of the green, which is about 2 to 3 feet above you. If the ball is sitting reasonably well, your first option should be to putt the ball, provided that the ground is not too uneven nor the grass too long (Fig 17.1). This would be almost like putting to the top level of a two-tier green (see Chapter 16). If the ball is sitting badly or the ground and the grass are too uneven, then chip the ball. Set up with the ball back of centre in an open stance, your weight more on the left side, your shoulders parallel to the target line and hands well ahead of the ball. From this set up just remember to hit down slightly on the ball and you will

strike it correctly. Make the swing using your forearms rather than your hands.

You would also use this set up and shot if you had missed the green by more than 10 yards when to putt may be impossible but you still want to run the ball rather than pitch it (Fig 17.2). You must make allowances for the roughness of the ground between you and the pin when deciding how hard to hit the ball. I would recommend an 8 or 7 iron for this shot to give you enough forward roll and elevation.

In each of these instances, even the lower handicap player should consider playing a running shot rather than always trying to pitch the ball. Whatever standard of player you may be, the shot that is the easier and has the greater degree of tolerance of a mis-strike is the best choice.

When faced with a shot from just beside an elevated green, which is perhaps 5 to 10 feet above you, you might be able to play either of the two shots just mentioned. If

Fig 17.1. If the ground and grass are not too uneven, your first option should be to putt to an elevated green

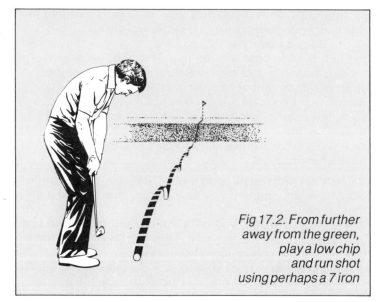

Fig 17.2. From further away from the green, play a low chip and run shot using perhaps a 7 iron

Fig 17.3. When playing from just beside an elevated green you could choose to hit the ball into the bank, which will stun it, leaving it to roll gently onto the green

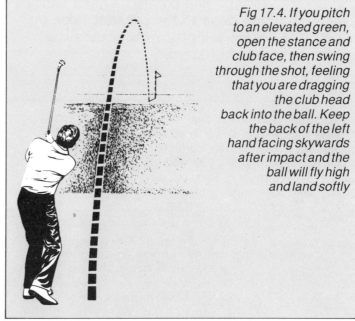

Fig 17.4. If you pitch to an elevated green, open the stance and club face, then swing through the shot, feeling that you are dragging the club head back into the ball. Keep the back of the left hand facing skywards after impact and the ball will fly high and land softly

the grass on the bank is cut quite short you could chip or putt the ball but you will have to hit it quite hard. Whilst the outcome from these shots may be less than perfect, if you are a high handicap player, then getting the ball onto the green, even if it is not too near the pin, is your principal aim.

If you are a low handicap golfer you should consider two other options. You could choose to punch the ball into the bank, which tends to stun the ball, making it jump up in the air and then run onto the green (Fig 17.3). This is often a good shot to play if the hole is cut near to your side of the green. However, it does need practice since you will have to hit the ball fairly firmly into the bank, and should you misjudge the shot it might prove costly. Set up as for the chip and run shot already described in this chapter and, using a medium iron, punch the ball into the bank, about half-way up. This will kill most of the power in the shot and the ball should then roll onto the green with little force. The nearer you are to the bank, the easier the shot. If you have missed an elevated green by, say, 10 to 15 yards and the pin is cut close to your side of the green, this shot could still be considered, but judging the power

and elevation so that the ball hits the bank at the desired spot becomes more difficult.

The other option you have is to pitch the ball onto the green (Fig 17.4). This is the more difficult shot to play, often requiring a delicate touch, which can lead to quitting on the shot if you are not careful. You also need a reasonable lie where the ball is neither sitting on bare ground nor nestled down in thick rough. You should use your most lofted club, i.e. the sand iron, and set up slightly open with your stance and shoulder line, ball forward of centre and with the club face just open.

'My playing partners say I stand too close to the ball, but I don't agree with them, how far away should I stand?'

Reason

The problem with golf is that 99 per cent of the time we address the ball and swing in what feels a comfortable manner. We also translate comfort into correctness, as no golfer would purposely try to address the ball or swing incorrectly. For most golfers, standing close to the ball, usually with their arms quite close to the body, gives a sense of safety and security. Sadly it denies them room in which to swing their arms at maximum speed, or on the ultimate in-to-straight-to-in swing path. Standing too close encourages the arms to lift up too steeply in the backswing on an outside path, creating a weak chopping action at the ball, together with the occasional shank.

Remedy

To help you stand the correct distance from the ball, and also to attain good posture, stand upright, and, with your hands at waist height, hold a club out horizontally in front of you. Do not stretch your arms away from your body — keep them relaxed. Now lower the club head to the ground by bending forward from the hip bones. As your shoulders come forward, you should feel your seat going out behind you as a counter-balance. Once you have grounded the club, flex your knees. Your weight should be distributed between the heels and balls of your feet, rather than just on your heels. As a guideline, with medium irons there should be about a fists gap between the butt end of the club and your thighs. This gap increases progressively for the longer clubs, and decreases slightly for shorter irons. You will most likely feel that you are stretching considerably for the ball, but this is to be expected, since you have been standing too close. Carry out this address drill using a mirror to check your final position. Remember that what you feel and what is actually happening, are quite often two entirely different things. Another guideline to use on the course is to sight your left forefinger knuckle down to an imaginary line across your feet. Make a note of where this should be when you have addressed the ball correctly — using the mirror to help you — then refer to this in your set-up on the course.

Stand erect with your arms comfortably extended, hands at waist height and the shaft horizontal. Lower the club head to the ground by bending forward from the hip bones, then flex the knees. This will indicate how far away the ball should be, and also give you correct posture. Sighting your left knuckle in relation to an imaginary line across your feet, may help you on the course

'To keep things simple, I play all shots with the ball opposite my left heel. Is this correct?

Reason

The ball position should change according to which club you are using. Since iron shots should be hit with a descending strike, it makes sense to position the ball opposite your stance at a point just prior to the lowest point of the arc. A fairway wood shot should be swept from the turf, so the ball should be positioned at the lowest point, or base, of the arc. Since you tee the ball up for a driver, it is best struck whilst the club head is at the base of its arc, or just starting to ascend, so it follows that the ball is positioned at the appropriate point.

Remedy

Irons: stand with your feet together, so that the back of the ball and the inside of the left foot are in line. Move your left foot approximately 3-4 inches to the left, and the right foot the appropriate amount to the right, depending on which club you are using. This process should ensure that the ball remains in the same position in relation to the left foot, i.e. about 3-4 inches inside the left heel for all normal iron shots, allowing the right foot to change the width of the stance.

Fairway woods: adopt the same procedure, but place the left foot about one inch less to the left.
   Driver: adopt the same procedure but move the left foot about 2 inches less to the left, so that the back of the ball is just inside the left heel.

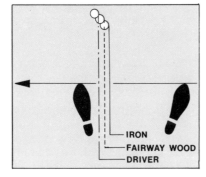

'I grip the club quite tightly because I am scared it will come out of my hands. Does grip pressure affect the swing?'

Reason

Whereas it is very difficult to be exact about grip pressure, gripping too tightly will definitely be detrimental to the swing. Muscles need to be in a reasonably relaxed state to work at maximum efficiency, and a tight grip does not promote relaxed muscles. If there was a scale of 1 to 5,

with 1 being light, and 5 being tight, then the best grip pressure would be about 3-3½.

Remedy

Grip the club in your left hand only, then place your right hand on your left forearm. If you tighten your left-hand grip you will feel the muscles in your forearm tense; that is what you have to avoid. Experiment by swinging the club with a progressively lighter grip without hitting a ball. I can assure you that you will not let go of the club. Moreover, you will find that the relaxed hand and forearm muscles will work more efficiently, creating increased club head speed in the impact zone. As you swing the club back, it is most likely that your grip pressure will increase, due to the swinging weight of the clubhead. If you start with too tight a grip, by the time you reach the top of the swing, you will be gripping too hard. If you held an empty glass and then water was poured into it, as the weight of the glass increased, you would naturally adapt your grip pressure to accommodate this extra weight. The same is true of the golf swing: your hands will cope with the pressure throughout, but you must guard against strangling the club.
   Feel that your hands are light and firm, rather than tight and firm, with the grip pressure mainly in the last three fingers of the left hand, and the middle two of the right. Once you are confident, your hands, your arms and hands will work in a freer and faster manner.

'I feel my wrists cock too early in the backswing. When should they cock?'

Reason

The problem for most beginners is to appreciate that golf is played by using the entire body. Beginners often feel that it is played solely by using the hands and arms. Sadly this incorrect preconception encourages a weak, narrow and inefficient backswing, which results in erratic and powerless shots. The fact that the hands and arms commence the backswing without the support of movement from the body, leads to an early wrist cock, which sets the club on an incorrect plane and path, and incorrect attack on the ball.

167

Remedy

Take your address position, facing a mirror. Note that your arms and shoulders form a triangle, which should move away as a unit. If you initiate the backswing moving your left shoulder, arm and club shaft away together, you will feel your upper body turning to the right. As this takes place, the clubhead will remain closer to the ground for a longer part of

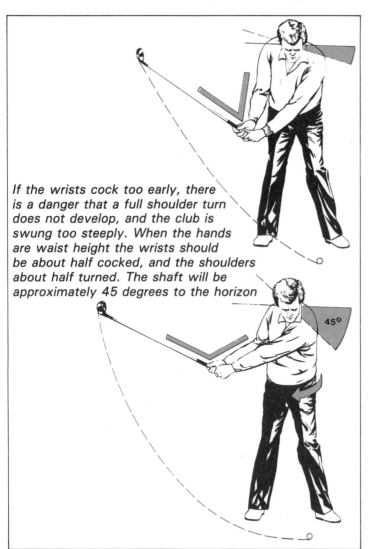

If the wrists cock too early, there is a danger that a full shoulder turn does not develop, and the club is swung too steeply. When the hands are waist height the wrists should be about half cocked, and the shoulders about half turned. The shaft will be approximately 45 degrees to the horizon

the arc than has been the case until now. Stop the backswing when your hands are about hip height, and the right arm has begun to fold so that the elbow is pointing downwards. You should find that the wrists have started to cock automatically, but have not yet cocked sufficiently to form a 90-degree angle between the shaft and left arm. The shoulders will have turned through about 45 degrees, and the hips also should have begun to turn to the right.

I believe that the wrists cock gradually throughout the backswing in response to the swinging weight of the clubhead. To the player whose hands have been too active too early, the correct action will create width in the backswing, with a greater emphasis on arm and body action. With shorter clubs you will be more aware of an earlier wrist break, because there is less body action, but the wrists cock must develop after the arms have started the backswing.

---

5   **'On the backswing my club head moves on a sharply curving inside path. Is this correct?'**

Reason

No, it is not correct. If the clubhead moves immediately inside on the backswing, this will probably encourage the downswing path to be too much from the inside, which can result in pushed or hooked shots. However, it can also encourage the real beginner, who suddenly feels too much on the inside, to incorrectly use the right shoulder area. This action will force the downswing onto an outside path, resulting in a slice or pull. Either resultant swing path from this incorrect backswing movement, does not produce the ideal shot. The move can be traced either to an address fault, combined with the ball being positioned too far back in the stance, a poor initial movement away from the ball, or simply having the wrong concept of the ideal backswing path.

Remedy

Check the ball position, read Section 2, page 167 and see that your shoulders are aligned parallel to an imaginary line from the ball to the target. Have a colleague place a club across them to check this. Now place a club just outside the ball, parallel to the ball to target line. This will give you a good guide to the correct path. Using the clockface principle, with a 5 iron, swing the clubhead away towards 3 o'clock. If you do this correctly, the clubhead will remain close to the club on the ground for about 6 inches, but this does depend on your height and the length of your club. With longer clubs, it will not remain in a straight line so long, and thus your driver will tend to swing to the inside sooner than your wedge.

However, regardless of which club you use, the clubhead should stay close to the club on the ground for a short distance; it should *not* move immediately towards your right foot. Having set the club on the correct path initially, it then swings inside between 3 and 4 o'clock as your body turns.

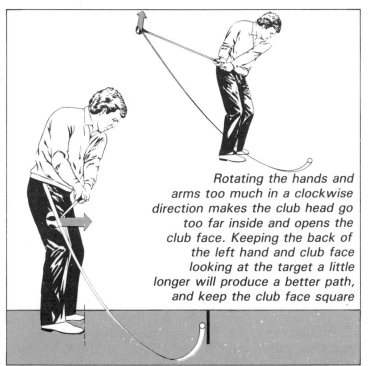

Rotating the hands and arms too much in a clockwise direction makes the club head go too far inside and opens the club face. Keeping the back of the left hand and club face looking at the target a little longer will produce a better path, and keep the club face square

If the fault remains, you are rolling your hands and arms too much in a clockwise direction as you swing the club back. Whilst there is a little clockwise rotation, if this movement is exaggerated the clubhead will move almost immediately towards 4 o'clock as the backswing commences. To correct this ensure that the body is turning as it should be

then keep the clubface and the back of the left hand facing the target a little longer.

'I do not seem to be able to make a good shoulder turn. Why?'

Reason

1 Excessive, exaggerated and early hand and wrist action tends to subdue and discourage a decent shoulder turn.
2 Open shoulders at address, which makes it difficult for even the most supple of golfers to turn fully. The angle of the feet, and lack of hip turn can also create problems.
3 General lack of mobility around the waist will prevent a full or complete turn.

Remedy

1 Refer to Section 4, pages 167-168, noting the correct address position, and initial backswing movement.
2 Check shoulder alignment, ensuring that when a colleague places a club across your shoulders they are parallel to the ball to target line. To assist the turn, just prior to the backswing, rotate your head slightly to the right, so that you are looking at the ball predominantly with the left eye. Jack Nicklaus has used this action throughout his superb career to help him achieve a good turn, so it must be worth a try. Turn the right foot out about 20 degrees, which will enable the hips, and thereby the shoulders, to turn more readily.
3 Warm-up exercises will be the answer to increased mobility. Place a club behind your neck, across your shoulders, and bend forward from the hips as in the address position. Now turn to the right, then the left. Repeat this action regularly, especially prior to the 1st tee.

Although you see that top professionals have an extremely full shoulder turn, even past 90 degrees, not everyone is able to emulate that. By working on the points outlined above, your turn will undoubtedly improve, but your full turn may still not quite reach 90 degrees. These are the handicaps that golfers have to work around, and if you have trouble turning, be sure to swing back *slowly* enough to give the larger, and slower moving, back muscles *time* to turn.

'My left wrist seems to be very buckled and weak at the top of the backswing. Is this right?'

 'At the top of the backswing I can see the club head down below my left shoulder. Why does this happen?'

Reason

The wrist needs to be in a good supportive position at the top, so that the clubhead can remain under control. When the back of the left wrist folds back, i.e. collapses towards the back of the left arm, control is lost. The clubface is turned from a square to an open position, which will require well timed independent hand action on the downswing for the clubface to be square at impact. If the hands are behind the clubface at address, the wrists can buckle at the top.

Remedy

Take normal address position. Without moving your arms, cock your wrists straight up in front of you. Complete backswing and check that the back of your left hand, forearm and clubface are in line, facing between the horizontal and vertical. You will see creases in the skin at the base of the left thumb. The thumb will be in a good supportive position, you will have better club control, and your hands can provide maximum power.

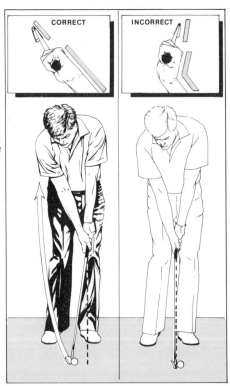

Reason

Length of backswing varies from player to player, but if you see the clubhead at the top of your swing, it has almost certainly gone too far. Unfortunately, women often have this problem, which can sometimes be blamed on releasing the last three fingers of the left hand at the top. If a player collapses the left elbow too much so that it bends almost at right angles during the swing, the clubhead goes too far. The sheer momentum created by too fast a backswing is another culprit, as is too upright an arm swing.

Remedy

Check that the 'V's formed by the thumb and forefinger of each hand are parallel and point between your right ear and shoulder. Keep a firm but not tight grip pressure with the last three fingers of the left hand and middle two of the right, and maintain that pressure, especially at the top of the swing. The swing will now feel restricted, but this is to be expected. During the backswing, turn the shoulders and arms away together, keeping the left arm as straight as possible, but not stiff. At the top it should be slightly bowed, not absolutely straight, as this would create tension. Also check that the right hip turns out of the way; if not, it can restrict shoulder turn, and cause the left elbow to bend. Slow down your backswing so that it feels like three-quarter pace, and consequently three-quarter distance. Try to feel that your arms and shoulders stop moving at the same point in your backswing. You will gain better club control, and quality and consistency of strike. It is also possible to swing the club too far when the arms are swung too upright, so check in a mirror, and if necessary feel that your hands and arms swing more behind your head than above it. When the arms swing too upright the distance that separated the elbows at address increases, so try to keep this constant.

'My body seems to impede a free arm swing through impact. How can I rectify this?'

Reason

Usually movements on the through swing reflect movements made on the backswing. Consequently the player who in the backswing fails to turn the right side out of the way and who often tilts rather than turns the shoulders, experiences trouble in getting the body out of the way through impact and beyond. This situation is often created by someone who feels that the club should be swung on a straight line back and through the ball for as long as possible.

Remedy

The first point to understand is that the club has to be swung inside the straight line from the ball to target, quite soon after the backswing commences, and soon after impact. In clockface terms, the club must swing initially towards 3 o'clock, then inside between 3 and 4 o'clock as the body starts to turn. The club moves towards 9 o'clock at impact, then inside towards 8 o'clock as the through swing progresses. As the backswing commences, you must allow the right hip and the right side of the body to turn out of the way. This creates a space into which the arms and club can swing. Through the impact zone, the left hip and left side of the body will respond by turning out of the way.

One point to check in your address position is that your seat is pushed out behind you. If the hip bones are pulled forward at address, it is very hard for the hips to turn out of the way, and instead they tend to slide laterally to the right. This sliding action of the hips tends to prevent the clubhead swinging correctly to the inside; instead it swings more on a 2 to 8 o'clock line, producing weak, slicing shots. A good exercise is to place a club behind your neck and across your shoulders, then bend forward from your hips and flex your knees. Now turn to the right, then the left, and you should find that your body moves more correctly than before.

Bad posture prevents correct body action. Good posture allows the right hip to turn out of the way in the backswing, and the left out of the way in the downswing

'My husband says that my swing should be shorter like his. Is he right?'

Reason

Because men are innately stronger than women, they can usually make shorter backswings and still hit the ball a long way. However, many would improve their game by making a full backswing with a 90-degree shoulder turn, rather than swinging the club just with their hands and arms and making a three-quarter length swing. Most women lack the power to create enough clubhead speed from a purely hands and arms swing, and sensing this take the club back further than most men. They are easily capable of making a shoulder turn in excess of 90 degrees because they are more supple and have slimmer waists than men, and this bigger shoulder turn will tend to make the clubshaft aim right of parallel at the top of the backswing.

A longer backswing offers them more time to build up club head speed, and therefore hit the ball further. However, if you have a long backswing, it will be detrimental to your game if you lose club head control, or lack accuracy through poor timing.

Remedy

Read Section 8, page 170 and check that your long backswing is not caused by any of the swing faults mentioned there. You may benefit by experimenting with the three-quarter swing exercise mentioned there, as this will concentrate your thoughts more on the downswing than backswing. The quality of strike and consistency may improve with a slightly shorter swing. If your right foot is angled out at address, square it to the target line, which will restrict your hip and shoulder turn a little, and give you a more coiled feeling in your swing. Alternatively, if your length of swing does not result from any swing faults but is due more to your suppleness, do not worry, but concentrate on swinging rhythmically, and leave the quick short swings to the men.

 'I seem to throw the clubhead from the top of the swing. Why does this happen?'

Reason

Throwing or casting the club from the top of the swing, usually occurs because the hands are working out of sequence in the swing. This often happens because the player is too keen to hit the ball hard, and consequently forgets about rhythm and timing and uses brute force instead.

Remedy

During the backswing the arms swing the club back and the hands respond to the swinging weight of the clubhead, until at the top of the swing there is a 90 degree angle between the left arm and the shaft. From this position the hands can be used to add extra power to the swing. However, this power must be contained until the clubhead starts to approach the impact zone.

Therefore, from the top of the swing as the left knee moves towards the target, the *arms* must swing down, so that most of the angle between the shaft and left arm is initially retained. Having done that, you can use your hands to apply their power where it counts, i.e. at impact. For the right-handed player, it is usually the right hand that causes the throwing action, so a good drill is to slide the right hand up the grip until it completely overlaps the left, and is not on the grip at all. Now make a few swings, and you will find that as you change direction from backswing to downswing, because the left arm is in command, the angle at the base of the left thumb will remain virtually the same. The change of direction is one of the most crucial parts of the swing. Keep it *smooth*, and give your arms a chance to play their role before your hands contribute.

Using your normal grip, hit some three-quarter paced shots, concentrating on the rhythm of the swing. Make sure that as your arms swing through impact, your right knee moves towards your left, so that at the completion of the swing the weight is mainly on the outside of your left heel, and only your right toes remain in contact with the ground. The player who casts from the top, often has too much weight on the right foot at impact, so do spend some time trying to improve both the rhythm and leg action. Read pages 40/41 which will help you synchronize and improve your leg action.

Practise gripping the club with the right hand on top of the left. This should prevent you from throwing the club, and the angle between your left arm and the shaft should be retained.

'However hard I try I cannot make my legs work in the swing'

Reason

To hit the ball your maximum distance, good leg work is essential. So often the beginner believes that golf is played simply by swinging the hands and arms. Leg action is then neglected, and distance and accuracy are lost. Legs help to provide the rhythm in the swing, and enable the weight to transfer correctly in both the back and downswings. Apart from not helping your swing, lack of leg action also puts extra strain on your lower back as you swing.

Remedy

First check your set up to ensure that your weight is spread between the heels and balls of your feet. If you have too much weight on your heels you will not be able to use your legs correctly. Shift your weight towards the inside of each foot, with your knees knocked slightly inwards. As the backswing is made, allow the left knee to point behind the ball, letting the left heel rise if you are not very supple. In the throughswing, make the right knee move towards the left, with the right heel coming off the ground completely.

To improve leg action take your normal address position, using a 6 iron and the ball teed low. At the completion of the backswing lift your foot entirely off the ground, then replace it in the same spot at the start of the downswing. As you swing through impact lift your right foot completely off the ground so that you finish the swing balanced on your left foot only. This drill over-emphasises how your weight transfers back and forth, and how your legs must work to accommodate this action. You may also like to try this without a club or ball; it will help to highlight what your legs are doing. You can then gradually reduce the leg action back to its correct proportion during the swing, holding the finish position balanced on the outside of the left foot, with the right heel completely off the ground.

'I get frozen over the ball, and am taking longer and longer to start my backswing. What should I do?'

Reason

This sort of problem can suddenly creep in to the game of quite experienced players. You may have had a fault in your swing that you have been trying to cure, and end up standing over the ball thinking of too many things, not knowing which thought is most important. Too much competitive golf can also make you a very careful golfer, rather than hitting the ball with a devil-may-care attitude.

Remedy

If you have been curing a fault by a number of swing changes, try to work on them in practice so that they can gradually become subconscious movements on the course. Allow yourself only one swing thought, so that your mind is uncluttered. Develop a strict pre-shot routine whilst practising and playing. You should start behind the ball looking towards the target, and pick out an intermediate target about two feet ahead of the ball on the target line. Set your clubface square to an imaginary line between the ball and this spot, and then position yourself accordingly. Keep your hands and arms relaxed, and do not let your grip tighten. As you stand over the ball glance towards your target, but keep the clubhead just off the ground, and waggle it back and forth over the intended backswing path as you focus on the ball. Whether you feel totally prepared or not, hit the ball. Eventually you will feel perfectly comfortable.

It may help you to get the clubhead moving by saying 'One', then 'Two' as you waggle the clubhead, then 'Go' or 'Swing', as a trigger. Do this first on the practice ground rather than the first tee, so that you feel more familiar with the routine. One other good drill is to tee-up several balls in a row, about 6 inches apart, then, without re-gripping or stopping, hit them one after the other.

 'I lack the power in my long shots. How can I overcome this problem?'

Reason

There are three distinct areas to look at with this problem:
1 Technique
2 Strength
3 Equipment

Remedy

1 The player who attacks the ball from an inside path, is best able to hit the ball the maximum distance. Providing the clubface is square at impact, you should be able to promote the desirable draw flight characteristic of a well struck ball. So the set up must be checked for squareness, and the clubface delivered into the ball from the 3.30 direction. You are then looking for good clubhead acceleration through the impact zone, which is promoted by lively hand and arm action. If you are gripping too tightly this will prevent the hands working as fast as they can, so read page 9 on grip pressure. Through impact you should feel your wrists straighten so that they are in virtually the same position as they were at address, and also that your right hand begins to turn over the left.

One way to improve your hand action is to swing your hands back to hip height, making sure that your wrists are fully cocked. Now hit the ball as hard as you can. To create clubhead speed you have to use your hands, allowing the right to cross over the left. Do this using a 6 iron with the ball teed low. Also read page 184, which will help with the swing path and clubhead speed.

2 Whereas you do not need to be muscle bound to hit the ball a long way, well developed golfing muscles will

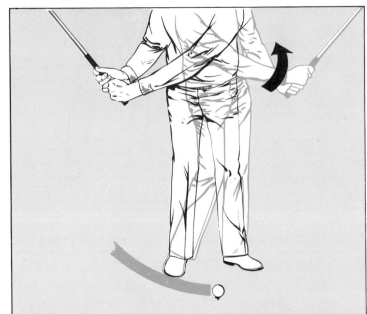

To improve hand action make a short backswing where the wrists fully cock by waist height, and the end of the grip points to the ground. Swing to a similar position on the throughswing, using your hands to accelerate the clubhead.

inevitably be very valuable in hitting the ball your maximum distance. To improve muscle strength try the following exercises:

a. Swing a weighted club, try leaving the clubhead cover on your driver (just to start with), then build up. Your professional may be able to add some weight to an old club for this purpose.

b. Squeeze a squash ball in each hand.

c. Holding dumb-bells, rest your forearms on your thighs, then raise and lower the weights. Do this with your hands above and below the weights. This will strengthen your forearm muscles.

d. Practise swinging a short iron through grass about 8-12 inches long.

3 Fortunately today's equipment does enable you to buy yards. Be certain that you have the correct shafts for your strength, i.e. L for ladies, and R for the average man. Try some of the new graphite or boron shafted and headed clubs — although more expensive than steel, they usually add length. Solid golf balls should be tried. The feel with them has improved, and the little you lose in that department, is certainly compensated for by the yards added to long shots.

'As a beginner, I find there are so many things to think of that I stand over the ball and get tense. How can I get over this?'

Reason

Even for the most naturally gifted sportsman or woman, golf is a very difficult and demanding game to learn. It is easy to try to take too much knowledge on board at one time. Your ego demands that you hit the ball well, but during the early learning months, you may often have to be prepared to hit the ball quite indifferently; until your movements start to resemble the smooth ones required in a subconscious manner.

Remedy

If you take lessons or read instructional features, try to incorporate one set of actions before moving on to another part of the swing. I encourage my pupils to break golf down into two sections: the set-up, and the swing. Invariably as a beginner you will be trying to improve some aspect of your set up for each shot. However, once you have done that, forget it, and focus your mind on one or at most two aspects of the swing on which you are currently working. On the practice ground, try to focus your attention on the specific parts of the swing that you are trying to improve. Do not be tempted or misled into thinking that you are there just to hit the ball well. If you improve the component parts of the swing, then the ball strike should improve as well.

You will soon learn whether you are the type of player who can cope with thinking consciously about movements in the swing whilst playing a round, or if you are better leaving most of your conscious thoughts to the practice ground. If you fit into the second category I would still encourage you to concentrate on smoothness and rhythm during your round. If you find yourself getting tense, develop a pre-shot routine and stick to it, so that you invariably take the same length of time over each shot. Incorporate this into your practice sessions as well, so that you quickly become familiar with the routine. You will also find that your body will relax if at address you take a deep breath and then breathe out slowly.

Why do I swing too upright, and how can I change it?'

Reason

In all swings there is an inward and an upward element. The former is provided mainly by the body turning, and the latter mainly by the direction of the arm swing. Most upright swings are caused by the shoulders tilting instead of turning, which may be due to bad posture. If you stand too far away from the ball, with your back angled too far forward and your arms stretching, you set the pattern for your shoulders to turn on too steep an angle, and thus create an upright backswing. It could be that you visualize the swing on a straight line, which leads you to tilt rather than turn the shoulders. You might hit some iron shots successfully, but your drives will not be very satisfactory. This is because your swing creates a steep attack on the ball, which suits some iron shots, but not a driver, which requires a shallow approach.

Remedy

Check your set up, particularly the distance from the ball. Re-read page 166, which explains this in some detail. You should stand closer than before, with your spine more upright, and your weight distributed between the heels and balls of your feet. Have a clear picture of where the clubhead will swing, i.e. straight back for a few inches but then it must swing inside between 3 and 4 o'clock. Place a club on the ground parallel to the target line, just outside your clubhead, and use this to check your backswing path. Once the clubhead leaves the straight line, the clubface *will*

Stretching for the ball causes bad posture and the shoulders turn on a too upright plane. By hitting balls from above your feet or swinging at a ball on an imaginary high tee, your spine will be more upright, and you will feel how your shoulders turn on a flatter plane, with the clubhead gradually swinging to the inside

start to look to the right of the target. Your shoulders will respond by turning on a flatter plane instead of tilting. A good way to practise this is to hit balls from a sidehill lie with the ball above your feet. This lie requires your spine to be more upright at address, thereby helping the shoulders to turn and the swing to become flatter. If you cannot find a suitable lie, imagine the ball is on a high tee and make your swing. Try to keep your elbows the same distance apart throughout the swing. It is quite possible that your right elbow has been flying out behind you, so keep it pointing more towards the ground, and the same distance from the left as at address.

'However much I keep my head still, I still hit poor shots. Why?'

Reason

Most beginners quickly learn one or two golfing adages. 'Keep your head still,' is one of the best known and unfortunately one of the most misunderstood. Many golfers mistakenly believe that if they keep their head still, the rest of the swing will fall into place. What happens, in reality, is that the swing becomes restricted. A decent shoulder turn is unlikely, and the correct amount of weight transference is lacking. The result is known as a reverse pivot, where the weight at the top of the backswing is too much on the left side. As the downswing commences, the weight shifts to the right side, so that very often fat shots occur, and cleanly hit shots lack length.

Remedy

The golf swing is made around a central hub which must remain steady. This hub is not the head, but the large bone at the top of the spine. Using a 5 iron, start your backswing with your head positioned behind the ball, and weight evenly distributed. Prior to swinging the club back, rotate your head to the right so that the left eye is closer to the ground than the right eye. This will assist you to make a complete shoulder turn. During the backswing, allow your weight to shift more onto the right side. This will feel like a swaying motion, which is to be expected if your weight has been

By restricting head movement you will encourage a reverse pivot. The swing should pivot around a central hub at the top of the spine so that weight transfers to the right side

gauge if your head moves either way. Swinging with the sun behind you will also enable you to see what is happening. Once the ball has been struck, allow your head to rotate towards the target, so that your throughswing continues to accelerate through the ball, guaranteeing maximum clubhead speed.

'As a right-handed person playing golf right-handed, I feel my left hand and arm contribute little to the swing. Is this correct?'

Reason

A very high percentage of golfers are right handed and indeed play the game that way. All their lives they have performed most tasks of strength and dexterity with the right hand, and so, understandably, it has become stronger and better trained than the left. The question is often asked, 'Is golf a right-handed game?' I believe it is a double-sided game, with both hands and arms playing an important role, whether you are right- or left-handed, and regardless of which side of the ball you stand. What the very right-handed player must do is to train the left arm to cope with, and direct the power of, the right.

Remedy

I believe the right-handed player should put more emphasis on the left side throughout the backswing, which helps to get the body turning correctly, leading to the desired top of the backswing position where the back faces the target. To appreciate how the left arm should work, at address place your right hand over the left — *not* on the grip. Now make the backswing and you will feel the correct action and the role that the left side plays.

At the top of the swing, the change of direction should be made by the left side, which is in a better position than the right to start pulling the club back to the ball. Once this change of direction has taken place, then both hands and arms should contribute power and clubhead speed to the swing. The left arm must continue swinging through the impact zone, with the left elbow gradually bending towards the ground after impact.

moving previously in the opposite direction. From this correct position your weight can now transfer back to the left side, thereby moving towards the target as you strike the ball. Think of swinging around that central hub, and allow a little head movement to develop on the backswing if necessary.

To be clear, I am not saying that you should sway on the backswing so that the hub moves laterally to the right, but when the incorrect action has been ingrained, then this is what it will *feel* like. Ask a friend to hold a club horizontally just outside your right ear; then when you swing you can

By practising the right hand over left drill, and also swinging with the left arm only, gripping down on a 7 iron, you will quickly improve the power and control in this arm. One word of warning, however: so that you do not damage your arm, start with just a few one-armed swings, and then gradually increase the number.

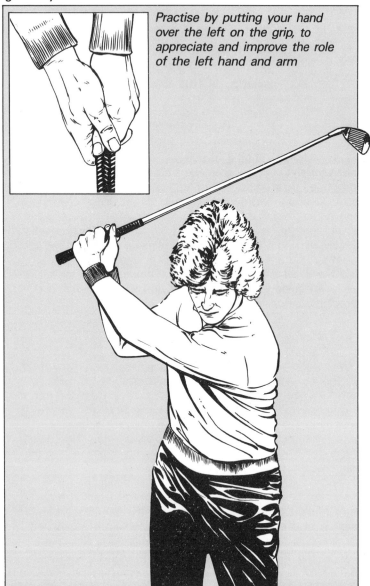

Practise by putting your hand over the left on the grip, to appreciate and improve the role of the left hand and arm

'I'm told I lift my head when I hit the ball. How can I stop this?'

Reason

I have seldom seen even total beginners lift just their head on long shots. What happens is that they use their body incorrectly and it rises up through the shot in an effort to impart power. Since the head is attached to the body it is inevitable that the head comes up as well. Whilst the head should remain at virtually the same height throughout the

You must retain the spinal angle set at address until well after impact. Alter that angle and obviously your head will rise as well

swing, on any long shots there has to be a degree of flexibility from side to side, otherwise the swing is too restricted. It is only on the shortest of pitches, chips and all putts that the head can or should be kept absolutely still.

Remedy

The answer lies in learning to swing your arms more freely, allowing your body to move to accommodate the arm swing. This is often difficult at first because the body feels so much stronger than the hands or arms. The most important factor in hitting the ball a long way is clubhead speed (provided that the face and swing path are square to the target at impact), and as the hands and arms can move much faster than the body, they are best employed for the task. Practise hitting shots with your feet together and the ball on a low tee. If you use your body you will over-balance, so you will quickly learn and feel how your hands and arms should perform. When you swing, try not to over-power the ball, but cultivate a smooth balanced swing, letting your body follow rather than lead. Keep your head steady, and certainly watch the ball until it is struck. Then allow it to rotate towards the target. At address your spine is angled forward, and you must learn to retain this angle until well after impact. At the beginning, your swing will feel rather cramped and restricted, but you will undoubtedly start to hit the ball better.

You will also find it helps you to appreciate how the swing should feel by making shadow swings, i.e. swinging without the club, just interlocking your hands together. You will be better able to sense a free swinging arm action if your body is more passive. Consequently it will not lift up during impact and neither will your head.

 'I have often read that to hit a ball low you move the ball back but keep the hands forward. When I do this the ball still goes too high and way to the right. What am I doing wrong?'

Reason

What you have read is absolutely correct, and indeed you will read that same advice in this book. Where you are going wrong is that when you slope the shaft towards the target, you allow the clubface to open, causing it to be open at impact. Any time this happens the ball will fade or slice to the right depending on the degree of openness. When the ball is back in the stance it is contacted when the club is still approaching from the inside; if the face is square the ball draws back, but if it is open the ball starts right, then curves right.

Remedy

Survey the shot from behind the ball, and pick out an intermediate target about 3 feet ahead on the target line. Align the clubface at right angles to an imaginary line between the ball and this closer target (a). When you take your stance with the ball positioned further back than normal, the shaft slopes noticeably forward so that your hands are still opposite the inside of your left thigh, but the clubface must become *hooded* (b), not open. This de-lofts it, making a 7 iron more like a 5 iron, depending on how far back the ball is played. But the clubface remains *square* to the target line, and consequently it should be square at impact. When you allow the face to open (c), you add loft, so that in effect you negate the act of playing the ball back.

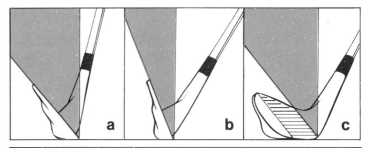

 'I top a lot of iron shots or push them. Why?'

Reason

To strike iron shots crisply, it is necessary for the club to be descending still as the ball is struck, taking a divot after impact. However, when someone is pushing and topping a lot of shots, the problems arises from too shallow an attack on the ball, brought about by the clubhead approaching too much from inside the target line. The base or lowest point of the arc of the club then occurs prior to impact, and thus the ball is not struck while the clubhead is still descending.

Remedy

Check the address position, ensuring that when a club is placed across the shoulders, it does not aim at, or right of, the target. It should point parallel left of the target. If your shoulder alignment is significantly right of the target, this causes the exaggerated inside and shallow attack. Be sure to have the ball forward of centre, about 3-4 inches inside the left heel. From the corrected set up, you should be able to produce more crisply struck and straighter shots almost immediately. However, if your shoulder line is satisfactory, you have a swing fault that needs correcting. You need to imagine and then create a different swing path into the ball. In clock face terms, your club approaches too much from the 4-5 o'clock direction, and needs to come more from the 3.30 line. Make sure that the club swings back between 3 and 4 o'clock, and that at the top of the swing your hands and arms *feel* more above your head than behind it.

Check this new position in a mirror. From this more upright backswing, the club will be descending more steeply than before, resulting in the clubhead descending onto the ball just prior to the base of the arc, which will now occur just *after* impact. The club head will be approaching more from the 3.30 than 4 o'clock direction.

 'I hit a lot of my iron shots thin, and the better ones lack distance. Why?'

Reason

In the address position the left arm and the shaft form a fairly straight line, which should be likened to the radius of a circle. During the backswing this radius is broken by the wrists cocking. If this angle is not fully restored at impact to resemble almost exactly its address position, then the radius

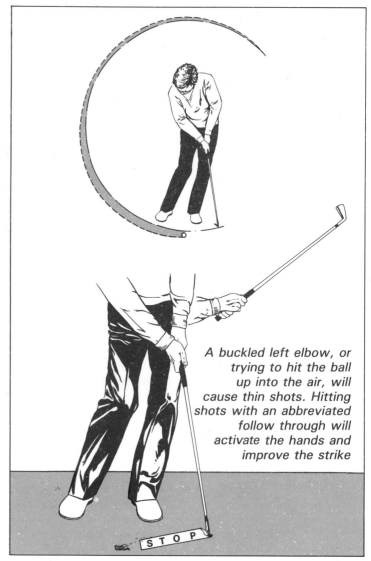

A buckled left elbow, or trying to hit the ball up into the air, will cause thin shots. Hitting shots with an abbreviated follow through will activate the hands and improve the strike

is not completed and the clubhead will not strike the bottom of the ball, but will instead produce a thin shot. Lack of distance even on the better struck shots tends to suggest that the grip may be too tight, thus inhibiting a free-flowing hand action. It is also possible that you have the wrong mental picture of how the ball should be struck, perhaps trying to hit the ball *up* in the air, rather than allowing the clubhead to descend on the ball.

Remedy

Provided that the clubhead is descending onto the back of the ball, the loft of the club will apply backspin, which will get the ball airborne. Any attempt to hit up on the ball causes a thin shot, imparting topspin, which causes the ball to nosedive. Hitting up on the ball also makes the left arm buckle, thus shortening the radius and thereby producing the very situation you want to eradicate. To help improve hand action and speed, first be sure that you are not gripping the club too tightly (read page 167 on grip pressure). Take a 6 or 7 iron and experiment with using a lighter grip to see if you can get better clubhead speed. Practise without a ball and you will be able to hear if the speed improves.

Practise hitting balls but try to stop the club quickly after impact. Although your arms can drop fairly quickly, the swinging weight of the clubhead will activate the hands. Also use the drill on pages 174-175.

'Why do I hit my iron shots fat?'

Reason

When you hit an iron shot fat, you take a small amount of turf *before* the ball is struck. If your drives are hit well you might have a set-up fault with your irons. If your drives are also unsatisfactory, perhaps lacking power or hooking uncontrollably, you may lack left-side control throughout your game.

Remedy

1 Check that you do not have the ball too far forward in your stance. Hit a few shots with the ball more central and you may be pleasantly surprised at the results. The ball should be positioned just prior to the base of the arc. If you play it forward of this point, the clubhead will quite readily strike the ground first. Also check that your hands are ahead of the ball at address, with the left arm and shaft forming a straight line. The shaft should slope towards the target. Re-read pages 166–167 to get some good guidelines.

Imagine a piece of rope tied between your left knee and wrist. As you start the downswing try to keep the rope taut; this will improve left side control and your timing

2 Crisp iron shots require good timing. In the swing, your top half, i.e. the hands and arms, are out-racing the lower half, i.e. the legs. From the top of the swing change direction smoothly, pulling down with the left arm and moving the left knee towards the target. There should be a tautness in the left arm and side at the top of the swing, and the correct move from the top will preserve that tautness into the first part of the downswing. You must initially have a feeling of pulling the club head back into the ball with your left arm, rather than throwing it with the right. Try to swing through to a finish, with your body facing the hole, and the right heel released from the ground. To help preserve the tautness, imagine at the top of the swing a length of string tied between your left knee and left wrist. The two must move together to keep the string either from breaking or sagging. Read pages 176–177 because you may also be lacking correct weight shift due to keeping your head too still.

181

'I shank a lot of my irons, and the better shots start left. Why?'

Reason

A shanked iron shot is hit from the area called the shank, where the hosel blends into the clubface. Any ball hit from this area shoots quite alarmingly out to the right. It is possible to shank with the clubhead approaching from either inside or outside the target line, but the fact that your better shots start left indicates that your shank is caused by an out-to-in swing path.

Remedy

Read page 184 which details how to correct the out-to-in swing path, and in addition check at address that there is at least 4-5 inches space between the end of the grip and your thighs with a medium iron. One good practice drill is to put 2 tee pegs in the ground about 2 inches apart, one nearer to you than the other. Address the outer tee, then swing the club and try to hit the inner one. This will train you to keep the club on the inside on the downswing, instead of re-routing it onto an outside track. It is most likely that your right shoulder area has been too active from the top of the backswing, so concentrate on swinging your arms and using your hands, and do not try to swing too aggressively. You should feel that your arms swing more to the right of the target than before.

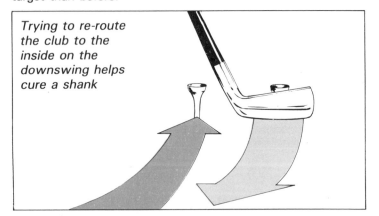

Trying to re-route the club to the inside on the downswing helps cure a shank

'I have great difficulty playing long irons. How can I improve'.

Reason

Because long irons do not have much loft; any sidespin imparted by an open or closed club face is highlighted; the ball curves more violently than when playing a middle or short iron. The lack of loft also makes you try to help the ball into the air. When this happens you fall back onto the right foot and top the ball along the ground. Long irons also have a small head which does not inspire confidence and combined with the longer shafts make the clubs much more difficult to use.

Remedy

If you badly slice or hook the ball, the best advice is to cure that first before you use a 1, 2 or 3 iron. You may be able to play a 4 iron with some success, but your swing needs to improve. The answer could be to make more use of lofted fairway woods as they are more forgiving clubs. If you hit your middle irons reasonably well, then you should be able to manage the 3 and 4 iron, but only the straighter hitting low handicap players should expect to hit 1 and 2 irons well.

Hit about twenty 6 iron shots, then, using the same rhythm and pace, hit a few long irons. Play the ball in the same position in relation to the left heel and just move your right foot more to the right. Either place the ball on a low tee, or give yourself a good lie to help build up your confidence. Keep the swing smooth, and as you change direction at the top of the swing ensure that your weight starts to move back to the left side. You will then be assured of striking down slightly on the ball. Because of the longer shaft, the swing will be a little flatter, so you will not take a large divot. Keep practising, using alternately long and medium irons.

26 'I always thin shots from tight lies, and am now very scared of them. How should I play them?'

Reason

The main problem with tight lies is contacting the ball in exactly the right spot. When the ball sits on a cushion of grass it seems easy to hit down and through the ball, but when there is only compacted earth, or very little grass beneath the ball, the temptation is to try to hit it up into the air. Professional golfers often prefer a tight lie, as no grass intervenes between the clubface and ball, and so they are better able to spin and control it as they wish.

Remedy

First you need to practise these shots off the course, so go to a spot on the practice ground that is particularly bare and fairly hard. Using a 5 or 6 iron, play the ball further back in your stance, perhaps a ball's width. You may need to experiment to find the best position that allows you to strike the ball readily with a more downward blow. Keep your hands ahead of the clubface, and a touch more weight on your left side; then, from a normal backswing, concentrate on hitting *down*, keeping the back of the left wrist very firm. The swing will feel more punchy than usual, and the ball will fly lower because you de-lofted the club at address. Once you can hit the iron well, try a few shots with a lofted wood, using the same technique. If you need extra height on a shot, play a fade, by aiming your shoulders and feet left of target and opening the clubface. Where this shot differs from a normal fade is that you must still play the ball back in your stance to accommodate the lie. Take enough club for the shot, because the ball will go high and land softly. The left hand must lead through the shot, keeping the blade a little open.

For those formidable pitches over bunkers from tight lies, do not be over-ambitious. The higher handicap player might be better playing away from the pin if it offers an alternative shot such as a chip and run. For the better player and when there is no alternative shot, you would find the shot easier with a wedge or 9 iron, but the ball will not fly very high. Play it in the same manner as the fade shot, keeping the

On tight lies play the ball back in your stance. From the normal position there is a likelihood of thinning the shot Concentrate on hitting down on the ball

head very still and your weight on the left side. The wrists must remain firm and ahead of the clubface through impact and, above all, stay down on the shot.

183

27

'My shots nearly always start left of target. Some curve back to the right whereas others stay left. Why does this happen?'

Reason

These flight characteristics indicate that, at impact the clubhead is travelling left of the target, instead of towards it. When the shot continues flying left of target, it indicates that the clubface was square to the direction in which it was travelling. Where the ball starts left and then curves to the right, this indicates that at impact, the clubface was looking to the right of the direction in which it was travelling, i.e. open at impact. You will also find that shots with the straighter faced clubs, i.e. the driver, and 1-5 irons, will curve more than the lofted clubs. This is because the lofted clubs impart more backspin which tends to override unwanted sidespin.

Remedy

First check that your shoulders, hips and feet are aimed parallel left of the target. Also check that the ball is not positioned too far forward in your stance — the back of the ball must be inside the left heel for the driver, and about 3-4 inches inside for iron shots. Ensure that your grip is strong enough, the 'V's between thumb and forefinger on each hand should be parallel and pointing between the right ear and right shoulder. Do not grip too tightly; maintain pressure on the club with the last 3 fingers of the left hand, and the middle 2 of the right. However, do not strangle the club, but hold it with just enough pressure to control it. You must now concentrate on the direction in which you should swing the clubhead; in clock face terms, more from 4-10 o'clock, as a corrective measure.

Lay down a club in that direction and, while standing parallel to the target, try swinging the clubhead parallel to the club on the ground. You should feel that you are swinging to the right of the target. You may well find that most of your shots now fly towards the target, but if some are still drifting to the right, your hand action needs improving. Through impact you must have the feeling that the right hand is starting to turn over to the left. Concentrate on getting the back of the right hand parallel to

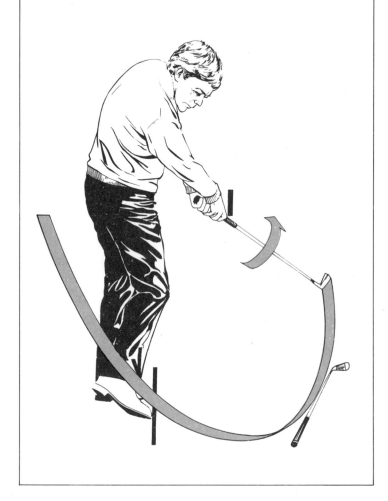

Lay down a club in the corrective 4-10 o'clock direction, then while standing square to the target, try to swing the clubhead parallel to this club, allowing the hands to rotate anti-clockwise through the impact zone

the target line as soon as possible after impact. Two drills will help: for swing path and hand action see the right foot behind left drill on the opposite page; and for hand action see page 174.

28 'I always take a divot with my driver. Why does this happen?'

Reason

This indicates that the clubhead is approaching the ball from too steep an angle, usually as a result of an out to swing path. Because the ball is teed up, best results will be gained if the club head approaches from a shallow inside path, with the ball being struck either at the base of the arc, or when the clubhead is just ascending, which will give maximum distance to the shot.

Remedy

First I would suggest that you refer to the opposite page and, in addition, to the address checks there, place a little more weight on the right side, as this will help you strike the ball with an ascending clubhead. Flex the right knee inwards more than usual which will help lower the right shoulder, and put your head well behind the ball. Also be sure that the ball is not too far back in the stance — it should be just inside the left heel, and you should have a strong sense of looking at the back of the ball. This set up will help you to swing the club back and down on an inside path, but do not make the mistake of trying to hit the ball too hard. This often happens when you use the part of your body that feels strongest, i.e. the right-shoulder area, which unfortunately throws the clubhead onto an outside path. Keep the change of direction from back to downswing smooth, and gradually accelerate through the ball.

   A simple drill that will help with the swing is to place your right foot almost directly behind your left at address. With the ball on a low tee, and using an iron, you will find it very easy to keep the clubhead on an inside path approaching more from the 4 o'clock than 2 o'clock direction, and therefore from a shallower angle of attack. This will illustrate how the correct swing path should feel.

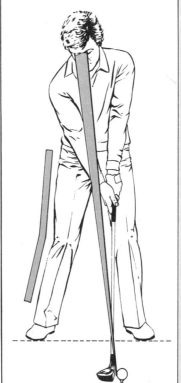

Place more weight on the right leg and flex that knee more than usual. This will drop the right shoulder, and position your head well behind the ball, which will help you to make a shallow inside attack. Look at the back, not at the top of the ball.

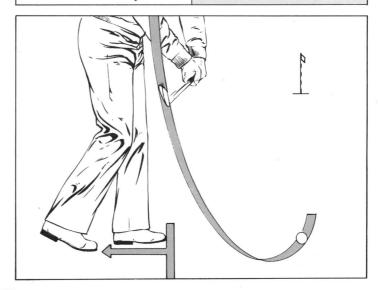

Hitting shots with the right foot almost behind the left will help you to ingrain an inside attack

'**I hit my driver low and sometimes with a slight fade. Why?'**

Reason

This combination of shots is caused by moving too laterally towards the target from the top of the backswing. The sway tends to de-loft the face of the club, and since a driver has only about 10 degrees to start with, it will hit the ball naturally very low. The lateral sway means also that the hands can get significantly ahead of the clubface and leave it slightly open, hence the low fade. The lateral sway can also cause too steep an attack on the ball, and the occasional skied drive may result.

Remedy

Check there is a little more weight on the right side at address. The right knee should be knocked in towards the left, which will help to lower the right side and put your weight in the correct place. You should have the feeling of looking very much at the back, and not at the top of the ball (see page 185). At the top of the backswing, you must feel even more weight on the right side than the left, and the shoulders should be fully turned. Now feel that your arms swing down without your legs moving first. I stress the word 'feel' since anyone who has over-used their legs, needs to feel that they remain passive in the swing.

A great deal has been written about transferring the weight to the left side, but this must be done around a steady central hub in the swing. Feel that you keep the central hub, i.e. that large bone at the top of your spine, very steady as you swing down — do not allow it to move towards the target. You will now get the feeling of hitting the ball away from you towards the target, at the correct height. A good practice drill is to hit balls teed up, preferably with a 3 wood, but keep your left heel off the ground throughout the swing. This prevents you moving laterally, but do not hit the ball too hard as you may hurt your back. Just try to appreciate how the swing feels, and how much more behind the ball you are at impact.

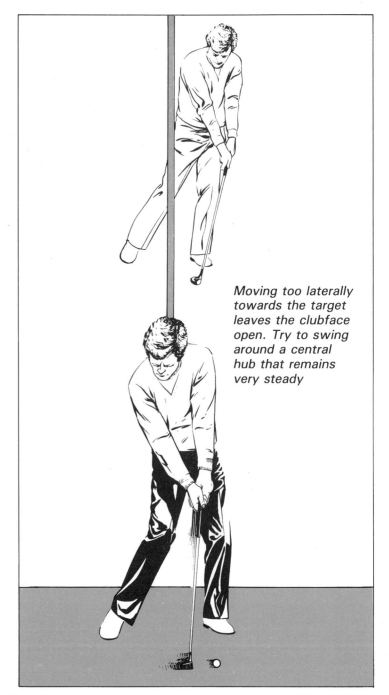

Moving too laterally towards the target leaves the clubface open. Try to swing around a central hub that remains very steady

30 **'I either thin my chip shots, or hit them fat. How can I stop this happening?'**

Reason

As with all golf shots, one of the most important points in chipping is to set up correctly. The majority of poor chippers set up with the ball too far forward, and the hands and weight too far back. This being the case, there are two likely mishits: hitting a fat shot, i.e. contacting the ground before the ball (likely since this is where the base of the arc will occur); or hitting a thin shot, i.e. striking the ball near its equator while the club head is ascending (likely since it is positioned forward of the base of the arc).

Remedy

All chip shots should be struck whilst the clubhead is slightly descending. This imparts gentle backspin, which will initially loft the ball over the fringe before it rolls towards the hole. The ball must be positioned so that it looks well back in the stance, near the right foot. Remember that for chip shots you need a narrow, open stance, so if the ball is placed about 2 balls' widths inside the left heel, it should look near the right foot. The weight must be about 70:30 in favour of the left side, and the hands must be opposite the left thigh so that the shaft slopes towards the target. From this position it is easy to strike the ball while the club is still descending. The swing should be made primarily with the forearms, so that the angles at the back of the wrists do not change. As you address the ball, your hands are ahead of the clubface, and that is how they must remain throughout the stroke. You should feel that you are dragging the clubhead back into the ball, keeping your hands ahead all the time, even after the ball has been struck. To keep the back of the left wrist firm, allow the right knee to ease towards the target. Try to make the back and through-swings the same length, and the whole action as smooth as possible. A good practice drill is to set up and hold the shaft of another club near the head, so that the shaft extends under your arm and to the left side of your body. If you swing through correctly, the shaft will not touch you, but allow the left wrist to buckle, and the shaft will hit you in the side.

By holding a second club so that it extends under the left arm and to the side of the body, you can develop the correct chipping action with a firm left wrist

31 'I use my 7 iron for chipping. Should I use a variety of clubs?'

Reason

By only using your 7 iron for chipping, you will find some shots that are more difficult, i.e. those where the pin is cut close to your side of the green. Having said that, the 7 iron is a good club for many shots, and by using that club only, you should at least become familiar with how hard to hit the ball for any specific shot. However, to become even more proficient at chipping, I believe that you should use more than one club.

Remedy

When chipping with a 7 iron, the ball will tend to spend one-third of its journey in the air, and two-thirds on the ground. To vary the overall distance, you vary the power of the stroke. Ideally, when chipping you want to land the ball just on the green, then let it roll up to the hole. So if the pin is only 3 or 4 yards on the green, and there are 10-12 yards between you and the edge of the green, the 7 iron is not ideal, since you would have to land the ball on the fringe. This is acceptable if the fringe is smooth and firm, but winter conditions or an uneven surface make it unacceptable. A better club to use in these circumstances is a wedge. A ball hit with this club will spend about two-thirds of its journey in the air, and one-third on the ground. By learning to use even just two clubs, e.g. 7 iron and wedge, you will be able to cope with most situations.

To learn more about how the ball reacts with different clubs, practise chipping using the same strength swing, but hit each successive shot with a different club, working from the 5 iron through to the sand iron. The lower numbered clubs hit the ball lower and it runs further. Whereas the higher numbered clubs hit the ball higher with less roll.

32 'When the hole is at the top of a two-tier green, I pitch the ball, but without much success. How can I improve this shot?'

Reason

The answer is not really to improve the shot, but to play a different one. Pitching the ball is harder to judge than chipping it. Often the upper tier is shallow, so there is little room for error. Hit the ball too far and it runs off the back; hit it too short and it lands on the up slope and rolls back down. All but the lowest handicap players would be better playing a chip shot.

Remedy

To play the long chip and run the better clubs to use are the 5-7 irons, which should ensure that the ball will roll quite readily. Of course, you still have to judge how hard to hit the ball, and this is made more difficult by the slope. Perhaps one of the best ways to assess the shot is to imagine that the green is flat, but that the pin is, say, 2-3 yards further away, depending on the degree of slope. Set up with the weight favouring the left foot of a narrow open stance, the ball central, and the hands ahead of the ball. Keep the swing smooth and have a couple of practice swings so that you have given yourself a chance to experience how the swing should feel. If playing this shot from, say, 20 yards short of the green, allow the right hand to start to roll over the left through impact which will give extra roll to the ball.

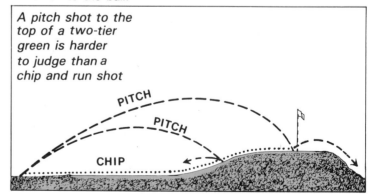

A pitch shot to the top of a two-tier green is harder to judge than a chip and run shot

33 'Why can't I judge successfully the length of my short pitch shots?'

Reason

Once you have to hit shots that are less than a full swing, and this happens mainly with the 9 iron wedge and sand wedge, then you must manufacture a part swing. If you are someone who has very active hands, these part swings can become extremely difficult to judge, because trying to use your hands actively but slowly, requires precision and practice. Without this, the swing becomes either very short and flicky or, from a longer swing, the ball is hit too far. Either way, it becomes difficult to be confident about how far back to swing or how hard to hit the ball.

Remedy

The answer is to play the shot with a more passive-handed swing. Set up with a wedge, hands just ahead of the ball, weight 60:40 in favour of the left side. Now swing your *forearms* back and up, without any conscious wrist or hand action, stopping when your hands are waist high. Look at your hands, and you will see that a certain amount of wrist cock has naturally taken place, but the shaft should be no more than about 45 degrees to the horizon. With this swing you have not created power through an excessive wrist cock. Swing your arms down, keeping your hands ahead of the clubface, and finish with your hands about waist height on the follow through. Your wrists will naturally uncock, and to prevent the right hand rotating over the left, swing your arms to the left of your body after impact. Include a little weight transference and leg action so that the swing develops rhythm.

Hit several shots with this length swing, and you should find that the balls all go a similar distance, provided that you use the same *paced* swing. Once you sense that your arms and not your hands are providing the power, experiment by lengthening and shortening the swing. The pace, and consequently the length of shot, will vary accordingly, but you will be able to develop a consistent shot pattern. For instance, you may learn that when you swing your hands to waist height with a wedge, the ball goes 25 yards, and

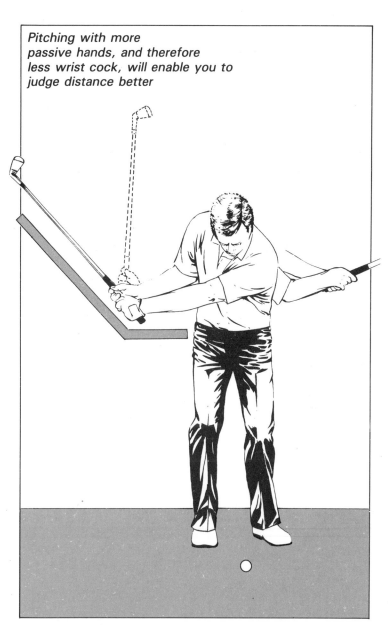

Pitching with more passive hands, and therefore less wrist cock, will enable you to judge distance better

you can use that as a guideline. Pace out some of your shots, and practise to a variety of targets, so that you become familiar with judging the distance. The swing should feel wooden to start with, but keep your knees moving to provide the rhythm, and leave the hands out of the action.

'Some of my chip shots from light rough around the green seem to fly out and others come out dead. Why?'

 'I hate hitting short shots over bunkers, and always play them badly. How can I cure this?'

Reason

Shots from light rough can be unpredictable. When grass intervenes between the club face and ball, it impairs control of the shot, because it is almost impossible to put backspin on the ball. The amount of grass and the way it lies also have a bearing on the result. When the grass lies in the same direction as the shot, the ball tends to come out quite fast and run a lot. If the grass lies against the direction of play, then this can severely retard the club head speed, obviously making the ball come out in a dead manner.

Remedy

By being able to recognise how the ball will react in different lies, you should be able to play the shot more successfully. Always have a practice swing at a spot where the grass is lying in the same direction as the shot to be played. You will feel the different effects on the club head. When it lies in the same direction as the swing (a), the club will be more likely to slide through the grass, and the ball comes out lower than expected. This, plus the fact that you will not be able to put backspin on the ball, means that you should play the shot delicately, perhaps opening the face of a wedge for extra control. When the grass lies against you (b), it is difficult to swing the club through, so use a little more force. The ball usually pops up in the air from this type of lie, so play it boldly. The best way to become proficient is to practise from each of the lies.

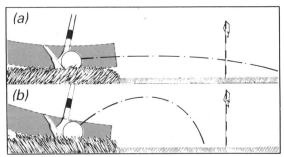

Reason

Most golfers fear this shot, mainly because if it is mishit, the outcome can be very penalizing, with the ball landing in the bunker. The mere fact that you dislike the shot usually means that it will be rushed so that you get it over quickly. This may lead to carelessness with your set up and the swing can deteriorate into a short jab at the ball.

Remedy

First practise short pitches without an intervening bunker. Place the ball on a good lie, and choose a target about 20 yards away. Using your wedge or sand wedge, set up with the ball inside the left heel, and your weight just favouring the left side. Choke down on the grip so that you can swing the club a little longer and more rhythmically without gaining distance. Swing your arms up and keep your hands leading the club head into impact. Do not try to hit the ball up into the air — the loft of the club will do that. Feel that you drag the club head back into the ball as you smoothly move your weight onto your left side. Keep your head steady until the ball is well on its way.

Once you can hit these shots successfully, practise hitting over a bunker, or your trolley. Build up your confidence, and when faced with the shot during your round, you will recall how well you have played it. When on the course, do not be tempted to rush this shot. Visualize the ball going over the bunker and then running up to the hole. Have a practice swing, rehearsing the length of the swing, and feeling the rhythm of the shot. Carefully address the ball, then hit it. Imagine yourself back on the practise ground, where you know how easy it was to play the shot. Make your mind work for you, not against you.

36

'I am afraid of bunker shots as I have no success playing them. The clubhead seems to come to a sudden halt in the sand. Why?'

Reason

Lack of success makes all golfers fearful, and usually the shot is then rushed. When the clubhead stops in the sand, it is often because it is digging in too deeply as a result of the wrong set-up. Moreover, greenside bunker shots are usually not very long, so it is easy to be tempted into taking too short a backswing, forgetting that sand offers great resistance to the clubhead. So there must be enough power in the swing to enable the clubhead to cut through the sand.

Remedy

First check your grip and alignment. The flange on the bottom of the sand iron comes into maximum effect when the club face is turned open, enabling the club to bounce through the sand. So be certain to first turn the face open slightly, then grip the club. Take your stance, with the club face aimed just right of the target, and your body and feet aimed a similar amount left. Wriggle your feet into the sand, working the left in a little deeper than the right, and keeping a little more weight on the left foot to encourage a downward attack on the ball. Position the ball opposite the left heel, and look at a spot about 2 inches behind it. This is where the club head should enter, so hold the club above this point, and not above the ball. From this set up, you can naturally swing across the ball from out-to-in in relation to the target, creating a cutting action on the ball.

Make the backswing primarily by swinging your arms up. Your hands should reach at least shoulder height, with your wrists fully cocked. As you swing down, keep your hands ahead of the club face, and move the right knee towards the left as you swing through. Maintain an open club face after impact by keeping the back of the left hand facing more towards the sky than the ground, and the left arm in control. Your arms should swing very much across your body, finishing with your weight mainly on your left leg, and your body facing the target. With the correct grip and set up, have the confidence to swing the club through to a full finish, much as you would for other full iron shots. Make the

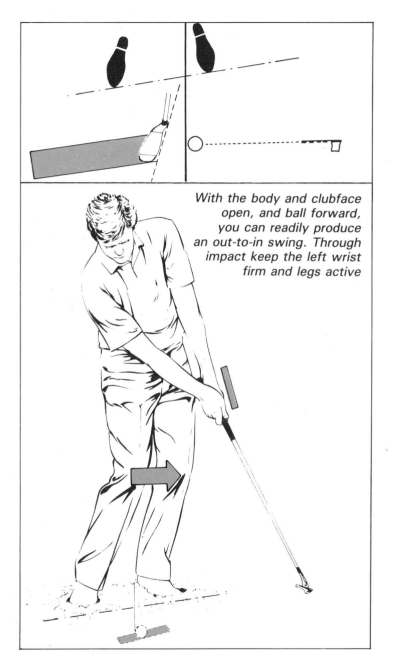

With the body and clubface open, and ball forward, you can readily produce an out-to-in swing. Through impact keep the left wrist firm and legs active

swing full and easy, rather than short and stabby. The exercise on page 192 will help to give you confidence.

191

'My greenside bunker shots are erratic, I hit some too cleanly, while others fail to get out at all. Why does this happen?'

Reason

As a general rule, the club must enter the sand about 2 inches behind the ball. Erratic shots are an indicator of lack of club head control and thus the club enters the sand at varying points behind the ball, producing a variety of shots.

Remedy

Lack of club head control is often due to too much independent hand action. It is true to say that the wrists break earlier, and more noticeably, on bunker shots, but the arms must continue swinging throughout. Concentrate more on swinging your *arms up* away from the ball, letting your wrists cock naturally. Swing your *arms down*, keeping your hands just ahead of the club face, through impact and beyond.

A good practice drill is to draw parallel lines in the sand, about 6-8 inches apart. With your weight favouring the left foot, stand so that the right-hand line is about two inches inside the left heel. Now try to remove a divot of sand from between the two lines, making the clubhead enter the sand at the right line, and exit at the left. In this exercise you can easily concentrate on the sand and not the ball, and, allied to a greater emphasis on arm action the results should improve. I would also suggest that you read page 191 to be certain that your grip and set up are correct.

Practise taking a divot of sand about 6-8 inches apart from between two lines

'Why does the ball often hit the lip of the bunker on long fairway bunker shots?'

Reason

Long bunker shots are not difficult, but never be too greedy in trying to gain distance. By taking a club with too little loft, it is easy to catch the lip. Furthermore, since you are trying to hit the ball cleanly, it is easy to catch it a little thin, probably hitting it into the face or lip of the bunker.

Remedy

It is always a good idea to look at the shot from the side, so that you can see exactly how quickly the ball must rise. In fairway bunker shots you should play the ball slightly further back in your stance than for fairway shots, so this will reduce the effective loft of the club. Having taken this fact, and the height of the bunker face into consideration, grip down slightly on your selected club as this will tend to restrict any excessive wrist action and assist clubhead control. I also think a slightly firmer grip than usual, helps to the same end. Get a firm stance, but try not to wriggle your feet too deeply into the sand, as this makes a clean contact more difficult.

One usually advises a pupil to look at the top of the ball rather than the back in order to make clean contact more likely. However, if you are thinning the shot, experiment with looking at the back of the ball to see if the results improve. Although ideally you should be trying to sweep the ball off the top of the sand and just taking a shallow divot, this may result in thinned shots, in which case just think of hitting down a little more until you get the desired contact. Swing in an unhurried manner, and try to finish balanced. Do not be in a rush to see where the ball has gone — just stay down on the shot a little longer than usual. Always err on the side of caution: better to take a 7 iron and get out rather than risk a 6 and hit the lip.

'39' 'How should I adjust my bunker shots when the texture and depth of the sand varies?'

Reason

Sand texture varies from course to course and from bunker to bunker, and this makes it difficult to judge shots. When sand is first put into bunkers it can take a time to settle down, and until such time it is very light and fluffy and makes accurate shots more difficult. Depth of sand also varies, but, in this respect, forewarned is forearmed.

Remedy

Your best friend in bunkers, apart from your sand iron, is your feet. Quite legitimately you are allowed to wriggle your feet into the sand to take your stance, and it is at this moment that you can best gauge the texture of the sand.

If your feet sink in very easily, obviously the sand is deep and quite light. In this situation, you should have the club face fairly wide open bringing the flange into play, so that the club head will not dig too deeply into the sand. As it is easy to do this with this type of sand, provided that the ball is sitting fairly well, try to take a longer shallower type of sand divot. To this end you may find it helpful to set up a little further from the ball than normal, weight evenly distributed, and then swing your arms slightly wider than usual.

In bunkers with coarser sand, your feet probably will not dig in so deeply, and neither will the club head. Still open the club face, and with your weight favouring the left side, concentrate on hitting down and through the sand, taking a divot starting about two inches before the ball.

When the sand is wet, firmly packed or shallow, do not open the club face too wide, as the flange will tend to bounce off the sand and you could thin the shot. Try to dig your left foot deeper into the sand than your right, then swing your arms up steeply, and think more about hitting *down* than forward, making the entry point closer to the ball. In extreme circumstances, either use the sand iron with the club face square to the target, or take the sharper bladed wedge.

Therefore as a general guideline, the deeper and more

In soft, deep, powdery sand, open the face fairly wide, and take a long shallow divot of sand

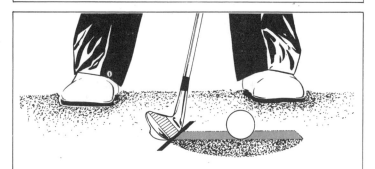

In coarser sand, do not open the blade as wide, and you will take a shorter deeper, divot

In wet, firm sand, square the clubface and hit nearer the ball

powdery the sand, the deeper the club head will penetrate, so try to adjust the type of swing you make and the divot you take.

193

40

'I have no confidence with 2-3 foot putts. Why do I miss the hole so regularly from such close range?'

Reason

A high percentage of golf shots require confidence, and none more so than putting. Once technique is reasonable, confidence can bring most encouraging results. However, faulty technique will mean missed putts even from close range, and most cases of poor putting are caused by too much independent hand action. The best putters in the world putt using a firm-wristed action, which allows them to reproduce a repetitive stroke quite readily.

Remedy

I would advise checking the grip first, and if you do not use the reverse overlap grip, I would recommend that you try it. With this grip all the fingers of the right hand are on the grip, while the left forefinger overlaps the fingers of the right hand. Both thumbs should be at the front of the grip, which ensures that both palms are at right angles to the target line. This grip helps to keep the back of the left wrist firmer throughout the stroke. Keep the wrists slightly arched and the grip firm enough to have a steady control of the club. You must bend forward from the hips, so that the arms have room in which to swing, and position the ball just inside the left heel. Carefully line up the face of the club square to the hole, then make a smooth stroke, ensuring that the angles at the back of each wrist and forearm do not change. Try to make the backswing and throughswing the same length, keeping the clubhead and clubface moving towards the hole. Keep the body and head still, until you hear the ball drop or it has finished rolling. A good practice drill for short putts is to lay down clubs on either side of the hole, parallel to each other, forming a track between which your putter will fit. Just practise the 2-foot putts, and you will soon develop a sound technique, which will lead to you becoming a confident and successful putter.

Practise short putts with two clubs forming a track back from the hole. Use the reverse overlap grip, and maintain the angles at the back of the wrists throughout the stroke

'I have great difficulty judging long putts: they finish either well short or well past the hole. How can I improve this?'

 'I have trouble lining up my putts accurately. How can I improve this?'

Reason

To hit long puts well, you must strike the ball consistently off the sweet spot, and be able to assess the effect of the pace and slope of the green.

Remedy

Take 4 balls and practise on a level green just trying to hit the balls consistently into a cluster about 15-20 feet away. This will indicate if you are striking the balls correctly out of the sweet spot. If not, be sure that the back of your left hand is not stopping at impact; it must remain firm well into the through swing. Length of swing is important too — the correct length should enable you to accelerate the putter smoothly through the ball. Too short a backswing will make you jab at the ball; too long a backswing will cause you to decelerate. So work on what feels a smooth rhythm, which will allow you to increase the length of the putt purely by taking the putter back further. Practise the cluster putting with your eyes shut, and you will heighten your awareness of feel.

On the course, before putting have a look at the putt from the side. This gives you a better idea of the true distance, which can easily become foreshortened. Imagine how fast the ball needs to leave the putter in order to reach the hole. Walk from the hole back to your ball; look at the grass to see if it is longer or shorter than the previous green, and use your feet to sense any slope. Take a couple of practice putts looking at the hole and imagine the pace at which the ball must leave your putter in order to die at the hole.

Trying to sense the strength of any short game shot is vital, and pre-shot visualization must be integrated into your game. Also watch your partners' putts, and imagine how hard you would have hit the ball.

Reason

Because in golf we do not look directly at our target, whether putting or hitting longer shots, aiming accurately is quite a difficult part of the game. If you asked a snooker or pool player to pot a ball standing to the side, rather than behind the target, he too would have trouble aiming. If your eye-line is not parallel to the target line, this also gives a distorted view.

Remedy

Check that your eyes are parallel to the target line by addressing the ball, then, keeping your head still, hold the putter shaft under the bridge of your nose and across both eyes. This will indicate if you should adjust your eye-line or not. Also make sure that your eyes are almost directly over the target line by dropping a ball from under your left eye. It should fall on or just inside the object ball. You can also check this by suspending your putter from under your left eye. When you have read the line of your putt, pick out a point about two to three feet ahead on the target line, and use that as an intermediate target. All you have to do then is to set the ball rolling over that point, and if you have read the putt correctly, the ball should finish in or near the hole. If the borrow means aiming two inches right of the hole, try to focus on that area, rather than the hole.

One last tip: line up the manufacturer's name in the direction of the putt, then set your putter head at right angles to that name. Remember to aim the name in the initial direction the ball must start, which may not be at the hole.

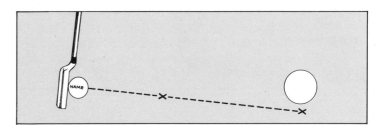

'However straight I take the putter back, I miss too many putts on the left. Why?'

Reason

Although when putting you are standing closer to the ball than for any other shot, you are still standing to the side of, rather than directly over, the ball. Consequently, even though the putter may go back and through on a fairly straight line with short putts, for longer putts it must start to move inside the target line. If you take it back in a continuous straight line, you are in effect taking it outside of the path it should be on.

Remedy

There are three ways to correct this. When practising, lay a club down just outside the putter head, and make a backswing allowing the putter head to leave the line of the club as the backswing progresses. To help to this end, soften your right elbow at address, so that it rests on or very close to your right hip bone. Most golfers putt with a square or open stance. To help you visualize the correct inside track on the course, adjust your stance so that your right foot is withdrawn, giving you a closed stance, but keep the shoulders parallel to the target line. You will now be able to swing the putter back straight but then allow it to move inside as the length of putt increases.

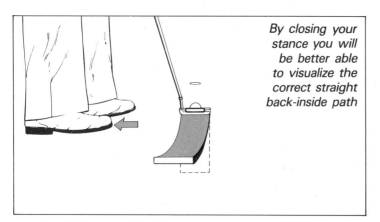

By closing your stance you will be better able to visualize the correct straight back-inside path

'As an older person playing golf, I am losing length. What should I do?'

Reason

Once you get older, it becomes more difficult to make as full a turn as a younger more supple player, and you may lose some length. It could also be that the equipment that suited you 10 years ago, may not be helping you now.

Remedy

You can help yourself make a better backswing turn by closing your stance, i.e. withdrawing and angling out your right foot, and also aligning your shoulders just right of parallel to the target. This enables you to make a better turn, and also sets you up to draw the ball, thereby adding distance to the shot. Do not let your stance become too wide as this will restrict whatever turn you can still make (page 169 gives more detail about how to make a good turn). You also need to practise and concentrate on good hand and arm action. Practise with a narrow stance, choking down on the grip of a medium or short iron. Make a very short backswing where your arms hadly move, but your wrists fully cock by waist height, and the end of the grip points to the round. As you accelerate the club through to a similar position on the through swing, use your hands predominantly (see illustration on page 174). This can be done with or without hitting balls, and will keep your hands and arms active and strong.

Do not allow your backswing to become too fast or it will get shorter and shorter. Rely on good rhythm allied to correct hand and arm action to produce well struck shots. Consider using lighter clubs with whippier shafts — ladies' clubs may be most suitable. You will not only be able to swing and control these more easily, but will also create more clubhead speed — because of their lightness and the whippier shafts. Graphite shafts would also be worth considering, because these do help to hit the ball further.

45 'Whenever I play into the wind I cannot keep the ball low. What am I doing wrong?'

Reason

The most common fault when playing into the wind is to hit the ball too hard. This makes the ball spin faster and therefore go higher. Many golfers fail to take enough club, but instead select the usual club for the shot in hand and try to hit the ball harder. Adjustment in swing technique is needed also, so that wrist and hand action become less active.

Remedy

The wind's strength must dictate which club you use, but always take at least one club more than usual. I would rather see a player take two clubs more, and then choke down on the grip. This will give you more control, and will naturally help to restrict the wrist action in the swing. The less lofted club will also quite readily hit the ball much lower. Play the ball more centrally in your stance, which should be a few inches wider than normal, but keep your hands forward, so that the shaft slopes more obviously towards the target. This address position also deducts loft from the club face. (See page 179 for more information on this.)

With this set-up and club choice, you have given yourself a good chance of hitting a low shot, but a swing adjustment is advisable. Make what feels like a three-quarter length backswing, where the wrists do not fully cock, then drive the club through impact, keeping the hands ahead of the clubface. The follow through should be abbreviated, so that the whole swing has a rather wooden feel to it. It is a good practice drill, even in calm weather, to hit some full 6 iron shots and then to hit your 5 and 4 irons the same distance. When driving, tee the ball a touch lower, and play it about a ball's width further back in your stance, which should be a few inches wider than normal. Also stand a little further away, as this will encourage a flatter swing, producing a lower drawing flight. Choke down the grip a little, and make the same swing adjustments as above, but above all, do not try to hit the ball too hard. A strong wind can knock you off balance, so swing smoothly, and try to finish balanced.

To keep the ball low, choke down on a straighter faced club, and play the ball back. With a wider stance than normal and your hands forward, make a shorter backswing with restricted wrist action

46 'As I seem capable of beating better players in matches, why do I play poorly in medal rounds?'

Reason

In match play you can have two or three very bad holes, but will only have lost those holes and not the chance of winning the match. You may be a cavalier golfer who goes for broke on every shot. This is fine on a good day but on a bad day in a medal round, a 9 or 10 on a hole will end your chances of playing to your handicap. Remember also that the better players will be giving you shots, and will be expected to beat you.

Remedy

First assess whether or not you take too many chances. I am not suggesting that you play totally defensively, but realistically. Taking your full handicap, assess the true par values of the holes on your course, e.g. a par 4 where you get a shot is really a par 5, then try to play the holes accordingly; you will probably find you make more gross pars. Do not attempt to carry a distant ditch or bunker if it requires a perfect shot.

If you have a bad hole early on, try to dismiss it from your mind. This is harder in medal than match-play, because it is more damaging, but work at it. Most golfers do not warm up or practise before they play, so it is wrong to think that you should play immaculately from the start. However, do have some practice swings before you play, or disaster may strike very early. Use your 3 wood on the first few holes, and then if you are swinging well move to the driver.

Do not try to keep up with a longer hitting player if he/she happens to be your partner; concentrate on your own smooth rhythm. Your putting strategy may need to be changed. In match-play you tend to 'go for the hole' more often than not. This philosophy in medal play can lead to knocking the ball a long way past the hole and then missing the one back.

47 'When the greens are wet I always leave my chip shots short. How can I learn to judge the pace?'

Reason

When the greens are wet, naturally the ball will not run so freely, so you must adjust accordingly. No one can tell you how hard to hit the ball — this comes only with experience. What you should consider, however, is changing the shot you play from around the green.

Remedy

On all short shots from around the green in wet weather, if possible walk at least halfway between your ball and the hole. Each green is likely to be different in its softness, and you may not be able to see if casual water intervenes between your ball and the hole unless you go onto the green. If there is casual water on your line, you have to play the ball as it lies. It is only when the ball is *on* the green that you may move it. When the grass is wet it is better to choose the air route. At least if you loft the ball two-thirds of the distance to the hole, you should not have too long a putt. So instead of using perhaps a 7 iron to chip and run, use your wedge or sand wedge.

There is no need to play a wristy type of shot, especially as in wet weather if the club contacts the ground even fractionally before the ball, the shot is dampened. You can use a firm wristed chipping action, allowing the club's loft to send the ball into the air. To ensure that you do strike the ball first, play the ball slightly further back in your stance, and open the clubface a fraction so that you still have plenty of loft. If you use a sand iron, make sure that there is a cushion of grass beneath the ball, otherwise the flange will bounce off the ground. Using either club you will have to hit the ball harder than a 7 iron, but you are playing a more predictable shot. Depending on how wet the green may be, play the shot boldly, as the ball will not run very much when it lands.

'What thickness of grip and type of shaft should my clubs have?'

Grips

It is now possible to get quite a wide variety of width of grips. To check if you have the best for your size hands, when you take your left-hand grip, there should be only a small space between the ends of your middle two fingers and the base of your thumb. If the space is considerable, indicating that the grips are too thick, you may experience problems getting sufficient hand action into your swing, and also have insufficient control of the club. If your fingers tend to overlap your thumb, indicating that the grips are too small, you may well get excess hand action and/or lack of control. If you change your grip thickness, remember that using a thinner grip will make the club feel heavier and will encourage hand action, whereas a thicker grip will lighten the feel of the club and possibly reduce hand action.

Shafts and swing weight

The three main shaft flexes in use are: 'L' — Ladies; 'R' - Mens; and 'S' — Stiff. Shaft flexes and swing weights are inter-related - the heavier the clubhead and longer the shaft, the stiffer the flex needs to be.

Ladies' shafts are suitable for most lady golfers, since the fairly flexible shaft helps increase clubhead speed. The swing weight range of clubs with these shafts is from about C0-C8. Some less athletic or older men players often find that ladies' clubs are more help to them than men's, as the lighter weight and shorter shaft are easier to control, and the additional shaft flex provides extra distance.

Men's shafts are suitable for most men players, with the slightly longer but less flexible shaft giving added control and distance. The swing weight range of clubs with these shafts is from about C9-D2. Stronger women may find men's clubs in the lighter end of the range more suitable than ladies' clubs. However, they do need sufficiently large hands to cope with the thicker grips, and enough strength to get sufficient clubhead speed from the stiffer shaft.

'S' shafts are for the stronger man who hits the ball further than average. The stiffer shaft will increase control of

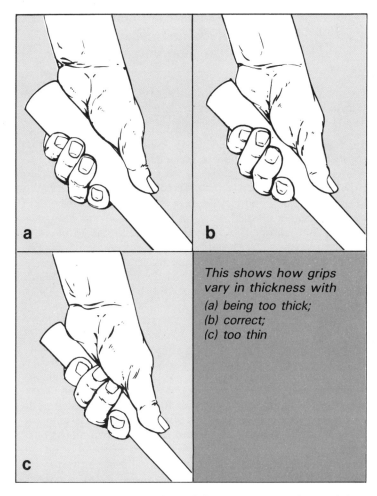

This shows how grips vary in thickness with
(a) being too thick;
(b) correct;
(c) too thin

the clubs, which will be about D3 onwards in swing weight.

Beginners should guard against using clubs that are too heavy. Clubhead control is the name of the game, and for beginners, especially ladies who have less strength than the average man, a heavy club makes that control even more difficult.

Swing weight can be reduced by removing weight from the head, shortening the shaft or using a thicker grip. Swing weight can be increased by adding weight to the head, lengthening the club, or using a thinner grip. A good professional or club maker will be able to advise you which club is best for you, and, by a combination of the above adjustments, can tailor your clubs to your liking.

'As a beginner I am confused about which golf ball is the best one to use. Can you advise?'

There is a wide choice of golf balls, and the beginner can be forgiven for being confused as to which is the best. Golf balls really fall into two categories: wound or solid.

The wound ball consists of a small inner core, around which a long thin length of rubber is wound. The ball is then covered in one of two materials, balata, or surlyn. Balata is a soft cover, which permits the club to gain a better purchase on the ball, thus imparting more spin. The top professionals and top amateurs would be more likely to use this ball, because they can control it better. They are able to utilize its qualities to impart the desired spin, and consequently shape shots very readily. Higher handicap players unfortunately more often than not impart unwanted sidespin on the ball, and so their shots would hook or slice more violently. The soft cover also marks and cuts easily, and thus does not last very long. The surlyn covered ball has a slightly harder feel to it, but is resistant to cutting, and will not spin as readily as the balata ball.

The solid ball, sometimes known as a two-piece ball, has a solid core and a surlyn cover, and has an altogether livelier feel than the wound ball. It travels further and, because of its solid nature and surlyn cover, is virtually impossible to cut. It is a more difficult ball to spin, and to control around the greens, although there are now solid balls which offer as much, or indeed more, spin than wound balls. For these reasons the better player is less likely to use it, but it is the ideal ball for beginners and most club golfers. The extra length gained by using it, and the fact that it will not curve as much as a balata covered ball, more than outweighs the slight loss of control around the greens. Almost every ball manufacturer now makes a solid ball, and the feel aspect continues to improve with each subsequent model. You may find one particular make that you like more than another, but make sure that you compare like with like, i.e. solid ball with solid ball.

 'Why is the lie of my irons so important?'

When you strike the ball, ideally the sole of the club should be parallel to the ground, which enables you to retain the club face in a square position whilst it penetrates the soil. Consequently you are more likely to hit straight shots.

To check the lie of your irons, address the ball, and if the lie is correct the toe end will sit slightly off the ground. This is to offset the fact that through impact your wrists will tend to arch upwards slightly and so the whole of the sole will then be in contact with the ground.

If, when you address the ball, the toe end sits so far up in the air, that only the heel is in contact with the ground, then the lie is too upright. Through impact the heel will catch on the ground and cause the blade to close, sending the ball to the left.

If, on the other hand, the heel sits off the ground at address, then the club is too flat, and the toe is likely to catch on the ground through impact, opening the clubface and sending the ball to the right.

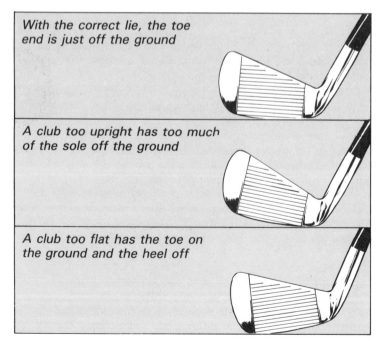

With the correct lie, the toe end is just off the ground

A club too upright has too much of the sole off the ground

A club too flat has the toe on the ground and the heel off

CHAPTER ONE

The right equipment can help you

Many beginners start playing golf with an inexpensive, and often an unmatched, set of clubs, but if you have reached the stage of being reasonably competent, and wishing to break 90, then it is possible that you may wish to upgrade your equipment. This does not mean buying the most expensive set in the shop – far from it. What it does mean is buying a set that suits you. In recent years, technology has improved golf club performance, and most professionals have a stock of trial clubs which you can test before you buy, so do invest some time before you buy new clubs. The following advice should also help you to know what to look for in a new set.

Which clubs are right for you?

Below is a table showing which swing weight and type of shaft suit different categories of players (Fig 1.1).

Swing-weight	C0-C5	C6-C8	C9-D2	D3-D5
Shaft	L	L or R	R	S or XS
Category of Player	Lady beginner and average lady player. Slow swing and hand action.	Strong lady and weaker man. Reasonable hand and club speed. Man may feel that a lighter club is easier to control and L shaft helps clubhead speed.	Strong lady and average man. Good hand action and clubhead speed.	Strong man. Very fast hand action and clubhead speed.

Fig 1.1. The various swing weights and shaft flexes available, and which category of player they suit.

Swing weight

Swing weight is the system of measuring the balance of a club, and refers to how heavy the club feels when swung. As you progress with the game, it is quite feasible that you will become stronger, and thus can play with slightly heavier clubs than those with which you started. However, always guard against playing with clubs that are too heavy. When you try out a club, it may be when you are feeling quite fresh, but remember that towards the end of your round, you may begin to feel a bit weary, and the clubs may start to feel too heavy, causing you to lose control.

Shaft flex

The main shaft flexes available are L (ladies'), R (men's regular), S (men's stiff), and XS (men's extra stiff), each one being progressively stiffer than the last. The lighter the swing weight, usually the more flexible the shaft. Nowadays there are so many new materials being used for shafts, such as graphite and boron, which are all designed to help you hit the ball further. Although these are usually more expensive than steel shafts, if distance is one of the factors lacking in your game, you may well feel that the investment is worthwhile.

Grips

The two main grip thicknesses are ladies' and men's, the former being thinner than the latter. However, many companies make a greater variety of grip widths, and you can always have an additional layer of adhesive tape under the grips to make them thicker. So what is the importance of the grip thickness? Ideally when your left hand closes around the club, the tips of the middle two fingers should be quite close to the pad at the base of the thumb, which should enable you to have good control (Fig 1.2). Someone who slices may be using grips that are too thick, thereby preventing free hand action through impact. A player who hooks the ball could find that slightly thicker grips will stabilize over-active hands. Remember, however, that if you should alter your grip thickness, thinner grips make a club feel heavier to swing, whilst thicker grips will have the opposite effect.

Always keep your grips clean by washing them regularly with soapy water to keep them grease-free, and, if necessary,

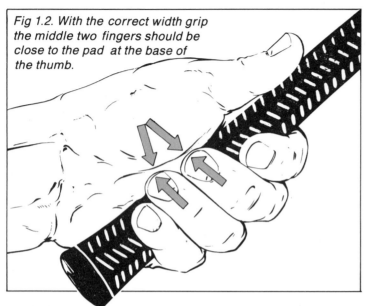

Fig 1.2. With the correct width grip the middle two fingers should be close to the pad at the base of the thumb.

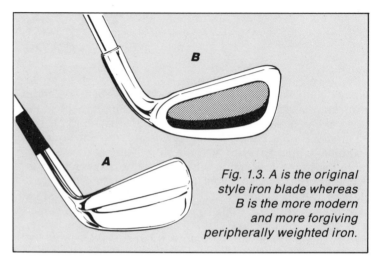

Fig. 1.3. A is the original style iron blade whereas B is the more modern and more forgiving peripherally weighted iron.

rough them up using sandpaper or a file. Grips do not last for ever, and once they become shiny and feel hard, then you will have to grip tightly to keep control, which will inevitably restrict good hand action. So if your grips reach this sad condition, then the time has come to have them re-gripped.

Club head choice

There are two main shapes of club head for irons, these being *blade* and *peripherally* weighted (Fig 1.3). The blade is the original shaped head where the weight is distributed fairly evenly. It is best used by the lower-handicap golfer or professional, who often likes the feel and look of this type of club. The *blade*-type head has a small optimum area of strike, known as the sweet spot. On the *peripherally* weighted club, this is much larger, giving the less consistent higher-handicap golfer a much better chance of hitting the ball 'out of the middle'; thus it could be described as a more forgiving club. So the best piece of advice I can give you when buying clubs is to go for peripherally weighted ones, which most manufacturers now have in their range.

You can also buy woods that offer a similar advantage. Those that have heel and toe weighting have an enlarged sweet spot, as do metal woods, which consist of a metal shell filled with polystyrene.

The lie of the iron

When you address the ball the toe end of the iron should be just off the ground, so that through impact, where the wrists arch slightly, the whole of the sole will be in contact with the ground (Fig 1.4). If in your set the toe end sits up too much, the club is too upright, and can cause the heel to catch on the ground, closing the clubface at impact and thereby creating a pull or hook (Fig 1.5). If at address the whole of the sole touches the ground or the heel is off the ground, the club is too flat, and can cause the toe to catch the turf at impact, creating a push or slice (Fig 1.6). Check this on your current

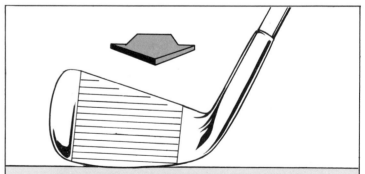

Fig 1.4. With the correct lie, the toe end sits just off the ground, encouraging straight shots.

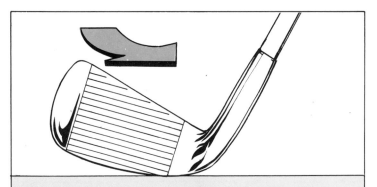

Fig 1.5. When the lie is too upright, the toe sits too far off the ground and promotes a pull or hook shot.

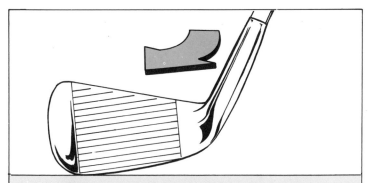

Fig 1.6. When the lie is too flat, the heel sits too far off the ground, and promotes a push or slice shot.

set, and especially if buying new irons. Most clubs can be adjusted to suit you, but be certain that this is done either by your professional or a good club maker. Because of the more rounded sole of a wood, and the fact that the ball is often hit from a tee peg when using them, the lie is perhaps less crucial, but do get the professional to check them as well.

Which number clubs to buy

If you buy a set of clubs, this can consist of 9 or 10 irons, and 3 or 4 woods, plus a putter. Most off-the-rack sets consist of 3 through 9 irons, pitching wedge, sand iron, driver, 3, and 5 wood. Very often you will have to buy the complete set of irons, but may not have to

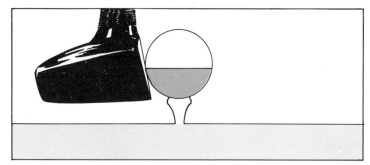

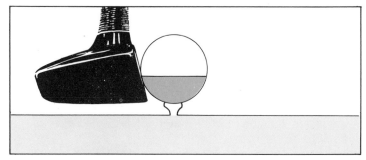

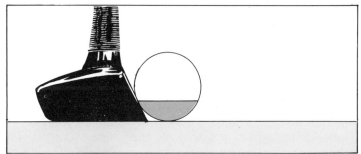

Fig 1.7. The straight-faced driver contacts the ball near its equator, imparting maximum sidespin. The more lofted clubs contact the ball lower down, thereby imparting more backspin and resulting in straighter shots.

buy all three woods. In which case I recommend the clubs you should carry are 4 iron to sand wedge (leave the 3 iron indoors) and a 3 and 5 wood. My reasoning for this choice is based on the fact that the less lofted clubs, such as the 3 iron and driver, are more difficult to hit well. Their lack of loft means that the ball is contacted near its equator and thus more sidespin is imparted (Fig 1.7). This means that a slice or hook is accentuated. The 3 wood has more loft than the driver, and will enable you quite adequately to hit the ball far enough off the tee. Likewise, a 3 iron has little loft, and unless you can hit yours consistently well, I recommend that you either leave it out of the bag, or include it only in case you need to hit a low shot under a tree. You would be better served by using the 5 wood, and women especially would benefit from using a 7 wood (roughly equivalent to a 3 or 4 iron) which many companies now make. Each of these lofted woods is also so useful out of the rough when distance is needed.

If you do insist on buying or using a driver, be sure that it has at least 12 degrees of loft – anything less will be very difficult to hit consistently well.

Ideally all players who are endeavouring to break 90, should steer away from the less lofted clubs, settle for more consistent accuracy, and do not be fooled into thinking that you *have* to hit a driver off every tee because your friends do. If their ability enables them to use this club consistently, then that is fine, but if you analyse their round, you may well find that their driver gets them into trouble too often. It is better to sacrifice 10 or 15 yards in distance, in order to be consistently on the fairway.

When choosing a putter, I would also recommend a heel and toe weighted model, which, like the irons and woods, will have a bigger sweet spot. Again there are many to choose from, so pick one that lies with its base on the ground, and that is the correct length for you.

The ball to use

If your goal is to break 90, do help yourself by playing with a decent golf ball. By that I mean one that is round, and without cuts or other serious imperfections, although slight paint grazes should not make too much difference. I would also recommend that you play the 'two-piece' golf ball, which has a solid core, is covered with a very resilient material, and whose structure promotes distance. Most manufacturers make this type of ball, which has a livelier feel to it than the

alternative wound ball. For the higher-handicap player generally the extra control of the wound ball around the greens is worth sacrificing for the extra distance of the solid ball. However, for those who do prefer the wound ball, steer away from a Balata cover, which, since it is softer than the alternative Surlyn, promotes spin. Whilst this is fine for the better players who use this property to their advantage, it will exaggerate unwanted sidespin, making the ball slice or hook even more.

Summary

The above advice is not offered to make you dash to the professional's shop to spend money, but to make sure that you choose wisely. You may already have a good set of clubs, consisting of what I recommend, but I know from experience that once you have been 'bitten' by the game, you may wish to upgrade your equipment. The above advice will help, but always consult your professional, who will be only too willing to help you. The most expensive set of clubs will not turn a bad player into a good one, but if you have reached the standard of nearly breaking 90, then the correct equipment will start to make some difference to your play. Look after your clubs by keeping the grooves and grips clean, and at least then you will know that your clubs are not hindering you, but helping you to break 90.

CHAPTER TWO

Help for those who slice or hook

If you cannot quite break 90, the chances are that you either slice or hook the ball too often. Whilst this book does not set out to deal with badly struck shots in great detail, I want to give you some tips on how to minimize these faults, and learn how to live with them.

Help for those who slice

A slice is caused because the club face is aimed to the right of the swing path at impact, which imparts left-to-right sidespin on the ball (Fig 2.1). The reason for this is that the correct hand and forearm action through the impact zone is a far from natural movement for beginners, whose grip is seldom correct, and whose swing is often rather stiff and wooden. Their action fails to square the club face, leaving it open and creating left-to-right sidespin on the shot. To offset the ball veering to the right, the player then aims to the left, and in effect causes more sidespin by cutting even further across the ball. The sliced shot will go higher and travel less distance than it should for the club being used.

The grip

With the correct left-hand grip, where the club lies diagonally across the palm and fingers of the left hand (Fig 2.2), if you hold the club up in front of you, two-and-a-half to three knuckles should be visible (Fig 2.3). The 'V' formed by the thumb and forefinger should point to the right side of your face. When the right hand is placed on the grip, the 'V' formed should be parallel to that of the left, and pointing in the region of the right shoulder (Fig 2.4). Do not grip too tightly. The last three fingers of the left hand, and middle two of the right, should provide most of the pressure, which on a scale of one to five, with one being light and five being tight, should be about three to three-and-a-half. When you take your grip ensure that the club face is square to the target.

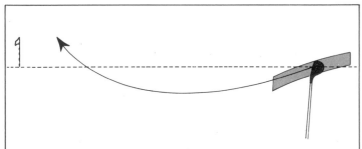

Fig 2.1. A sliced shot is caused by the club head travelling from out-to-in, with the club face aimed to the right of this path.

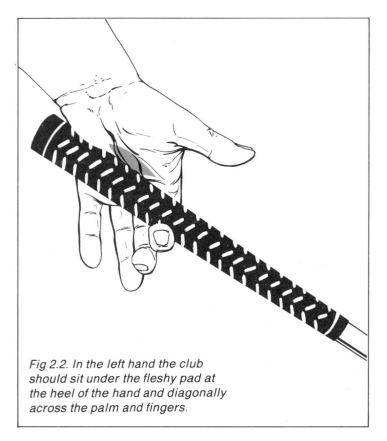

Fig 2.2. In the left hand the club should sit under the fleshy pad at the heel of the hand and diagonally across the palm and fingers.

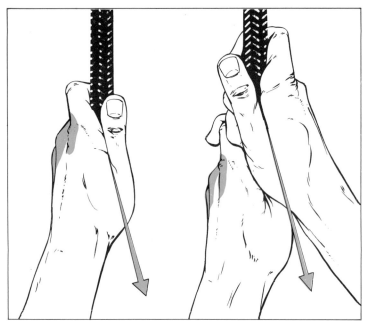

Fig 2.3. Those who slice should see $2\frac{1}{2}$-3 knuckles of the left hand, and the 'V' of the thumb and forefinger should point to the right side of the face.

Fig 2.4. On the right hand the 'V' will point in the region of the right shoulder.

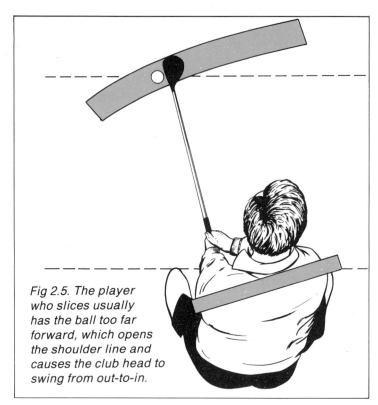

Fig 2.5. The player who slices usually has the ball too far forward, which opens the shoulder line and causes the club head to swing from out-to-in.

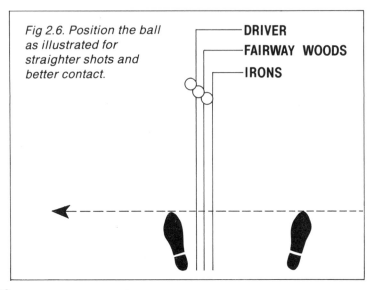

Fig 2.6. Position the ball as illustrated for straighter shots and better contact.

DRIVER
FAIRWAY WOODS
IRONS

The set up

Most players who slice, have the ball too far forward in their stance, which pulls the shoulder line open (Fig 2.5). For your iron shots, the ball should be about three to four inches inside your left heel; for the fairway woods, about two to three inches inside the left heel; and for the driver and 3 wood, about one to two inches inside the left heel (Fig 2.6). With the ball more central you should now be able to take your address position with your shoulders parallel to the target line (Fig 2.7). Your left arm should be comfortably straight, but the right should be slightly softened at the elbow. Your feet, knees and hips must also be parallel to the target line. Your posture is also important, which means that you should bend forward from the hip bones, allowing your seat to stick out behind you as a counter-balance. The weight should be more

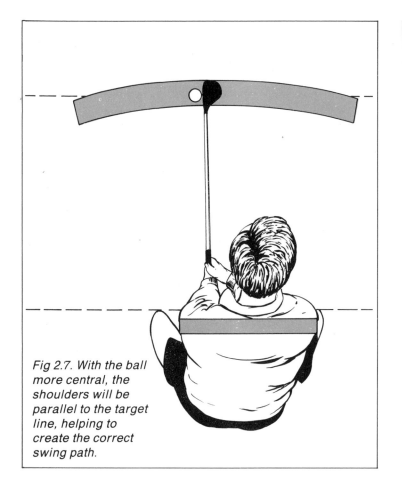

Fig 2.7. With the ball more central, the shoulders will be parallel to the target line, helping to create the correct swing path.

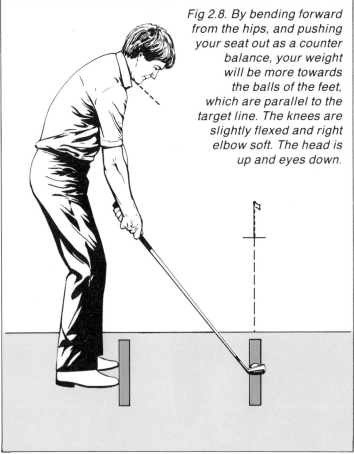

Fig 2.8. By bending forward from the hips, and pushing your seat out as a counter balance, your weight will be more towards the balls of the feet, which are parallel to the target line. The knees are slightly flexed and right elbow soft. The head is up and eyes down.

towards the ball of each foot, with the knees just flexed (Fig 2.8). Keep your chin up off your chest, and feel that your eyes are looking down at the ball.

The swing

This grip and set up will allow you to swing the club correctly to the inside of the target line during the backswing. Keep the club head fairly low to the ground for the first foot, which will encourage the body to turn, so that at the completion of the backswing your shoulders have turned 90 degrees. To help to this end, make certain that the right hip moves backwards, not laterally sidewards (Fig 2.9a). You must allow your arms and

hands to dominate the downswing. Change direction by gently pulling down with the left arm, then allow both hands to strike the ball.

For the player who has sliced for some time, the wrists and hands will have to play a greater part in the swing, where the right hand and forearm will start to turn over the left just after impact (Fig 2.9b). Swing through the ball, not at it, so that you finish with your body facing the target, and the weight mainly on the outside of your left foot. To understand a little more how the hands and arms should work through the impact zone, stand with the club held horizontally in front of you, as if the ball was on a very high tee peg. Now swing to the right, then the left, and you will notice that just after the

Fig 2.9b. Allow the right hand and forearm to begin to rotate over the left just after impact.

Fig 2.9a. Turn the right hip backwards, not sideways, to create space in which the arms can swing.

club head passes your face, the right hand and forearm start to turn over the left (Fig 2.10). This action, which resembles a baseball swing, is similar to that in the correct golf swing.

Help for those who hook

The hooked shot is caused by the club face being closed, i.e. aimed to the left of the swing path at impact (Fig 2.11). This imparts right-to-left sidespin on the ball, causing it to curve in that direction. It also deducts loft from the club face, so that the ball flies lower than normal for the club being used. Since the ball finishes left of target, the player tends to aim to the right to allow for it, but this encourages an exaggerated inside attack on the ball, creating more hook spin (Fig 2.12). Players who are plagued by this type of shot are really not that far from hitting the ball very well. They at least are able to attack the ball from inside the target line, and may well find that most of their problems are caused by a poor grip, and lack of good leg action.

208

The grip

Check that the two 'V's formed by the thumb and forefinger are not pointing too much to the right – ideally they should point slightly less to the right than recommended for the player who slices. Because you have good hand action, you should be able to see only two knuckles on the left hand rather than two-and-a-half to three (Fig 2.13).

The set up

Check that the ball is not played too far back in your stance, as this will tend to close the shoulder line. The ball should be positioned as explained in the slice section. The same goes for the rest of the set up (refer back to 'Help for those who slice').

The swing

When you swing the club, concentrate on keeping your arms and body swinging in unison. The golfer who hooks violently, often stops the body turning through the ball, which prevents a good arm swing and forces the right hand to cross over the left too abruptly (Fig 2.14). Try to swing to a balanced finish so that through the impact zone, your right knee works towards your left, with the right heel releasing from the ground. This keeps your body turning and enables your arms to continue swinging through the ball. Finish with your body facing the target, and your weight on the outside of the left foot (Fig 2.15). Concentrate on *pulling* the club head back to the ball, feeling that the heel of the left hand leads. Never try to hit the ball too hard, as this will emphasize the closing club face. Take enough club, and swing smoothly.

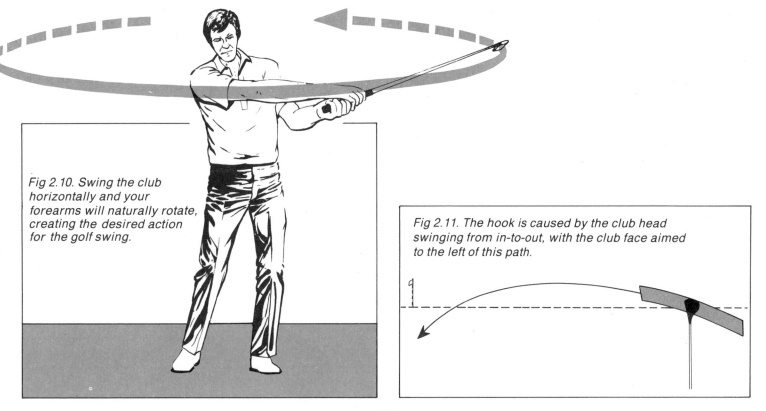

Fig 2.10. Swing the club horizontally and your forearms will naturally rotate, creating the desired action for the golf swing.

Fig 2.11. The hook is caused by the club head swinging from in-to-out, with the club face aimed to the left of this path.

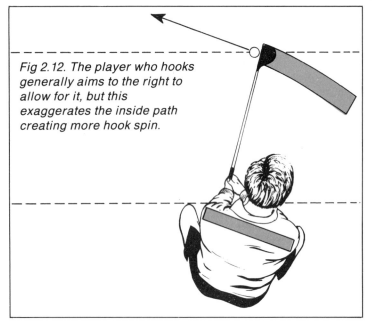

Fig 2.12. The player who hooks generally aims to the right to allow for it, but this exaggerates the inside path creating more hook spin.

Fig 2.14. When the body and legs fail to move through impact, they cause the hands and arms to rotate too suddenly and violently, closing the club face.

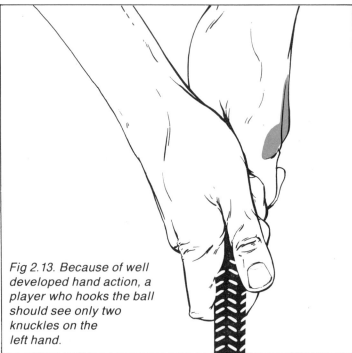

Fig 2.13. Because of well developed hand action, a player who hooks the ball should see only two knuckles on the left hand.

A set routine

Whether you slice or hook, you must always make allowances. The information above is designed to help you hit the ball with less sidespin, be that hook or slice. I have tried to help you *improve* the bad shot, but inevitably you will still spin the ball on many shots. However, I hope that your shots progress from slice and hook to fade and draw, each of these being a diluted form of sidespin shot. Whatever shaped shot you hit, the best way to cope is to allow for the curve. If you regularly hit the ball so that it curves 10 yards right to left, there is no use aiming at the pin only to see the ball finish 10

Fig 2.15. By finishing facing the target, with most of the weight on the outside of the left foot, your legs and body will be more likely to move correctly through impact, and enable you to keep the club face square.

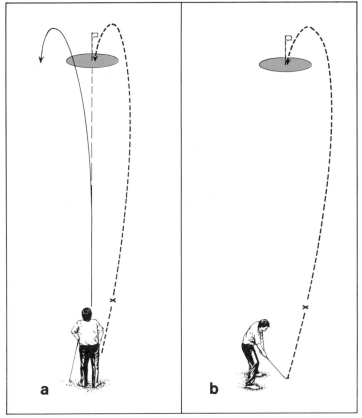

Fig 2.16a. If the ball generally curves to the left, do not aim at the target, because the ball will finish off-line. Use a routine where you stand behind the ball, visualize its flight, and then pick out an intermediate target just ahead of the ball on a line that allows for the curve.
Fig 2.16b. Aim the club face in line with this target and yourself parallel to the new target line.

yards to the left. Better to aim off where possible, so that the ball finishes on target.

The best way to go about this is to have a set routine, which will ensure that you set up to the ball as well as any professional. This is the stationary part of the game, so there is no reason why you cannot improve this aspect quite easily. Approach your routine as follows (Fig 2.16):

1 Stand facing the target and imagine the flight of your ball, so that it lands on target.

2 Pick out an intermediate target about three feet ahead of the ball on the line of flight.

3 Set up, ensuring that the club face is correctly aligned and that you are standing parallel to the initial line of flight. Remember that to break 90, you do not have to hit every shot straight. Try to decrease the amount of curve on your shots, and aim off to allow for this. Fairways and greens are not so narrow that only a straight shot will find them – you have some leeway, so do not despair.

211

CHAPTER THREE

Help for the ragged shots

You may not only hit shots that hook and/or slice, but also too many that are either topped or hit fat, or lack direction and distance. Golf is a demanding game, and having swung the club head about 20 feet through the air before impact, if it is as little as a quarter of an inch or a couple of degrees out of position, the shot is less than perfect, and often most disappointing (Fig 3.1).

There are a few points worth remembering about the golf swing that will help you break 90:

1 Under pressure, players tend to tighten their grip too much, and to swing too quickly. So take a firm but not vice-like grip, and try to keep the pressure constant throughout.

2 Use your practice swing to set the pace of swing for the shot, always being aware that you will tend to get faster as the pressure builds.

3 The rhythm of the swing is so important, but easily neglected. How often have you decided to play short of a hazard, taken an easy swing, and hit the ball so well that it is in danger of going into the hazard? That has happened to us all, and is a great lesson for demonstrating that when you swing smoothly, and in an unhurried manner, you strike the ball better, and it consequently goes further.

4 How many times has someone told you that you lifted your head when you hit a bad shot? Although this may be well-intentioned advice, it is seldom wholly correct. In an effort to hit the ball hard, the higher-handicap player will tend to use the body too much through the impact zone. This results in the original spinal angle set at address being raised,

Fig 3.1. If the club head is a couple of degrees or a quarter of an inch out at impact, the shot is less than perfect.

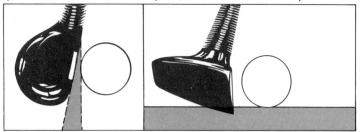

Fig 3.2. If the original spinal angle set at address rises, naturally the head must also be raised. Usually the ball is topped, or sometimes missed completely.

causing the ball to be topped (Fig 3.2). Naturally your head came up because your body came up. So try to keep the original spinal angle constant until the ball is struck. Swing your arms and hands, and let your body respond to that action. Certainly keep your head steady, trying to maintain its original height set at address, until you have struck the ball. Look at the ground long enough to see the tee peg or divot taken, but then allow your head to rotate towards the target. Trying to keep your head absolutely still is usually counter-productive, resulting in a very restricted action.

5 Do not rush the shots. So often if they are playing badly, golfers will rush to hit the next shot, not giving themselves a decent amount of time to aim and address the ball. The best professionals in the world would not play well if they did not take care at address. By all means walk quickly between shots, but take your time when you reach the ball. A few extra seconds on each shot will probably result in you hitting the ball less often, so the time taken to play the round will, in fact, be reduced.

CHAPTER FOUR

A better short game lowers scores

There is no question that the short game is the easiest part of your game to improve. It does not require a large open space in which to practise, nor does it need great strength. If you have a garden or can find a small area in which to work on this aspect of your game, then I assure you that your handicap and scores will come tumbling down. By spending even five minutes whenever possible, you can improve your action, and start to lower your score consistently.

I want to give you a few good tips on your technique. The following advice is for all short shots, excluding putting:

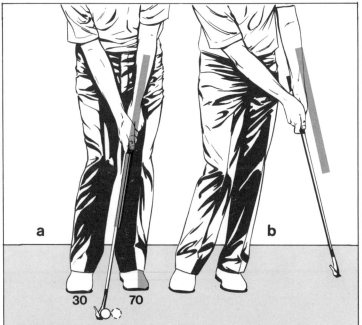

Fig 4.1a. For chips and pitches set up with a narrow open stance, the weight favouring the left side, and the left arm and shaft forming a straight line. This sets the hands ahead of the ball and club face. Play the ball inside the right foot for chips, and the left foot for pitches.

Fig 4.1b. Keep back of left wrist firm throughout stroke.

Fig 4.2. For pitches, swing the club up steeply, keeping the hands leading the club head through impact.

1 Keep more weight on the left foot than the right. With your stance narrow and open, but shoulders square to the target line, place your weight more towards the outside of the left foot, so that it favours that side in a ratio of about 70/30 or 60/40 (Fig 4.1a).

2 Position the ball just inside the *right* foot for chip shots, and inside the *left* foot for pitches (Fig 4.1a).

3 Keep your hands ahead of the ball, so that the shaft slopes towards the target. The left arm and shaft should form a straight line (Fig 4.1a).

4 Use a firm-wristed action for all chip shots, keeping the back of the left wrist in its address position throughout (Fig 4.1b).

213

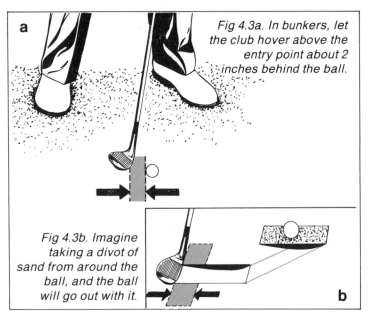

Fig 4.3a. In bunkers, let the club hover above the entry point about 2 inches behind the ball.

Fig 4.3b. Imagine taking a divot of sand from around the ball, and the ball will go out with it.

5 Try to swing the club back and through the same length.

6 For pitch shots swing the club back more steeply, but keep the hands leading the club face back into the ball (Fig 4.2).

7 *Never* try to hit the ball up into the air, or think of trying to *lift* it. Allow the club to descend slightly for chip shots, and more steeply for pitches, allowing the loft on the club to get the ball airborne.

8 For chips and pitches, feel that you are *pulling* the club head back into the ball, not *throwing* it at the ball.

9 Keep looking at the ground until the ball is well on its way.

10 In bunkers align your shoulders left of the target, be sure to swing back far enough, and endeavour to swing through the sand. Finish with your weight on the left foot, body facing the target, just as if it was a full swing.

11 For most bunker shots try to hit about two inches behind the ball, and let the club hover above that point at address, not at the back of the ball (Fig 4.3a).

12 Imagine taking a divot of sand from around the ball, and the ball will go out with it (Fig 4.3b).

13 Keep the swing long and smooth, rather than making it short and stabbing.

Putting

1 Use a firm-wristed action, where the angles at the back of each wrist remain constant (Fig 4.4).

2 Accelerate the putter through the ball.

3 Keep the body and head still. To prevent looking up too quickly, try to guess where the ball has gone. You may guess wrong, but your putting should improve.

4 To encourage a smooth action, try to keep the putter blade in contact with the ball for as long as possible.

All of the above points will improve your golf. You must be honest with yourself, and try to assess which points are missing from your game, then gradually incorporate them one or two at a time. If, for example, your chipping always lets you down, just check the points above and you may solve your problem. Do not expect to remember everything in one go. Take one or two points, and make a determined effort to work on them during your next round or practice session.

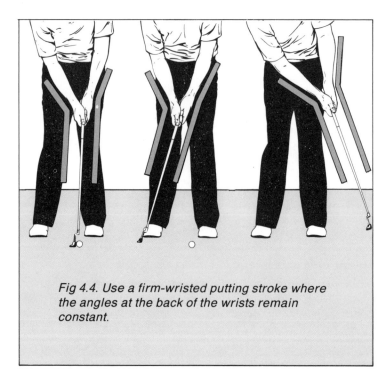

Fig 4.4. Use a firm-wristed putting stroke where the angles at the back of the wrists remain constant.

CHAPTER FIVE

Golf – the outdoor game of chess

The art of low scoring involves good planning as well as good striking. I do believe that it is as much a case of discipline as talent to get the best from yourself. Whilst we have all seen top-class professional playing, few of us are witness to their thoughts or plans on how to play the course. What I can tell you is that they put a lot of thought not only into each shot, but on how to play each hole. Regardless of the fact that they are quite capable of hitting their driver straight a high percentage of times, they will not pull that club from the bag at every par 4 or 5. They, and their caddy, will have worked out the best plan for getting the ball round the course in the lowest number of shots. Players of this calibre know that ego must give way to common sense, and striking the ball 250 yards with the driver may not put them into the best position for the second shot. Naturally their ability allows them to perform to a high standard quite easily and regularly, but you must adopt the same procedure, and put as much mental effort into the game as they do.

We cannot see their minds working, but I can assure you that the top players' minds are far more active and take in many more factors than those of any middle to high-handicap amateurs. So before you venture onto the course, here are a few words of advice about your pre-round preparation.

Warm up first

Try to arrive in time to warm up. Ideally you should hit some shots, but more realistically most people either do not have the time or the facilities do not permit this. Even before you swing a club it would be helpful to stretch your muscles, by just turning your upper body to the right then left, and gently swinging your arms in circles to either side of your body. The last thing you want to do is pull a muscle. Next swing a club, starting with a short iron and then working up to a wood. Some people benefit from swinging two clubs at once, the extra weight gently helping to stretch the muscles. If possible, chip a few shots, and have several putts, all of which will serve to give you an idea of the pace of the greens. Get your score card, tee pegs, ball, towel and markers organized so that you can go to the first tee knowing that you have prepared yourself and can concentrate calmly on the shot in hand.

Practise your hitting

At this stage of your progress you should also know how far you expect to hit each club. It would be well worthwhile spending some time on the practice ground in order to find out. Take about 20 balls, all similar to the ones you use. For instance, if you use a solid two-piece ball; and I recommend that you do, try to use 20 solid balls, not those of driving-range quality, or a wound ball. Try to pick a calm day, perhaps in the spring or autumn (fall) when the ground is not rock hard. Obviously the ball will run when it lands, but better to underestimate the total length of the shot than get flattering results during a long dry summer.

From a level, and good lie, hit your shots starting perhaps with a 9 iron. Do not try to hit the shots flat out, but at the pace and strength you would normally use. Then pace out to the centre of where the majority of the balls have landed. Ignore those you may have mis-hit and the one or two that have gone further than the rest. You want a good average yardage. Most people can readily pace a yard, but it would be worth checking your stride length.

If you continue this process for all the odd numbered clubs, you will then be able to gauge the even numbers from them. Depending on your strength, you may have a difference of about 10–15 yards per club. How far you hit each club is not that important, but being able to judge distances on the course and translating that into club choice is important. There is no point in hitting your 7 iron, say, 135 yards one minute, then 150 the next – correct clubbing will become impossible. This is why the professionals know the distance to the pin and are able to hit a ball yard perfect so often; good rhythm and striking enables them to hit the correct depth of shot time and time again.

If you are not able to go through this procedure, make use of the yardage at the short holes on your course. On a calm day, note which club hits the ball to the middle of the green, and use that as a guide. Some courses have markers at certain points on the course, say, 150 yards, to indicate distance, and many now have yardage charts, which may prove useful. If your course has neither, keep a note of which clubs you use from certain points (do this on a calm day), or make your own yardage chart of the course.

CHAPTER SIX

Planning your round

Most courses have a par value of between 68 and 72, with ladies' courses being perhaps one or two shots more. For the sake of practicality, I want to assume that par is 70, so that if you drop a shot a hole, you will break 90. In other words, playing to a handicap of 18 is a comparative standard to breaking 90. This means that the par values of each hole on the course must now be assessed differently, with the 3s becoming par 4s, 4s now 5s, and 5s now 6s. If you view the course in this manner, you will take pressure off yourself, and you can plan each hole more realistically (Fig 6.1).

Par 3s

Let us first look closely at how best to play a par 3 hole. Since these vary so much in length, you must first assess whether you can in fact reach the green. Whilst very few men have trouble with distance on a par 3, many ladies may be better off laying up short of the hole on the longer par 3s, especially

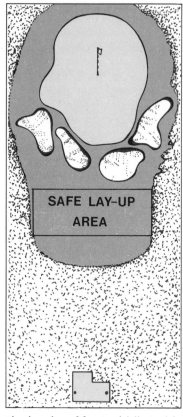

Fig 6.2. On a par 3, the shorter hitter may be wise to lay up in a safe area short of the green.

SAFE LAY–UP AREA

where there are cavernous bunkers placed to catch the short shot (Fig 6.2). If the last few times you have played a hole, you have landed in the front bunkers, then either take one or two more clubs, or decide to play short. I said earlier that golf required discipline, and it is not easy to make yourself play short of the green on a par 3, but ladies, where there is a grassy area for you to lay up, do that rather than plug the ball in the bunker. Most middle to high-handicap players would rather hit from grass than sand, so bear that in mind.

Do not think that I am going to turn you into a purely defensive golfer — I'm not. However, I want you to become an honest and thinking type of player. According to our earlier plan, this par 3 is now a par 4, so you can still be on the green in two, putting for a three, but with a greater chance of making four. Par 3s well within range, provide a golden opportunity to 'pick up' a shot if you can hit the green. You must first consider which club to use based on the tee and pin positions, the weather and your knowledge, perhaps newly found, of how far you hit each club. As a general rule, you should be aiming to hit the middle of every green, but on very

Fig 6.1. Mentally change the par values of each hole in order to take pressure off yourself.

							Stroke	Players Score		Won + Lost –
Marker's Score	Hole	Yards	Metres	Par	Yards	Metres	Index	A	B	Halved o
	1	423	387	4̷5	417	382	7			
	2	176	161	3̷4	160	146	13			
	3	389	355	4̷5	382	349	3			
	4	380	348	4̷5	354	324	9			
	5	147	135	3̷4	132	121	15			
	6	335	307	4̷5	326	298	17			
	7	392	358	4̷5	381	349	5			
	8	422	386	4̷5	407	372	1			
	9	505	462	5̷6	498	455	11			
	OUT	3169	2899	3̷5 4̷4	3057	2796				

COMPETITION .... DATE ....

PLAYER A .... PLAYER B ....

HANDICAP.......... STROKES REC'D.......... HANDICAP.......... STROKES REC'D..........

long greens, if the pin is at the back, you will need a longer club. If the pin is at the front, it may not be prudent to take a shorter iron if it means that a slightly mis-hit shot may land in a bunker (Fig 6.3).

If a hole is downwind, you may need one or two clubs less, depending on the wind strength. Into the wind always take more club than for the yardage, rather than trying to hit the ball harder, which only spins the ball faster, sending it higher into the air. Take one or two clubs more, perhaps grip down, and swing smoothly. Cross winds will obviously affect the ball, and may require you to take a longer club when the wind is strong. Always put the ball on a tee peg, which will give you the best opportunity of a clean strike. Take note if the greenkeeper has moved the tee boxes any considerable amount forward or back of the fixed yardage marker, since four or five yards difference here may just swing the balance of club choice.

One more point to remember about all tee shots, and that is not to be influenced by the direction in which the tee points, because it does *not* always aim directly at the green or down the fairway. By picking the intermediate target just ahead of the ball you should be able to disregard where the tee aims.

Par 4s

Your par 4 strategy needs more study. Under the plan of now playing it as if it was a par 5, you are allowed three shots to reach the green. On some holes this may be needed, but on

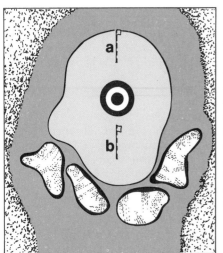

Fig 6.3. Generally you should aim to hit the middle of each green, but if the pin is at the back, take a longer club. If the pin is at the front, remember that if you mis-hit a shorter club, the ball could land in the bunker.

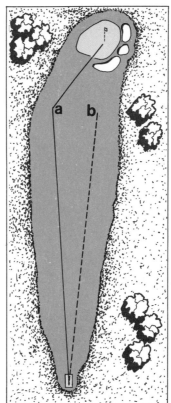

Fig 6.4. If you can see the pin position, aim your tee shot to give yourself an easier second shot avoiding the hazards.

others the green will be in range, provided that you put your tee shot into play. As you survey the hole, decide, being realistic, from where you wish to play your second shot, and indeed your third. You should base your plan on the layout of the hole, and even the pin position, provided that you can see the green. For instance, if the hole is a fairly short par 4, with no severe bunkers in play from the tee, if the pin is cut on the right side of the green behind a bunker, you would have a better approach from the left side of the fairway (Fig 6.4).

I realise that you may not have the ability to always hit the ball off the tee exactly where you wish, but where circumstances allow, consider from which side of the fairway it is better to approach. However, the one vital rule to follow is to avoid bunkers off the tee. If the fairway narrows down just where your tee shot lands, and there are bunkers either side, do consider playing a club that positions the ball short of these hazards (Fig 6.5). It is usually very difficult to gain much distance from a bunker, and you are putting yourself under extra pressure by subsequently having a longer third shot to the green. This is where your on-course discipline must prevail. If all your playing partners take their drivers and successfully hit the fairway, you may feel under pressure to follow suit. Keep to your game plan and you will prove to

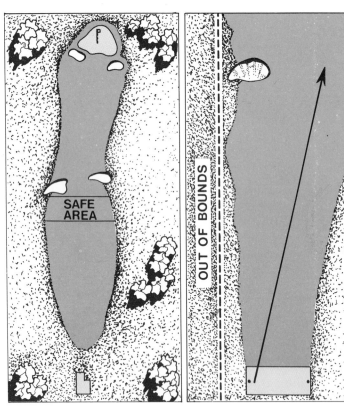

Fig 6.5. If there are bunkers in the landing area, lay up short of them.

Fig 6.6. Provided that you hit the ball fairly straight, tee upon the same side as any trouble, which will encourage you to aim away from it.

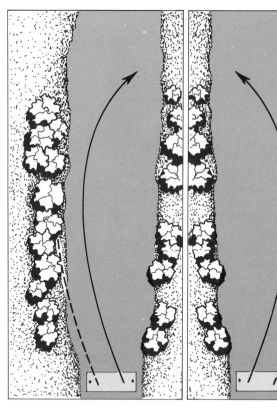

Fig 6.7. If your shots start left and then fade, on a tree-lined hole you need to tee up on the right side of the tee, or otherwise the ball will hit the trees.

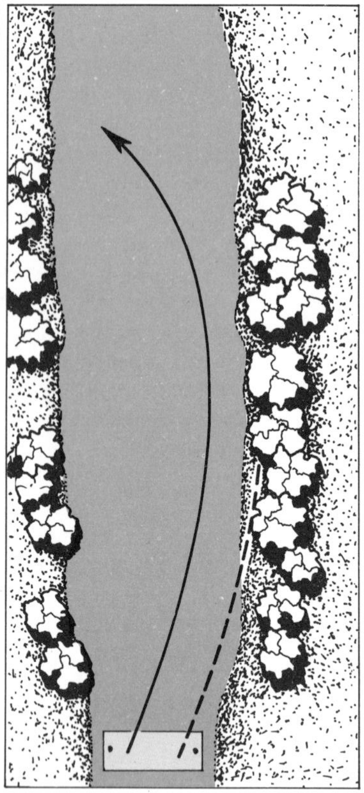

Fig 6.8. If your shots start right and then draw, on a tree-lined hole you need to tee up on the left side of the tee, or otherwise the ball will hit the trees.

yourself that you can score better by playing sensibly.

When teeing the ball, the general rule is to tee up on the same side of the tee as the trouble (Fig 6.6). In other words, if there is a bunker or out of bounds on the left side of the fairway, to help you to aim away from them, play from the left side of the tee. Whereas this advice works well on open courses and for the player who hits the ball reasonably straight, if your shots curve quite a lot, then you cannot follow this advice totally. If you play on a tight tree-lined course and your shots start left and then slice, by teeing up on the left

side you are more likely to hit the trees on that side (Fig 6.7). You must favour the right side of the tee, and allow your slice or fade to curve the ball away from the trouble. Of course, the opposite applies for players whose shots start right, then draw or hook. They should play from the left side of the tee, giving themselves room to aim well wide of trouble up the left, and to avoid the trees down the right side (Fig 6.8).

When playing dog-leg holes take care not to 'bite off' too much of the angle and land in trouble. Whilst taking the brave line on these holes may appear more spectacular, it is always

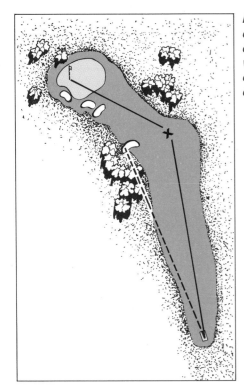

Fig 6.9. Avoid cutting off too much of the dog leg, or the ball will land in trouble, or leave you a more difficult second shot.

Fig 6.10. If you need to hit a 3 wood 100 per cent to carry bunkers, you would be wiser laying up short of them. Even a less than perfect 7 iron shot would be adequate.

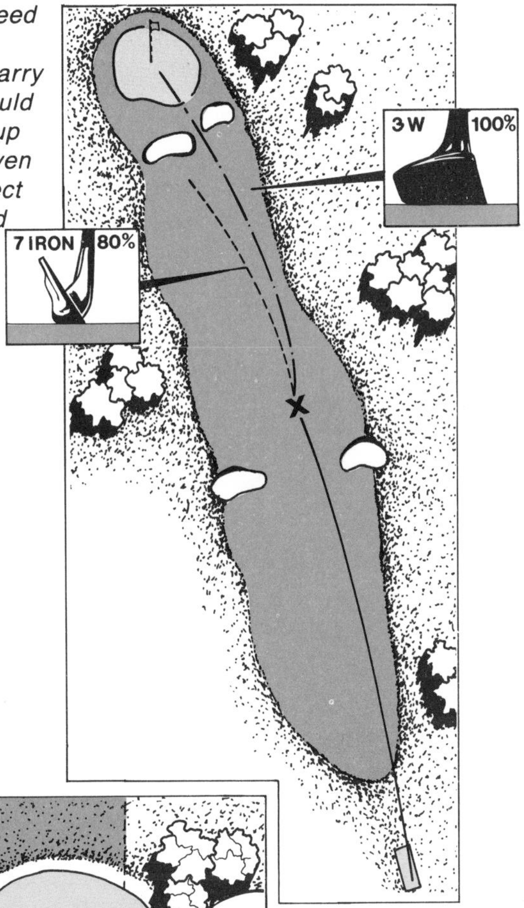

3 W 100%

7 IRON 80%

SAFE AREA

SAFE

WATER

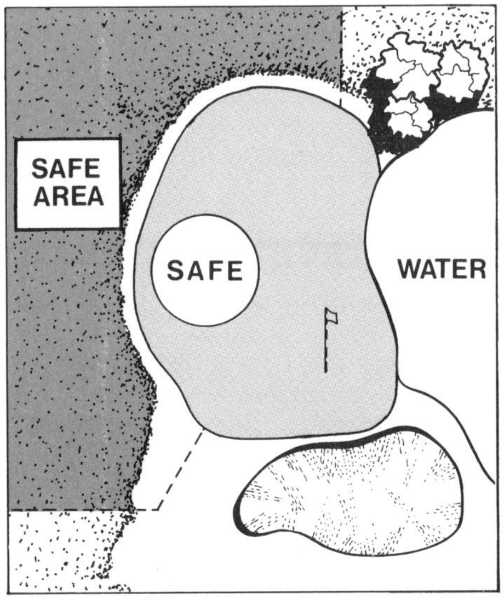

Fig 6.11. Do not always aim at the pin, because a mis-hit could land in trouble. Look for the safe areas.

a higher risk shot, so bear that in mind (Fig 6.9).

Once your tee shot is in play, your next decision is whether you can easily reach the green. If you need to hit your longest club very well to reach it, you should think carefully if this is the right choice. Are there bunkers short of the green to catch a slightly mis-hit shot, or are there no intervening hazards between you and the hole? If there are bunkers, I would suggest that you lay up short of them, then pitch on (Fig 6.10). Remember this par 4 is a par 5 in our plan. If you can reach the green easily, consider your club selection based on the same facts as described for the par 3 hole.

Do not blindly be drawn into aiming at the pin every time, because if it is cut to one side of the green close to a bunker or water, there is a risk that a slightly mis-hit shot will land in this trouble (Fig 6.11). If you can get the ball onto the centre portion of the green you will never be too far from the pin. More golfers under-club than over-club and, generally speaking, most trouble is at the front of the greens, so make a promise to yourself to take enough club.

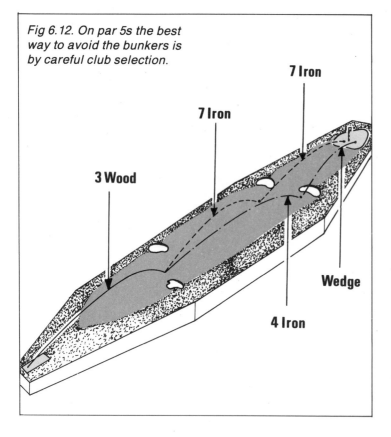

Fig 6.12. On par 5s the best way to avoid the bunkers is by careful club selection.

7 Iron

7 Iron

3 Wood

Wedge

4 Iron

Par 5s

Certainly for the longer hitters, these holes present a golden opportunity to pick up a shot. Our plan says that they are par 6s, but the longer hitter will have no trouble lengthwise in reaching the green in three shots, probably making a true par 5, and even a true birdie, a possibility. So let us examine how the longer hitter should approach this type of hole. Whilst I know that it does depend on the exact length of the hole, it is feasible that you could reach the green using a 3 wood, and then, say, two 6 iron shots. So do not be tempted to stand on the tee and thrash at the ball. Using the same principles as for the tee shot on the par 4, select your club and carefully aim the shot. Before you hit your second shot, consider the task and hazards before you. Very often on par 5s there is a second

set of bunkers short of the green, and you definitely want to avoid them (Fig 6.12). This is where the discipline of playing an iron, rather than a fairway wood, may be needed. Again, depending on your strength, select the club that will safely land the ball short of the trouble. You could play perhaps a 6 or 7 iron, leaving yourself a slightly longer shot to the green, or play a 4 iron, leaving only a short pitch shot (Fig 6.12). The choice is yours, and your ability at playing each of these shots must dictate and influence your choice. There is no one right way. You may love hitting your 7 iron, and hate the 4, in which case the former option would suit you better. If the lie of the ball is good, and you feel that you can easily carry the bunkers, then play that shot, and you will hopefully set up a birdie chance by leaving yourself only a short pitch to the green. For the longer hitter the most annoying thing is to take four shots to reach the green, so use your head, avoid trouble, and you should be putting for a gross birdie!

The shorter-hitting player has to plan to be on the green in four shots, which should not be too difficult. The chances are that the fairway bunkers will not be in range from the tee, and if there are further bunkers, say, 80–100 yards short of the green, you want to be short of them in three shots. Your lack of length in some ways makes planning easier because you are less tempted to try to carry distant hazards, and tee shots are less likely to reach the first set. By planning thus, you too should be on the green in four, in theory putting for a true par, so approach par 5 holes with pleasure and eagerness.

Perhaps a sobering thought for the more aggressive and less reliable player, is that most men could hit three 5 iron shots about 480 yards, enough distance to reach many par 5 holes!

Playing partners' influence

I wrote earlier that you must not be drawn into hitting your driver, just because your playing partners do. Always try to keep to your game plan for each hole, rather than being drawn into a long driving contest. But you can use your partners' play to good effect. If, for instance, you have all selected an iron to hit to a par 3, and all your partners' shots finish short, then maybe the wind strength or the actual distance have been misjudged. This is the time to consider whether to take a longer club. Of course it is possible that they all hit their shots very badly, but you may be able to learn from their mistakes.

To attack or defend?

The last chapter offered general advice on how to play different holes, but one of the most difficult choices on the course is knowing when to attack and when to defend. The fact that you are trying to break 90 means that it is a medal round, where you should err on the side of caution rather than reckless abandon. One high scoring hole in a match or stableford competition does not ruin the chance of winning, but a 9 or 10 in a medal round will undoubtedly make your original target much harder to achieve. But attack is not out of the question altogether; it is simply a matter of knowing where and when. The main points to consider are:

1 How the ball lies.
2 How you are playing on that particular day.
3 The outcome if the gamble fails.
4 Is the gamble necessary?

Apart from tee shots, the lie of the ball is purely a matter of luck. If you are wishing to hit a 3 wood from the fairway and the ball is in a divot or depression, then you have a problem, and hitting that club would not be wise (Fig 7.1). If, on the other hand, the ball is sitting up nicely in the rough, then you may even be able to use your 3 wood if a long shot is needed. So do not make up your mind about which club to hit until you have seen how the ball is sitting. If the ball is in the rough, the number-one rule is to get it back onto the fairway, using the club that has sufficient loft to make the shot possible. Do not try to carry a bunker perhaps 50 yards ahead if the ball is nestled down, because there is every possibility

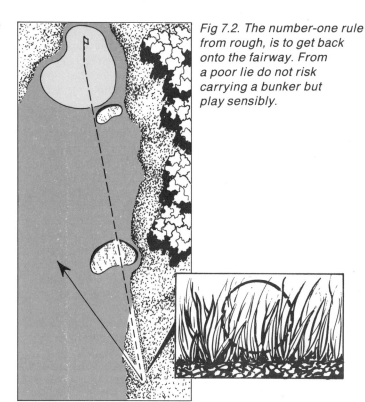

Fig 7.2. The number-one rule from rough, is to get back onto the fairway. From a poor lie do not risk carrying a bunker but play sensibly.

that it will come out low and run into the bunker (Fig 7.2). Aim away from the bunker and just accept that an errant shot means you must lose some distance. Do not compound the error by trying to play an impossible shot and risk a high score. Do not rely on trying to shape a shot from the rough, because the intervening grass between the club face and ball prevents you from imparting the desired sidespin. For this reason, those of you whose natural shots curve considerably, may find that you hit the ball straighter from the light rough.

No matter how much you may practise, your standard of golf will fluctuate, and certain shots or clubs that presented no problem a week ago can suddenly become quite unreliable. You may suddenly find that you have topped your favourite 5 wood all day. It would therefore not be prudent to try to carry a distant ditch or bunker with that club, but accept that, for today anyway, you must change your plan and hit a 5

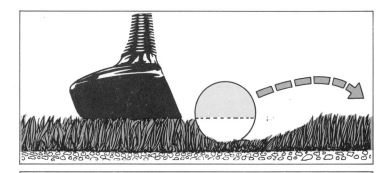

Fig 7.1. If the ball is lying in a divot or in a depression, then a 3 wood is not the club to use.

iron and then, say, a 9 iron. It is very difficult to put bad shots out of your mind, and, although I will deal with that subject later on, you should not put yourself under additional pressure by persisting in playing certain shots or clubs that are currently unsuccessful. Conversely, you may be having a day where you are playing much better than usual, in which case your quality of strike will allow you to be more attacking. But do not be lulled into thinking that anything is possible – try to maintain a realistic outlook and remember to adhere to your plan on how to play each hole.

Being realistic must be uppermost in your mind when you take any gamble on the golf course. It is not a negative attitude to consider what will happen if the gamble does not succeed – it will make you think better and help you to consider the perhaps less spectacular alternatives. It is probably not worth the risk of carrying a far-off ditch or bunker if you are not going to reach the green (Fig 7.3); better to lay up short and then pitch on. If the lie is good, and you have been playing your fairway woods very well, you may feel that it is worth the chance of being closer to the green, but this goes back to the previous points – that the lie of your ball and your play must both influence the choice of shot. If you were to go into the ditch, you would be penalized a shot, so think carefully before you play.

Despite the fact that you may not yet be a low-handicap player, there is no reason why you should not try on certain occasions to shape different shots. If your ball has landed behind some trees, you may decide to hook a shot round them. This is not a particularly risky shot in the right circumstances, but what would be the outcome should the ball either not curve enough or curve too violently (Fig 7.4). It may be wiser, though perhaps less exciting, to play a short

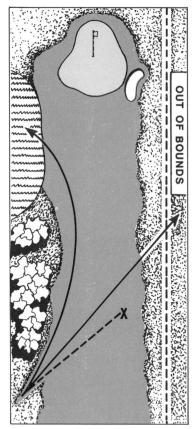

Fig 7.4. If you decide to curve a shot intentionally what will happen if the ball curves too much or not enough? Would it be wiser to play a less spectacular shot back onto the fairway?

shot to the middle of the fairway. If a shot is first of all considered a gamble, you must then ask yourself if the gamble is necessary or are you purely pandering to your ego. In many Pro-Ams I play, if one of my partners is in trouble I will point out their shot options. More often than not they will opt for the more spectacular, high-risk shot, which may involve threading the ball through quite a narrow gap in order to gain maybe a 30 yard advantage over the alternative choice. Whilst in a Pro-Am format, where it is a better-ball competition, this cavalier approach can be acceptable, I feel certain that most of these players would still go for the same shot in a medal round. This can be great fun, but not conducive to breaking 90 on a regular basis. Some people are gamblers by nature, and for them keeping their attacking spirit under control is paramount to consistency. Whilst they may excel in matchplay and stableford events, a medal round demands that they curb their gambling tendency until such time that better technique permits them to be more interested in breaking 80 than 90. If you keep to the par 4, 5 and 6 plan, you should start to produce better scores, and once you become more used to playing conservatively, it will not feel so restrictive. You must always guard against gambling just once too often, which could ruin your chance of a sub-90 round.

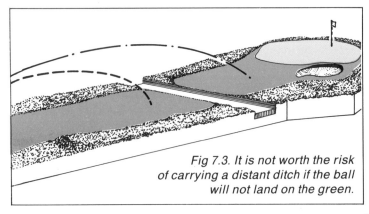

Fig 7.3. It is not worth the risk of carrying a distant ditch if the ball will not land on the green.

CHAPTER EIGHT

Short game strategy

I have already stated that one of the easiest ways to lower your score is to improve your short game, I have also advised you on how to play certain shots, but choosing the right shot to play is very important, too. The essential factor in the short game is being able to visualize the shot to play. If you have to play from 140 yards away, you will simply choose the club that hits the ball that distance. But when faced with a shot of, say, 75 yards, then you have several alternatives from which to choose (Fig 8.1). So let us consider how you should approach any short game shot.

1 Check the lie of the ball. This will determine which shots may or may not be possible. If the ball is sitting in a depression, then to play a high floating shot is not possible. If the lie is good, then your choice of shot is not too limited.

2 Are there intervening hazards or rough ground between your ball and the hole? If there are, then the ball must travel mainly through the air. If there are not, the ground route is the easier option (Fig 8.2).

3 How will the shape and contours and speed of the fairway, fringe and green affect the roll of the ball?

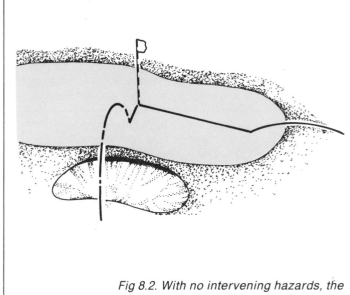

Fig 8.2. With no intervening hazards, the low running shot is the easier option, but the ball must take the air route when bunkers are on your line.

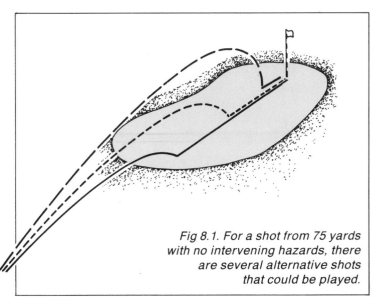

Fig 8.1. For a shot from 75 yards with no intervening hazards, there are several alternative shots that could be played.

4 Ideally if you do not hole the chip or pitch shot, and let us be honest and admit that although this is possible, it is not probable, then where do you want the ball to finish? Uphill putts are easier than downhill or sidehill ones, so if possible try to leave the easy putt. If the green is flat, then be positive and get used to 'seeing' the ball finish past the hole.

These are the main factors to consider *before* you select the club. The lower-handicap player will automatically tend to go through this thought process, whilst the high scorers will not. I played a round of golf with a pupil of mine, whose swing was really very good, but whose handicap did not seem to reflect her skill. I asked her to talk me through her thoughts about each shot before she played it. On the long shots she quite correctly considered the hazards and areas to avoid, but on those from 100 yards in, she failed to consider enough about how the ball was going to react when it landed, and therefore often played the wrong choice of shot.

Shot options must be determined by these factors, but they must also be governed by which shot you feel happiest with and are most successful at playing. I have played with many ladies who are deadly at running the ball onto the green with their 7 iron from all sorts of places. This, I would find more difficult and would choose to play a wedge or sand wedge so that the ball is lofted onto the putting surface, which will eliminate the chances of it getting a bad kick on the fairway or fringe. For me, my choice of shot is more reliable, but that does not make me right and them wrong. Whilst in text book terms the ideal shot to play is usually the one that avoids possible deflections from the area in front of the green, this must be balanced by your ability to play certain shots. Having said all that, I would like to offer some advice on club choice, which should help to clarify matters for you.

Situation 1

The ball is 3 yards short of the green, which slopes from left to right, with the pin at the back, and no intervening hazards (Fig 8.3). If the fringe is smooth and even, the first and easiest option is to putt the ball. You will be consistently more successful with this club in this situation, than chipping the ball. You will also do less damage score-wise if you mis-hit it – a badly hit putt is better than a badly hit chip. If the ground is uneven, or the grass is long or wet, then the ball needs to be lofted onto the front edge of the green so that it can roll up to the pin. The club choice for this shot is one without too much loft. You could use any club between an 8 and 5 iron quite successfully. Remember, the lower the number the lower the ball will go, and the more it will roll. I personally rarely chip with a club less lofted than a 7 iron, mainly because I find that I have a better control of the ball this way. However you should select a club within this range. The wrong club to use would be one with a lot of loft, such as a wedge or sand wedge. You would need to hit it harder to cover the distance, so if it is mis-hit the consequences are

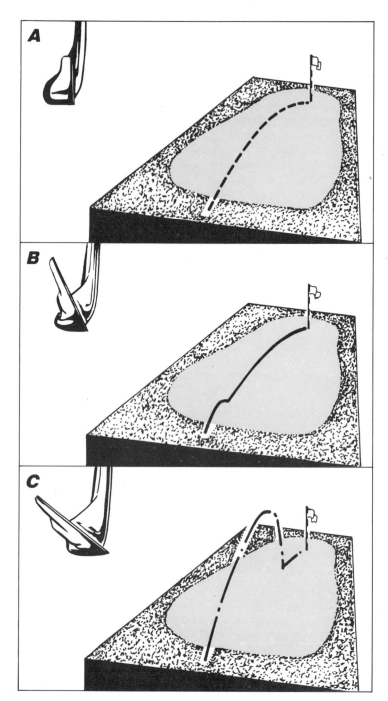

Fig 8.3. The ball is 3 yards off the green, which slopes from left to right:
A If the ground is smooth, the easiest option is to putt, aiming left of the pin.

B If the ground is uneven, chip and roll the ball with a club such as a 7 iron, aiming left of the pin.
C The hardest shot is a pitch or chip with a wedge.

more disastrous; it is also more difficult to judge how hard to hit the ball through the air than along the ground. Having selected your club, aim off to the left of the pin to allow for the ground to take the ball to the hole. If you find that your chip shots are almost always short of the hole, try chipping a less lofted club, i.e., use a 7 instead of an 8, but hit the ball using the same strength. The straighter-faced club will help the ball to roll further.

Situation 2

The ball is 20 yards short of the green, with the pin cut near the back. The green slopes up towards the back, and the pin is cut close to the back left edge, where there is also a bunker (Fig 8.4). This shot could be played in several different ways, but you must consider what could happen if the shot goes wrong. If you choose to pitch the ball all the way to the hole, using, say, a wedge or sand wedge, but pulled the shot slightly, the ball could land in the bunker. If you hit the ball on line but too long, you could be off the green – the only thing that could prevent this is the fact that the green is uphill from front to back. So if you opt for the air route, do not be drawn into aiming at the pin, but aim instead at the heart of the green. This way the bunker presents no danger, and you will leave an uphill putt.

You could choose to play a lower shot with a less lofted club so that the ball will run up the slope. Use perhaps an 8 or 9 iron, and play the ball just back of centre, so that you get a slightly more penetrating shot than normal. There are no real problems with this shot option, but your main task is to judge how hard to hit the ball. The fact that an uphill putt is preferable may persuade you to err on the side of being short rather than long.

If you are proficient at judging how far to pitch the ball, then you should choose the first option, but if you have problems judging pitch shots then play the alternative.

Situation 3

The ball is 15 yards to the left of the green, but a bunker lies between it and the hole. The ball is sitting quite well, with a cushion of grass beneath it. On the other side of the green, directly beyond the hole, is another deep bunker (Fig 8.5). Since the ball is sitting well, the best club to use is your most lofted, i.e., the sand wedge. The good lie will allow the deep

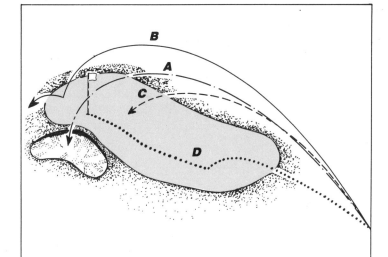

Fig 8.4. The ball is 20 yards off the green, which is slightly uphill, and the pin is cut near the back left edge:
A Using a wedge, if you aim for the pin, a slightly mis-hit shot may find the bunker.
B If you hit the ball too far, it could go off the green into trouble, and you will have a downhill shot back.
C Play a wedge shot sensibly for the heart of the green, leaving an uphill putt.
D You may prefer to play a lower running shot with perhaps an 8 iron, which is an easier alternative than shot C for the higher-handicap golfer.

flange to slide beneath the ball, so that the shot in itself is not difficult to execute. What is more difficult is to judge how hard to hit the ball so that it carries the first bunker but does not run off the green into the second.

Depending on your ability with this club and type of shot, you must decide where to aim. The very last thing you want is for the ball to land in either bunker, so if you decide to aim at the pin, do not try to be too clever by hitting the ball so that it barely clears the first bunker. With this in mind, it is obviously all too easy to hit the ball too hard so that it rolls into the far bunker. So this is a high-risk option and, as a general guide, I would suggest that by aiming slightly away from the pin you will be playing an easier and less risky shot. You will still have a chance of single putting, and, more importantly, you will have eliminated the possibility of dropping more shots than necessary. To get the ball anywhere on the green is better than putting it in a bunker. For those less confident with this type of shot, there is nothing wrong with playing the ball, even perhaps with a 7 iron, more towards the front of the green, so that it does not even have to carry a bunker. From there you can still two-putt and you will have avoided any great disasters. You must not allow the pin to act like a magnet, but instead allow your ability and discipline to be your guides.

If this situation occurred but the ball was lying badly, most players would be better playing towards the front of the green. The alternative could easily be to thin the ball into the face of the near bunker or a long way over the green.

The number of examples is endless, but I hope that these three serve to show the thought process necessary, whatever the options.

Bunkers

Ideally these should be avoided at all cost, but no matter how well you play, the ball will land in one at some time. Sadly, so many high-handicap players have poor bunker technique, so try to improve yours. The golden rule is to get out in one shot, ideally towards the hole, but if this is not possible, then either sideways or backwards will suffice. From a reasonable lie, where the bunker is not too deep, forwards should be possible, but in very deep bunkers, look to see if by playing sideways or backwards you stand a better chance of hitting your next shot from grass, rather than sand, which is what most golfers prefer. Again, do not let the pin distract or attract you too much; if you are not too good out of bunkers, settle for getting the ball on the green. I am always being asked how to play the ball when it has just rolled into the back of the bunker, settling onto a downhill lie, with a steep bunker face between it and the hole. The answer, if you cannot break 90, is that you do not play the shot. Even for the professional this is far from easy, so either play sideways or backwards.

Bunker shots of 30 yards and upwards are difficult, so guard against trying to hit the ball too hard and losing your footing. Consider what would be the worst shot that you could play, and then plan accordingly. Is the ball lying on top of or down in the sand? If you take too much sand will the ball land in another bunker just ahead? If you hit it a little thin and it goes too far, is there great danger over the green? How good are you at playing this particular shot? All these questions must be answered before the ball is played.

Similar questions should be considered before you play fairway bunker shots. If you decide to try for a long shot and it is not successful, will the ball go into another bunker or ditch, or just end up on the fairway short of the green. Try to assess the outcome, based on your ability, the lie of the ball, and the pressure you feel at the time.

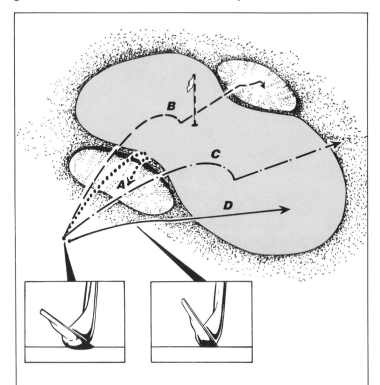

Fig 8.5. The ball is off the green with a bunker between it and the pin. It is sitting well, but the green is narrow with a bunker on the far side:
A & **B** Using a sand wedge and aiming at the pin, it is easy to under- or over-hit the ball, so it lands in a bunker.
C The safer shot is to use a sand wedge and play away from the pin, so that if the ball is hit too hard it will roll onto the fringe.
D You could use a 7 iron and play towards the front of the green rather than find a bunker.

CHAPTER NINE

Putting strategy

Many higher-handicap golfers neglect this department of the game. When you first decide on golf as a leisure activity, naturally your main task is to learn to hit the ball a decent distance and direction. This is quite acceptable and understandable, but once you have started to improve in that respect, you *must* look to your putting as one of the easiest routes to lower scoring. Most poor putters lack two things: a reliable putting stroke, and the ability to apply that stroke to its greatest effect.

Once your action is adequate, how can you use it to maximum benefit? Assessing a putt begins before you get to the green, because as you are walking along the fairway, you are better able to see if the whole green slopes in one particular direction or another. This is especially important when you play on hilly or undulating courses, where the true slope of the green can be difficult to judge. As a rule, the green will follow the slope of the surrounding land (Fig 9.1).

As you walk onto the green, look at the grass. Greens can vary from hole to hole, as well as from course to course, so try to assess if the green on which you are playing looks quicker or slower than the last green.

It is as important that you adopt a routine for your putting as your long game. Ideally if it is possible, and not too time consuming, walk from the hole back to your ball. As you walk, look at the line of the putt for any pitch marks that you can repair, and remove any stones or other loose impediments on your line. Whilst walking you can *feel* through your feet and legs if there are any slopes or contours. On very long putts I like to stop halfway, and then view the putt from the side, at this point trying to visualize how fast the ball must start, in order to be *dying* at the hole. Then take a look at your putt from behind the ball, carefully noting the borrows within one yard to either side of the hole, since these will have the greatest effect on the ball as it travels slowly at this point. Once you have chosen the line, have a practice putt to familiarize yourself with the correct strength. Meanwhile, look

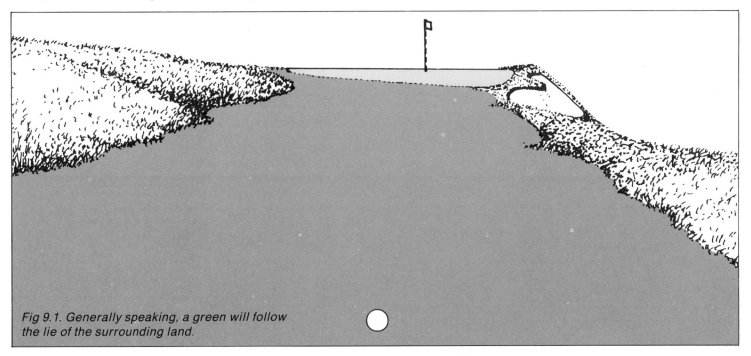

Fig 9.1. Generally speaking, a green will follow the lie of the surrounding land.

along the line of the putt, visualizing the ball rolling and then dropping into the hole. Where possible, pick a spot about two feet ahead of the ball and use that as an intermediate target – just as you did with the long game.

It is unlikely at this stage that you have become so good that you are able to hit the ball exactly where you wish all the time. The professionals may be able to putt the ball quarter-inch perfect, and so it is worth them taking plenty of time on their putts. I want you to take enough time, but not to take up residence on the green! Provided that you give yourself the opportunity of knowing whether the ball should be played straight at the hole, or whether you should allow, say, six inches borrow on the right, you are probably not proficient enough yet to worry that it should have been five-and-a-half inches on the right! Your aim is to avoid three-putting, and to be sufficiently positive to single-putt more often. So avoid slow play on the greens, but by taking enough time, you will undoubtedly take fewer putts and ultimately less time.

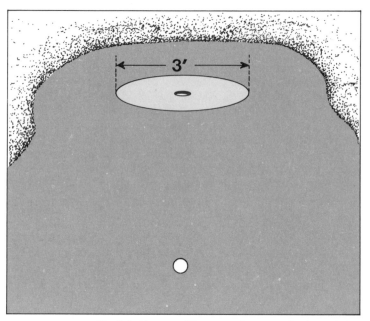

Fig 9.3. Your putting may improve by imagining you are putting into a 3-foot circle around the hole.

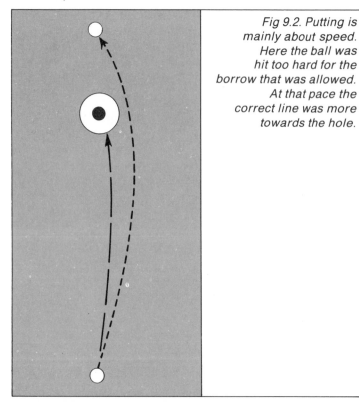

Fig 9.2. Putting is mainly about speed. Here the ball was hit too hard for the borrow that was allowed. At that pace the correct line was more towards the hole.

Good putting is firstly about correct reading of greens, and then the strength of the putt. Once you have read the borrow, concentrate on how hard to hit the ball. If you read a putt on the right lip, but hit it too hard, it will not take the borrow, and the putt will miss on the right. The correct *line* for that *speed* is straight at the hole (Fig 9.2). The way to become a good depth putter is to practise those longer putts, which most golfers seldom do. On the course it may help you to imagine rolling the ball into a three foot circle around the hole (Fig 9.3). I personally do not use this method, because I always like to imagine the ball rolling into the hole. no matter how long the putt. This, of course, is an unrealistic expectation on some putts, but I feel that it is certainly the more positive approach for the better putter. However, if your results improve by thinking of the three-foot circle, then so be it.

There are times to be aggressive on putts and times to be defensive. If your target is to do no worse than two-putt, then you need to plan where you would like to play your second putt from, should the first one miss. If the green is basically flat, then try to have the ball stopping about one foot beyond the hole. If the putt has left-to-right or right-to-left borrow, remember that especially in severe cases the ball will roll downhill in the last few inches (Fig. 9.4). You must allow for this when you judge the strength, but remember that the ball is better off finishing beyond and below the hole for two reasons. First, if it is not hit with enough strength to reach the hole it will not drop in (obvious really), and secondly, if it is below the hole at least you have an uphill putt remaining.

This then begs the question on whether you should attack uphill putts. These must be hit hard enough to finish just past the hole, and whilst this is easy to judge on short putts, from the 20–30 foot range this may present a problem. Realistically at this stage you may be unlikely to hole this length, so the safest thing to do is to try to leave the ball just short of the hole. This does not mean that you should be negative when you hit the putt – always strike it firmly, but not too aggressively. Remember that an uphill putt will not take as much borrow as one on the flat.

Downhill putts, which so often have borrow as well, are the most difficult to judge. On extreme slopes, you can easily just try to set the ball rolling, only to see it finish well short of the hole leaving another downhill putt. Therefore you must try to get the ball past the hole so that your second putt is uphill.

Always try to strike the putt well, rather than just timidly wafting the putter at the ball. Most right-handed golfers would prefer an uphill right-to-left putt, so try to hit the ball with sufficient pace and borrow that you have a chance of leaving yourself this putt if the ball does not go in.

Medal versus stableford and matchplay

If you have played a lot of stableford and matchplay golf, you may have become the type of golfer who is quite aggressive on the greens. By and large, this style of play suits these forms of golf, where the death or glory attitude can be beneficial, but it can become costly in medal play, where your main aim is to avoid three-putting. A later chapter has some advice on how to analyze your round, and based on this you should assess whether you putt too aggressively or too defensively. As I have already explained knowing when to attack and defend is part of the game.

Learn from others

Watch your partners putt, and by that I do not mean watch their action, but watch how fast the ball leaves the putter, and assess if that is how hard you would have hit the ball. This will give you a better chance of judging the pace and borrow of the greens. One last tip is to putt with a clean golf ball. A lump of mud or sand left on the ball is enough to send even the best hit putt off-line.

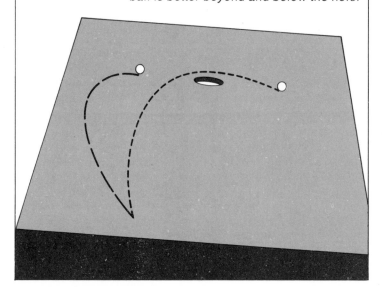

Fig 9.4. On sidehill putts, the ball is rolling downhill at the end, so allow for this when judging the strength of the putt. Remember that if you do not hole it, the ball is better beyond and below the hole.

CHAPTER TEN

The positive outlook

Having explained how the technical and strategic aspects of your game should help you to break 90, it is important that you appreciate just how much the right mental attitude will contribute to that goal. To progress to your best level, the sooner you view things in a positive light, then the quicker your technical and strategic improvements will bear fruit. It has often been said that the most important six inches in golf is that between the ears! Even for those in the middle- to high-handicap range this holds true, so let us examine how that six inches can help.

Self image

It is most important that you start to develop a strong mental picture of yourself succeeding at whichever shot you are about to play. How often have you had to play a pitch shot over a bunker, had the image of fluffing the ball into it, and then fulfilled this image (Fig 10.1)? This starts a chain reaction, so that when you are faced with a similar shot again, you think back to that failure and immediately have the wrong mental picture. Yes you are going to hit some poor shots – we all do – but you *must* start to build a better picture of yourself succeeding. You can even do this away from the golf course, by sitting imagining yourself on the first tee, swinging smoothly and hitting a good shot. Mentally see yourself playing the more difficult shots successfully, such as a chip over the bunker, or a three foot left-right putt for par. But do keep this mental image within the bounds of what is sensible and achievable. There is no point in thinking that just because you have *imagined* yourself carrying a ditch 250 yards in the distance, when your record for hitting a ball is only 190 yards, you are suddenly going to 'find' another 60 yards. That is not reasonable or feasible. But imagining yourself crisply striking the ball to your maximum ability is what you must start to envisage.

As you look from your ball to the target, you must not ignore the hazards ahead, since they will help to determine which shot you play. Having identified the areas to avoid, you must then get a positive picture in your mind of the ball's flight. If you address the ball thinking only of where it must not go then your body will not respond as desired. You must always feed in positive thoughts and pictures. So your

Fig 10.1. If you imagine failure, this will encourage bad shots.

pre-shot routine must begin by you 'seeing' the ball's flight, then 'seeing' and feeling yourself successfully playing the shot whilst you have a practice swing. When top-class skiers, who perform leaps and somersaults as they ski downhill, wait at the top of the run for their turn, they shut their eyes, and by their movements you can see them rehearsing what they are about to perform, although their skis never leave the snow at this point. They are unable to have a proper practice at their run, so they substitute a mental rehearsal for the physical one that is not possible. We are lucky in golf that we can have both, so make the most of your practice swing and your mental preparation.

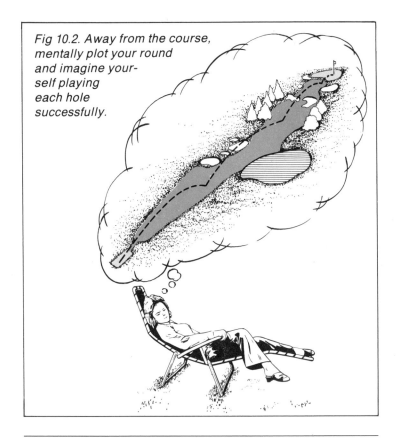

Fig 10.2. Away from the course, mentally plot your round and imagine yourself playing each hole successfully.

Seeing the round

You now know how to plot your way around the course, and you can endorse that plan by thinking about it before you play. The more vividly you can start to 'see' how you wish to play the course, the better your chances of so doing. If all you have in your mind is how badly you played last time, then you are preventing yourself from seeing success. This is especially important if there has been a particular hole or holes that have been troubling you lately. You must prevent the previous disasters from masking or clouding a new positive picture. By tackling the hole in a different manner, perhaps playing an iron from the tee instead of a wood, you will no longer view it as the hole that you just cannot play. Take time at home to sit and mentally play your round (Fig 10.2). This is especially therapeutic when bad weather or lack of time prevent you from being out on the course.

Self confidence

So many of the higher-handicap players whom I teach, seem to be apologetic for their handicap and their existence on the golf course. Anyone who plays golf does so for the enjoyment it brings, and whilst we all enjoy playing well rather than badly, it does not follow that a 3-handicap player gets more enjoyment from the game than a 23 handicap. Neither does it make the former a better person or super-human – he has simply learnt the art of getting the ball round the course. We all have to start somewhere; very few people break 90 in their first round of golf, and some never achieve that target but still enjoy the game. So do not go out on to the golf course thinking that you should not be there – it is your hobby and you have paid your green fee, so enjoy it.

Most golfers are interested only in their own game and are not really concerned about what other golfers are doing. You may feel that all eyes are upon you on the first tee, and it might be true in this instance, but once you have got off the first tee, no one will be bothered about how you are playing. You may watch others on the first tee, but when your round begins you are too concerned with your own game to worry about them. You do not have to forget that others exist – they certainly do – and by mending pitch marks, raking bunkers and calling faster players through, we give other golfers a fair chance to play well. However, do not be over-anxious about playing whilst others watch, and do not worry about what other people may think of your golf. If you have chosen to play short of a ditch when your partners have gone for the carry, do not worry if they make detrimental remarks about your defensive play. You must stick to your game plan.

Try to become a confident player, and get used to thinking in a positive manner. Walk down the fairway with your head up, even after a bad shot. By letting your head drop and by slouching you will not develop the best frame of mind for the next shot. Even if you are playing badly and breaking 90 seems out of the question, do not waste the rest of the round; try to learn something from it that will help you in the future. The sooner you learn to cope with, and recover from, playing badly, then the better your chance of *consistently* breaking 90. In trying to develop a more confident manner, it is important to repeat positive thoughts to yourself, but I would discourage you from getting over-confident and starting to boast about how good you have become. Outwardly boastful golfers tend to get brought back down to earth.

CHAPTER ELEVEN

Why where you play affects your play

So many golfers can hit the ball better at the driving range or practice gound than on the golf course. This is not difficult to understand; at each of the first two venues there is no pressure to score, you have the luxury of hitting shot after shot, and there are no hazards. If you find that your golf in a practice situation is far superior to that on the course, then by changing your mental approach you can maintain that higher standard on the course, too.

When you practise the chances are that you will be in a relaxed state, so that your muscles are able to perform to their maximum efficiency. When you play, relaxation is harder to achieve, but you can learn to control your muscles. On the practice ground, hit some shots with a grip that is tighter than normal. You will find that your arm and shoulder muscles will start to feel tense, and the swing will not be very fluid. Next start with a tight grip, but relax your hands just prior to your backswing. The grip should be firm but relaxed, and this will help to ease your arm and shoulder muscles also. By practising tensing and then relaxing in this manner, you can use the same technique on the course to great effect. It is also very relaxing to breathe deeply, taking one deep breath and exhaling just prior to the backswing.

I once sat on the practice ground at the British Open, and watched one of the world's top professionals have his caddy call out different hole numbers to him, and he would then hit the appropriate shaped tee shot. This is the next step for you. On the practice ground imagine yourself out on the course, perhaps at the first hole, where most people get tense. Picture where the hazards are as you look ahead, and where you want the ball to land; sense that there are several sets of eyes watching your every move, and imagine your friends waiting to tee off behind you. You may start to feel a little more anxious than for the your normal practice ground shot, but employ the above techniques to control this. Use your pre-shot routine, including positive imagery, and then hit the ball. By practising in this manner when the shots occur on the course, you will already have 'played' them successfully, and your confidence will grow.

The other way to approach on-course tension and lack of form during a round, is to imagine yourself in the situation where you perform best, which is usually your practice location,

Fig 11.1. To ease on-course tension, picture a practice ground target.

or even a favourite hole on the course. On the practice ground you may always aim at a yardage marker, or distant tree, so for each shot on the course just picture that object as your target (Fig 11.1). During my years as a tournament player, I carried in my mind one of the tee shots at my home club that I particularly enjoyed, and usually played successfully. In tight situations, or on days when my confidence and ability were not all that they should be, I would put myself back on that tee, and just imagine the ball flying off into the distance. I am sure that you have holes on your course, where you hit more good shots than bad. This may be because they are wide open holes with no danger lurking, so you relax and swing smoothly. Use this to your advantage and try to imagine that each hole is like these, with no dangers lurking.

Self-imposed pressure

When playing in Pro-Ams so often I hear partners announce that 'this is a difficult hole'. Instantly they are increasing the pressure on themselves, by saying that they will need to do something special in order to score well. This same attitude is not applicable to a practice situation, or even to a friendly round, where you are more casual and relaxed. If you are guilty of pronouncing shots or holes as 'difficult', then stop immediately. By using the practice ground drill already described of imagining yourself on different holes, you can start to conquer any fears. Build up a case history of successfully playing the hole, even if it is only in your mind on the practice ground, or in an armchair.

You may play a hole rather badly continually, and start to get a complex about it. The answer to this problem is to tackle the hole in a completely different manner. If the drive is particularly difficult, take a different club to your usual one, so that you can confidently get the ball on the fairway. Play subsequent shots with clubs that you can hit well, even if you just use medium and short irons. If the second shot has been landing in bunkers short of the green, from which you do not recover very well, be sure to lay up short of them so that the problem is removed. You need to regain your confidence, and to pose yourself a different set of problems on that hole, removing the original pressure.

Outside influences

Most beginners and high-handicap players are very self conscious, and often feel that they are in the way, or holding up play. Then they begin to rush round the course, giving themselves no chance of performing to their best ability. You never see top-class players quickly grab a club and hit the ball before they have had a chance to assess the situation, and take their address position in a precise manner. This, however, is what so many higher-handicap players do, and whilst I am the last person to encourage slow play, you will take more time by rushing your shots, because you will undoubtedly end up hitting more. You would not rush on the practice ground, so do not do it on the course. Learn to set up to the ball so that it becomes second nature. This you can do best indoors with a mirror to help you, so that you can check the ball position etc. Then once you are on the course, walk at a brisk pace, but give yourself time to survey the shot. Calmly select your club, and address the ball without any undue rush. Stick to your pre-shot routine, but if faster players behind are worrying you, then call them through. You need your full attention focused on the shot in hand, not on other players.

I strongly believe that to play good golf requires discipline, and if an outside influence distracts you, then you must deal with that influence. Your playing partners may distract you in some way, but do not let them affect your concentration. Once you have reached your ball, the discipline of your pre-shot routine must bring your attention back to hitting the ball and nothing else.

CHAPTER TWELVE

Keys to concentration

I am often asked, 'How can I concentrate for three to four hours during my round?' The answer is that you do not concentrate for three to four hours but for the amount of time it takes to prepare and hit each shot. You need to be in a relaxed yet controlled state of mind to play your best, and few people can concentrate at their peak for up to four hours. Golf requires an on/off concentration, so that between shots you can, and should, relax but be prepared to switch on the concentration when needed. For tee shots, start to get into your cocoon of concentration when you arrive at the tee; and for other shots, just before you reach the ball. For shots around the green, keep the concentration and alertness more constant, there is little time between shots and you should notice how your partner's ball is reacting on the green.

It is easy to forget key movements during the round, especially if one or two shots go astray. For instance, you may have been taking your club away *lower* to the ground, and then making certain that you swing through the ball. Remember that no-one hits every shot well, and if you have decided on using certain key movements for a round, then stick to them. Perhaps by using letters of the alphabet you may remember better. For instance for the two moves mentioned above you could say to yourself LT, which substitute for *low* back and hit *through*. Use letters that you can remember readily, but from personal experience I know that this method can help.

Some players respond better to thinking about one or more specific movements, while others prefer an overall swing feel. Top-class professionals employ one or two swing thoughts for as long as they work. Try to do the same, but do not allow these thoughts to prevent you swinging to a balanced finish, which, in itself, is a desirable on-course thought.

It is harder to concentrate when you are not playing well, and often you just want to complete the round as quickly as possible. Try to keep your attention on the game, because it is still good practice even if your score is above 90. Keep to the pre-shot routine, so that you at least use the round to incorporate that as a natural part of your game.

CHAPTER THIRTEEN

How the score affects your attitude

How you are scoring in your round will probably affect your attitude and your mental outlook. So many golfers start their round poorly, perhaps dropping nearly all their handicap shots in the first six holes. They then give up mentally, but often play the rest of the round in near par figures.

Most golfers fail to warm up sufficiently before they play. If top-class players need to hit practice shots to be totally on form at the first tee, then so do you. But I know that this is not realistic, and since few club golfers spend enough time warming up, expectations on the opening few holes should not be too high. That is not to say that you cannot score well, but you should not attempt shots that are difficult, or hit the driver. Give yourself a chance by playing the first three or four holes in a defensive rather than an attacking manner. If you still play them badly, do not give up – by being hard on yourself you will become miserable and will find it hard to get better. Try to have a positive outlook for the rest of the round, even if the score looks like being above the limit. If you can play some of the remaining holes well, it will have served as a lesson that you can play badly and then pick yourself up.

Score consciousness

If you are scoring well, you may be unable to cope with the prospect of a good round, especially if it is feasible that you could break 90 for the first time. For instance, you may know that you must play the last three holes in a total of 16 shots, find the pressure too great and go to pieces. If knowing your score seems to have a detrimental effect on your play, then do not add up the nine-hole total, and just tell your partners that you do not wish to know anything about your score. You will usually know if you are doing well or badly, but exactly how well may be enough to ruin the day. Fortunately I was never score conscious, by which I mean that I rarely knew my total score until I added up the card. This I believe is an advantage for most players, although there are a few people who give of their best with additional pressure. If you are scoring well, with just a few holes left to play, you may feel that you need to know exactly what you have to score to break 90, in order to know how attacking you should be. This could work in your favour if you have shots in hand, since you can play well

within yourself. It may work against you if you need to attack, as the additional demands may cause you to drop more shots. Only by experience and perhaps by experimenting, will you come to any firm conclusions about the score affecting your play, and you must then base your future rounds on this evidence.

If you are playing well and then have a few bad holes, do not give up. You may play the remaining holes very well, and still reach your goal. It is important to regard each hole as a separate entity, and do not let poor form at one upset you mentally. Think back to how your swing felt during those good holes, and reflect on your mental approach at that time. You can then direct your energies towards regaining your composure, instead of wasting time berating yourself, and possibly other people. Do not lose your temper because you will take several holes to calm down, by which time too much damage will have been done. Stay in the present, do not think back to the bad shots, or bad bounces you may have had; you can do nothing about them, but you can do something about the future shots in your round. Few top professionals play perfect rounds of golf; they too will make mistakes, causing shots to be dropped. However, their ability to put these errors out of their mind is what makes a good round of golf still possible. If you play well, then drop a few shots, you are likely to become tense, and deny yourself the chance to swing in a smooth relaxed manner. I have already dealt with relaxation in some detail, but one further way to help yourself to relax is to hum a tune quietly. I can testify to its benefit – find the right tune, and it may also help you to swing more rhythmically!

Practical application

I walked the course with a friend of mine, who felt he hit the ball well enough, but did not think that his scores were a true reflection of his ability. What follows is an analysis of my observations of his play, and my suggestions as to how he should have tackled the course.

Hole 1, par 4, 320 yards   (Fig 14.1)▶

Shot 1 John failed to warm up in any sense, and did not take time to plan how he would play the hole in five shots. He had no pre-shot routine, and, in his mind, a tee shot had to be hit with a driver. He should have given himself enough time for at least 10 to 20 practice swings, which, although not ideal, are better than nothing. If he had planned how to play the hole in five shots he would have known that he did not need his driver, but a 3 or 5 wood. If he had used a pre-shot routine he would have aimed better, and given himself a chance to calm down mentally and swing smoothly.

Shot 2 Playing sensibly was over-ridden by the desire for length. A 7 iron would have been a better club to use, which would have placed the ball in range of the green for the third shot. John rushed this shot too and again had no pre-shot routine.

Shot 3 The lie and situation demanded a more lofted club to be used. With the ball down in the sand, it could not be hit cleanly. The bunker face was only five feet ahead and three feet high. Again an obsession with length made John play the wrong club. He was also becoming aware of holding up players on the tee, and became anxious.

Shot 4 Again John tried to over-power the shot and had no pre-shot routine. He thumped his club back in the bag and charged off down the fairway.

Shot 5 John chose the more difficult shot, the pitch, when he could have played the easier chip and run with a 7 or 8 iron. So poor choice of shot contributed to his downfall. He seemed in a hurry to get out of the way of those following, and was already almost disinterested in his own efforts.

Shots 6, 7 and 8 At this point John just wanted to get out of the way and failed to look at any borrow or even have a practice putt.

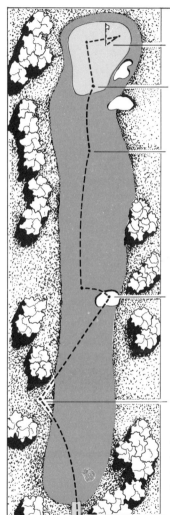

Shots 6, 7 & 8
John had 3 quick stabs at the ball, each in an uncontrolled manner.

Shot 5
A short pitch shot played with a sand iron, which John hit fat.

Shot 4
John played the 5 iron again, but struck it poorly. He was now very annoyed and angry with himself.

Shot 3
The ball was sitting down a little in the sand and John hit a 5 iron which caught the lip and went sideways out of the bunker.

Shot 2
The ball was nestled down in the rough. John topped a 5 wood into the right-hand bunker.

Shot 1
John rushed to the tee, and, without any practice swings, quickly grabbed his driver from the bag and duck-hooked the ball about 80 yards into the rough.

Conclusion John's actions were typical of many golfers, where one bad shot led to another. On-course discipline was non-existent, as was any thought about planning the hole or a pre-shot routine. I mentioned all these points, and we proceeded to the next hole.

Hole 2, par 5, 485 yards   (Fig 14.2) ▶

John took my words on board, had a few easy swings beside the tee to calm himself down, and then duly thought about how he could play the hole in six shots. He then went through his pre-shot routine.

Shot 1 The extra time, thought and discipline had paid off, and having hit a good tee shot, John walked down the fairway in a more positive frame of mind.

Shot 2 John did not stick to his plan of playing short of the ditch in two. True, he had hit a better than average drive, but the lie was bare, which increased the chances of hitting the ball thin and low – not the ideal shot to carry a ditch. If the lie had been good, the extra risk might have been worth the gamble if he could have reached the green in two; but since this was beyond the realms of probability, it would have been wiser to have laid up short of the ditch with a mid-iron.

Shots 3 and 4 John picked the ball out of the ditch, and dropped it into a bad downhill lie in the rough. If he had been more aware, he could have gone back another 10 yards to a flat and even part of the fairway. It was worth losing distance for a flatter and better lie. From the poor lie, the pitch was always going to be a difficult shot to control, and he should have aimed for the middle of the green, and not have been drawn to the hole.

Shot 5 Annoyed at having ruined a good drive, plus the fact that he did not like bunker shots, John rushed this shot. In this instance he should have calmly had one or two practice swings outside the bunker and taken his time.

Shots 6, 7 and 8 Another three putts were caused by the poor bunker shot leaving John in three-putt range. If he had cleaned his ball, he might have got the first putt near enough, but a lump of sand prevented this.

Conclusion John changed his game plan on the basis of one good shot. He failed to appreciate how the lie affects the shot, and how that must dictate the shot you play. If he had known and used the rules a little better he would have had a simple shot to the green, and would have been putting for a five. He tried to compensate for a mistake by going for the pin and not the green. His on-course discipline, rather than his lack of ability, let him down.

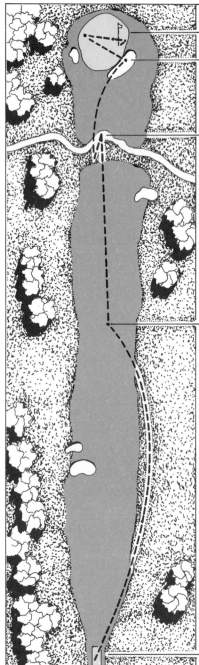

Shots 6, 7 & 8
Again John 3-putted. He did not read the green.

Shot 5
John thinned the ball from the bunker, playing in a very hurried manner.

Shots 3 & 4
Shot 3 was a penalty shot as John lifted the ball from the ditch. He then had 90 yards to the pin, with the ball lying poorly in the rough on a downhill lie. His 9 iron was pushed into the bunker and he was angry.

Shot 2
The ball was on a very bare lie, but John decided to hit his 5 wood in order to carry the ditch.

Shot 1
Using a 3 wood, John teed-up on the left of the tee, aiming right to allow his draw to bring the ball back to the fairway.

Hole 3, par 3, 150 yards
(Fig 14.3) ▶

Shot 1 The wind was quite strongly against at this hole, and John played a 5 iron, one more club than normal for the yardage. Because of the wind he decided to hit the ball hard, which sent it higher than usual. The strong wind affected it, and it landed short of the bunkers in front of the green, John should have taken a 4 or even a 3 iron, played the ball back in his stance and swung easily, thus keeping the ball lower.

Shot 2 John should have cashed in on his luck, finishing short of the bunkers and with a good lie, which meant the shot was more predictable. With the green sloping uphill, he should have kept the ball below the hole to leave an uphill putt, but his pitch shots ran well past the hole. However, he was playing the hole better than the previous two and was quite calm, positive and controlled.

Shots 3 and 4 John failed to strike the first putt with any authority. Although it was downhill, the grass was quite long and thus the ball did not roll very well. If he had hit it harder and missed, he would at least have had an uphill putt back. However, he then did well to hole the second putt, taking time to read the line.

Conclusion Club choice let John down in the first instance but, despite hitting his chip shot to a difficult spot on the green, he had still succeeded in his game plan because he had dropped only one shot. He had used a pre-shot routine on each occasion.

Summary

John made many mistakes on his first three holes. If you do not warm up, then you should not attack the course too early in the round. Instead, give your body a few holes to get going. The professional uses the practice ground to rid himself of the bad shots, and to practise any that he feels will be demanded of him that day: for example, hitting low shots into the wind. If you do not warm up sufficiently, you are less likely to strike all your early shots well, but you must get your brain working instantly, so that you do not squander and fritter shots away by bad thinking.

Analyze your rounds

By keeping a record or chart of your rounds, you will

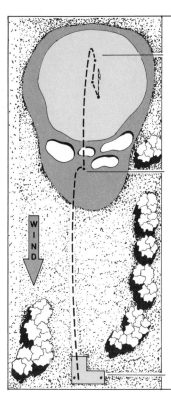

Shots 3 & 4
The first putt finished 3 feet short of the hole, but John did well to hole the next putt.

Shot 2
The ball was sitting well in short rough, John hit a wedge, and the ball finished past the pin.

Shot 1
Because of a strong wind against, John took a 5 instead of his usual 6 iron for the distance. The ball finished short of the bunkers.

inevitably discover facts and patterns in your play that may be very helpful in lowering your scores. It is all too easy to misinterpret the cause of high scoring, and unless you get to the root cause of the trouble, you·may never play to your best ability. Either during your round, or as soon as possible afterwards, make a careful note of how you played each hole, stating the club used and where the ball finished. It would also be helpful, although perhaps a little more time-consuming, to note your mental preparation and outlook on each shot – for instance, did you stick to your pre-shot routine and aim correctly; were you still thinking about a previous shot?

It is always easy to blame a poor round on bad putting, but if you put the ball in three-putt range all the time, you will certainly take three putts quite often. Hit the ball to 20 feet or less, and you will take fewer putts. So you might find that it is poor iron play that is putting extra strain on your putting. In turn, it could be bad driving that put extra strain on your iron shots, so you can see that a detailed and *honest* analysis of your round will help.

CHAPTER FIFTEEN

Make the rules work for you

To the beginner and high-handicap player, the rules of golf, which are drawn up by the Royal and Ancient Golf Club of St Andrews and the United States Golf Association, seem very complicated. Whenever possible read the rule book, because being able to find the appropriate rule quickly will prevent you getting flustered and making costly mistakes. Try to become familiar with where to find those most commonly used, which are probably:

Obstructions – Rule 24.
Abnormal Ground Conditions – Rule 25.
Water Hazards – Rule 26.
Ball Lost or Out of Bounds – Rule 27.
Ball Unplayable – Rule 28.

You do not need to know a rule by heart – carry a rule book to help you. But by knowing how to use the rules they can work in your favour, and you should avoid undue penalty shots. There are endless examples of the rules I could give, but two are worth explaining:

1 A ball lies close to a staked tree, which is considered by the club as an immovable obstruction (Rule 24.2), which means that you can move the ball **without penalty**. What many golfers fail to appreciate is that having found the nearest point of relief, so that the tree does not interfere with your swing, is not in a hazard or on the putting green, and is not nearer the hole, you should drop the ball **within one club length of that point**. The ball may then roll up to two club lengths from where it first hit the ground. In some cases this may mean that you play from the fairway and not the rough. This is quite legal and your good fortune (Fig 15.1). To help you, use tee pegs to mark the original position of the ball, the nearest point of relief, and one club length from that point.

2 A ball rolls into a lateral water hazard. Under Rule 26.1 a, b & c, you have five options (Fig 15.2):
(1) Play it as it lies. This is seldom chosen for obvious reasons, but if a ditch is dry and you do play the shot, remember not to ground your club.
(2) Stroke and distance. If you have hit the ball 200 yards, this is not a popular choice, but if the ball has not travelled very far, this could be the best option.
(3) Adding a penalty shot, drop the ball behind the hazard, keeping the point where the ball last crossed the margin of

Fig 15.1. When dropping from a staked tree. Find nearest point of relief, drop the ball within one club length of that point. The ball may then roll a further two club lengths away, meaning that in some cases you could play from the fairway even if the ball was in the rough.

STAKED TREE

NEAREST POINT OF RELIEF

BALL

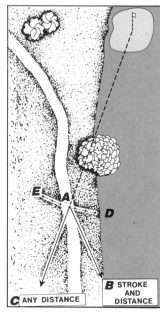

E A D

C ANY DISTANCE

B STROKE AND DISTANCE

Fig 15.2. Right: If the ball goes in a lateral water hazard, there are 5 options: **A** Play it as it lies. **B** Play from where the original shot was played adding one shot penalty. **C** Adding a penalty shot, drop the ball any distance behind hazard keeping the point where the ball last crossed the margin of the hazard between you and the hole. **D & E** Adding a penalty shot, drop two clubs' lengths either side of the hazard opposite the point where the ball last crossed its margin. If it was not in deep rough, E would offer the best shot.

the hazard between you and the hole, with no limit on how far behind the hazard the ball is dropped.
(4 & 5) Adding a penalty shot, on *either side of the hazard*, drop the ball within two club's lengths of where it last crossed the margin of the hazard, not nearer the hole. This option is not always used to its maximum advantage, as players rarely consider playing from the far side of a ditch. On occasions this may prove beneficial.

It may take you a while to work out where it is best to drop, but by keeping calm and being familiar with the full extent of the rule, you should make the right decision.